Stupid Things Parents Do to Mess Up Their Kids

Other books by Dr. Laura Schlessinger

The Ten Commandments

Ten Stupid Things Women Do to Mess Up Their Lives

*How Could You Do That?! The Abdication of Character,
Courage, and Conscience*

Ten Stupid Things Men Do to Mess Up Their Lives

Stupid Things

PARENTS DO TO

Mess Up Their Kids

Don't Have Them If You Won't Raise Them

(Previously published as *Parenthood by Proxy*)

Dr. Laura Schlessinger

Cliff Street Books

An Imprint of HarperCollinsPublishers

Originally published in hardcover by HarperCollins in 2000 under the title *Parenthood by Proxy.*

STUPID THINGS PARENTS DO TO MESS UP THEIR KIDS. Copyright © 2000 by Dr. Laura C. Schlessinger. All rights reserved. Printed in the United States of America. No part of this book may be used or reproduced in any manner whatsoever without written permission except in the case of brief quotations embodied in critical articles and reviews. For information address HarperCollins Publishers Inc., 10 East 53rd Street, New York, NY 10022.

HarperCollins books may be purchased for educational, business, or sales promotional use. For information, please write to: Special Markets Department, HarperCollins Publishers Inc., 10 East 53rd Street, New York, NY 10022.

First Cliff Street Books paperback edition published 2001.

Library of Congress Cataloging-in-Publication Data has been applied for.

ISBN 0-06-093379-8 (pbk.)

01 02 03 04 05 ❖/RRD 10 9 8 7 6 5 4 3 2 1

To all you parents
who treat your children
as the special gifts from G-d
that they are

Contents

Acknowledgments

I am grateful to the many people who care enough to sustain me through my journeys, missions, crusades, and battles. They are patient, understanding, inspiring, challenging, and lovingly critical when the moment most requires it.

Keven Bellows, my chief of staff, went over this manuscript with an ultrafine-tooth comb so many times that she remembers its contents even better than I do! Her editorial input was necessary and invaluable to the final presentation of this work. Her heart was in it as much as her intellect. I am eternally grateful not only for her literary expertise but for her personal sensitivity, sense of humor, and unflagging loyalty.

My radio office and broadcast staff not only helps me keep a tremendous amount of material organized, but due to their amazing commitment to mutual ideals and values, constantly keeps me hopeful for a better world: Cornelia Koehl, Lani Taymor, DeWayne McDaniel, Dan Mandis, Michelle Anton, and Amir Forester are the best group of folks one could ever imagine assembling into a fabulous team.

Kraig Kitchin, president of Premiere Radio Networks (my

radio syndication company) stands behind all of my efforts and copes (although I'll never know how) with all of my moods and sociopolitical on-air passions. He always tries to make things run smoother and be better. He is a godsend to all the people who have the privilege of working with him.

I would also like to recognize the folks I will be working with at Paramount Studios, as I bring my point of view and interests to television in the fall of 2000: Kerry McCluggage, Frank Kelly, Joel Berman, Bobbee Gabelmann, and Kim Schlotman. Most especially, I want to acknowledge someone who has become a dear friend in the strange course (another story entirely) of our bringing the "Schlessinger" television program to reality: Velma Cato (executive producer). Velma is an amazing combination of brilliance, energy, and tenacity combined with serenity, sanity, and spirituality. I am fortunate that she considers me a friend.

Rabbi Moshe Bryski, the spiritual leader of the Chabad of Agoura, California, is always there for me—for everyone— often even before I ask or know I need him.

Talk about people putting up with me! How 'bout my husband, Lew, and 5'10", fourteen-year-old son, Deryk! We are a family that has gone through more than most, and each endeavor hasn't always been "pretty." We've survived. We're tight. And they are a constant reminder that, next to only the privilege of life itself, family is the greatest gift of G-d.

Stupid Things Parents Do to Mess Up Their Kids

Introduction

For the duration of my career, I have been condemning full-time day care and championing a parent at home as being in the best interest of children, families, and, ultimately, society. Many critics, probably defensive about their own so-called lifestyle choices, have written to or about me imagining a "gotcha!" moment: "Well, how do you explain your hypocrisy, Dr. Laura," the letters or articles generally start, "when you're a working mother? How can you criticize? You do a radio show, you write, you go on book tours and lecture circuits and TV appearances. How can you possibly be an at-home mother with your schedule? You lie! You are a hypocrite!"

Here's the entire scoop. When I was re-singled (after a brief marriage and divorce in my mid-twenties) and teaching at the University of Southern California, I took graduate courses in the sociology department's Human Resources Center toward a postdoctoral certification in marriage and family therapy and a license as a marriage and family therapist. One of my friends, a married female graduate student, came to me and told me that she was pregnant. I replied, "Oh, I'm sorry," assuming, of course, that she had my feminist brainwashed perspective that becoming a mother was the original cop-out!

She was quite taken aback, but responded patiently, "No, I'm happy I'm pregnant. I want to be a mother. This is a wonderful thing."

I was embarrassed that I had had such a negative knee-jerk reaction and spent a lot of time thinking about my feelings and thoughts concerning marriage and children. Still, I was geared for accomplishment and success and wanted nothing and no one to impede my professional progress, certainly not a husband or a child.

Not only did the rise of feminism during my tenure in college have a negative effect on my thinking about marriage and family, the constant complaining of my mother when I was growing up discouraged any positive considerations I might have had about such experiences. My mother, an Italian immigrant from northern Italy, is a brilliant and talented woman who, for whatever inner lack of confidence or commitment, did not follow through on any of her unique, creative talents and abilities. She could paint, was clever about the stock market, and was able to budget, plan, shop, and create a beautiful home with the very modest financial resources provided by my hardworking father.

I remember my father always being very supportive about her taking art classes, for example, which she would eventually quit with some complaint I now recognize as specious about the teacher or the lessons. She was free during the day or evenings after dinner to pursue whatever interests and abilities she had. Yet she frequently admonished me about how marriage, and especially children, inhibit a woman's happiness and enterprise.

Nonetheless, when I was thirty-five, something took me over, in spite of my "woman of independent means" attitude. I was watching *Nova* on PBS. This particular hour was about conception, development, and childbirth. The incredible new technology could actually record on film the process of ovulation, the journey of the sperm from the vagina to the fallopian tube for fertilization, implantation of the embryonic mass in the uterine wall, the subsequent development of the fetus, and the birth of the baby. Nine months were telescoped into sixty minutes. I found myself sobbing—realizing that for all my bluster and accomplishments, something vitally important to me as a woman and human being was missing from my life: motherhood. All my successes simply moved the goal post back farther, and happiness continued to elude me. Then suddenly, this notion of being a mommy seemed transcendent and more important than any accomplishments.

Three years later, after I had my feminist-inspired tubal ligation reversed and married Lew Bishop, Deryk was born. Nonetheless, even through the pregnancy, I didn't really quite "get it." In spite of wearing maternity clothes the very first week of my pregnancy, I didn't yet understand what this experience ultimately means to a woman and a person.

I remember Lew and I watching yet another PBS program. This one was about lifeboat ethics—twenty-five people are on a boat fit for fifteen. The question—do you throw ten overboard so the fifteen can survive, or do you keep everyone aboard, hoping for a miracle but threatening the lives of all?

After seeing the program, I asked Lew what he would do if, after having a baby, all three of us were bobbing around the ocean, and he could save only one of us. Who would it be, the baby or me? Lew, not being dumb, refused to answer the question. I said, "Well, I'd save you because we are the primary relationship and we could always make a new baby."

See? I didn't yet get it.

Into about the second or third month, I woke Lew up in the middle of the night with one serious question, "Lew, how long can you tread water?" I finally got it. Something intense, unique, special, serious, and overwhelming naturally occurs between a mother and a child that becomes the focal point of the mother's life. She has created new life in her body—a life totally dependent upon her goodwill and good sense.

But bad ideas die hard. I made sure Lew knew that for every feeding or diaper change I did, he had to do one, and so forth. Once Deryk was born (and he was no easy baby), I cherished and selfishly protected all these special moments. I loved changing diapers and breast-feeding him. The sense of joy from watching him giggle as I wiped his bottom is frankly indescribable, as was the sense of significance I felt watching him take nourishment from my breast. I soon gave up the fifty-fifty nonsense and we settled into doing as a team whatever needed to be done.

I was home full-time while Lew earned a living to take care of us. I had been a local radio host prior to Deryk's birth, and I absolutely missed my radio work with a profoundly painful passion. I saw no way to work and to take care of Deryk myself. When Deryk was more than three years old, a very small radio station, KWNK, moved into the mall that was ten minutes' walking distance from our home—important because we could not afford two cars—and I was offered a radio job for $2,000 a month to work on-air live from noon until 3 P.M. Lew had been downsized, and we were struggling, so this money became the difference between paying the mort-gage or not.

Downstairs in this small mall was a place called KIDSTOP. It was run by former teachers and provided care for children while their parents shopped in the mall. KIDSTOP was adorable. It had more toys and instruction than could be imagined, and the owner was sweet with the children, who included her two sons about Deryk's age. I gave it a try to see if Deryk would enjoy the experience. He loved the playtime and managed to nap in the midst of the chaos. If he had reacted negatively to this environ-ment, I never would have accepted this part-time job.

After less than a year, I went to work for a small network, where I was able to work from our garage behind our home. Deryk would play at my feet while I broadcast 9 A.M. to noon—and during the five commercial and news breaks each hour, we would munch snacks and snuggle. I quit this network early on when it didn't pay for the broadcast equipment or my earnings, and I discovered that it was owned by a white supremacist group.

At this point, Lew's career seemed to collapse because of the lack of opportunities available to men in their fifties, and we were at risk of losing everything. We brainstormed. Lew suggested that our best option was to resurrect my radio career. We both committed to making sure that this never would interfere with my mothering and with our family. And it never has.

First, KFI in Los Angeles tried me out on Sunday afternoons. Then I got the job broadcasting Saturday and Sunday evenings. Essentially this meant that after Deryk and Lew went to bed, I'd go to work. After about a year, I was offered a full-time job Monday through Friday, 10 P.M. to 1 A.M. I was grateful and thrilled, and we had a decent income again. This meant that I would take care of Deryk all day, put him to bed at 9 P.M., and drive off to work. Yes, I was tired—but I had all week to take care of Deryk. We had the necessary income, and I was working at my first love: radio broadcasting—talking one-on-one to folks about life's issues.

Soon, Lew was working exclusively as my manager. There was some discussion at KFI about moving me to the more ratings-significant daytime hours because of the big audience I had in the evenings. I was panicked that they might offer afternoon drive (3 to 7 P.M.), because I would have to turn that down. I couldn't imagine Deryk coming home from school only to get a good-bye kiss from his mommy as she went off to work, not to return until it was time to put him to bed.

Fortunately for us, and for my career, I was assigned to noon to 2 P.M. While Deryk was in school, I did a radio show. This did not interfere with his life at all. I even wrote my first best-selling book, *Ten Stupid Things Women Do to Mess Up Their Lives*, in the wee hours of the morning when Deryk and Lew slept, and also after Deryk went off to school.

Our house rule is that Mom and Dad don't bring work home. The evening has always been strictly preserved as family time. Since the time we all converted and became observant Jews, from sundown Friday to sundown Saturday we observe Sabbath, and no work is done. Sundays, I write from 6 or 7 to 11 A.M. Then we all go out for lunch and have family day. I have always squeezed my career in around family life—never the other way around.

After my first book, I didn't go on book tours. For the first of my five bestsellers, Deryk came with me to five cities in four days. He did his assigned schoolwork on the trip and loved it. He travels well. I got sick (my sinuses hate airplanes and hotel air-conditioning). After that, I began to use TV satellite technology to avoid traveling. Twice for each book I get up at dawn and go to the satellite broadcast studio here in Los Angeles. We do fifteen- or twenty-five-minute interviews in as many cities around the nation—and that's that!

I do not do speaking tours. My only speaking engagements are the few I do to raise money for my Dr. Laura Schlessinger Foundation. Generally, Deryk and Lew come along—unless Deryk's in school. If I'm gone overnight, Daddy is with him full-time. Due to some emergencies, we had a brief experience with a part-time preschool in a Christian church, and had a baby-sitter for some hours once a week, but our basic, unwavering commitment has always been that one or both of us is always physically *there*.

It is amazing that I have become as successful as I have putting family and child first—always. If there were ever living proof that it could be done—I'm it. I have lived and continue to live what I nag.

It takes the value system, the decision, the commitment, and the sacrifice to do it. But our son has never felt neglected or less important than fame, fortune, or work.

So, contrary to what you often read or hear in the media, I really do practice what I preach, and so I know it can be done.

I got a letter not long ago from Chris Phillips in Escondido,

California, that warmed my heart at the same time it crystal-
lized my fear for our future.

*Yesterday my son and I were discussing the answer to an
interesting question posed to me by a questionnaire I received
from the Planetary Society, which is a space interest/education
organization. The question was: "If you could transmit one
picture or image to an alien civilization, what would it be?"
We agreed it would have to be something profound and something important. We discussed many things—the Statue of Liberty and such. My son suddenly shouted, "I know! I know!"
bouncing up and down. When I asked what, he said, "A family. A dad and a mom, and some kids, and a grandma and
grandpa." When asked why, he said with great conviction,
"Because it's the best thing. And aliens probably love their
families, so they would understand that."*

I'm afraid that by the time Chris's little boy's message gets a
response from somewhere out there in the cosmos, the reality of
family will have become an alien concept in our own civilization.

Divorces, full-time working mothers, stepfamilies, shacking
up, out-of-wedlock children, promiscuous reproduction, geographical fragmentation of the family, joint custody, and visitation are, to varying degrees, depending on the circumstances
and the child—a *disaster* to the lives and emotional well-being
of children.

It is now virtually impossible to make the above statement,
which would have been met with knowing nods in the 1950s,
without evoking a protest. People don't want to be told that
what they feel or believe they have to do (or simply want to
do) is wrong and may injure their children and society. While
compassion is an appropriate response for those who fall into
situations beyond their control through the death of a spouse,
severe illnesses, or abandonment, whitewashing the consequences to children is self-indulgent.

As a society we ignore what we know to be self-evident truths
about children, families, child rearing, commitment, and responsi-

bilities. We are willing to sacrifice what is noble and right for families to accommodate individuals who don't do right or behave nobly—all in the name of tolerance and the celebration of diversity. When this validation is reinforced by sources perceived as authoritative—mental health professionals or clergy—we are in deep trouble.

The May/June 1999 issue of *Psychology Today* features the "*new* rules" of parenting, under the title "By Any Other Name . . ."—a list of new vocabulary to describe the roles in rapidly changing family forms. These include binuclear family, social parent, serial parenting, distance parenting, nonresidential parent, and postdivorce family—just some of the examples of creative, nonjudgmental nomenclature used to identify the chaos adults choose to bring into the lives of helpless, dependent, vulnerable children.

"I am only twenty-one," writes Kristen Pietrowski, a future teacher from California, "but am I wrong in thinking this story in *Psychology Today* magazine is very sad? My classmates and my teacher (I am studying to be an elementary school teacher) told me to just 'accept this' as the norm. I have a broken heart thinking about all the students I will have in my future classes that have to deal with this as the 'norm.' Am I crazy?"

Contrast the *Psychology Today* list with a zoning ordinance in Sierra Madre, California (*Pasadena Star-News,* September 16, 1997): "People living together not related by blood, marriage or adoption, will not be defined as a 'family.' This was to change the pre-existing ordinance, which defined family as 'persons related by blood, marriage or adoption, living together as a single housekeeping unit in a dwelling unit.'" It also contained this astonishing corollary: "Family also means five persons or less, who need not be related each to the other, living together as a single housekeeping unit, in a dwelling unit. The redefinition was considered important because, as Councilwoman MaryAnn MacGillivray said, 'We didn't want to expand the definition of family into a garbage-can situation . . . The fact is this community takes a moral stand.'"

Don't think that this kind of stand isn't countered with hostility. The biggest weapon used in print media to dispense with common sense and values is the word "so-called." This word exists to mock what comes after it. I often see it written before such unacceptable and inflammatory concepts as "family values" or "traditional family."

A case in point was published in the *Wisconsin State Journal* on April 21, 1999, in a story about a (so-called) study conducted by the University of Michigan's Institute for Social Research. Without citing any independent or corroborating analysis of the study methodology or conclusions, the newspaper simply reported that "If you're a mother who works outside the home, you're no less of a mother than women who keep the home fires burning."

Now, how can that be? How can you be something to someone if you're not there all day to do it?

The article continues, "According to *Good Housekeeping* magazine, the study found that in so-called traditional families, parents spend an average of twenty-two hours a week with their children. In two-career families, children get nineteen hours of undivided attention."

It sounds like the reporter didn't bother to read the study itself but was relying on *Good Housekeeping*'s interpretation of the data (a scientific source?). The dreaded "so-called" only qualifies the "traditional family," not the "two-career families" whose children get their "undivided" attention. The traditional family only "spends" hours with their kids (presumably with divided attention?).

The reporter doesn't question how the researchers determined the number of hours, or even if the numbers make sense. What does it mean to "spend hours"? Does it include time sleeping, for example?

It is simply a fact that society's tolerance of virtually any "free choice," including illegitimacy, serial marriages, and divorced parents moving away from their children for job opportunities, has seriously jeopardized our children. Teen suicide has more than tripled. Juvenile crime is more prevalent and more violent. More children are diagnosed with mental illnesses and learning disorders. Overall school performance has declined. I would say this social experiment is a proven failure. Yet adults are so reluctant to give up self-gratification.

A stunning article by Barbara Dafoe Whitehead in the *Atlantic Monthly* (April 1993), ironically entitled "Dan Quayle Was Right," clarifies: "After decades of public dispute about so-called family diversity, the evidence from social-science research is coming in. The dissolution of two-parent families, though it may benefit the adults involved, is harmful to many children and dramatically undermines our society."

Ms. Whitehead points out that "family disruption is best understood not as a single event, but as a string of disruptive events—separation, divorce, life in a single-parent family, life with a parent and live-in lover, the remarriage of one or both parents, life in one step-parent family combined with visits to another step-parent family, the breakup of one or both step-parent families, and so on."

Many calls to my radio program concern some aspect of this "road to hell" for children. Though callers may mouth concern for the welfare of their children, they inevitably whine, "But what about *me*? What about *my* happiness? When am I entitled to what makes *me* happy? When am I going to get what *I* want?" Somewhere along the way the focus of American thinking shifted from respecting obligation and character (sexual fidelity, commitment to sacred vows, sacrifice for family) to seeking self-fulfillment and selfishness (sexual freedom, entitlement to perpetual bliss, nix the kids, spouse as oppressive constraint).

Lloyd Olivia Davis, AKA "Uppity Woman," wrote in her *Topeka Capital-Journal* column (February 2, 1995):

> You don't get to resign from parenthood. You don't get to tend to your "inner child" at the expense of your real ones. You

don't get to have the childhood you wish you had or wish you still had, while your children are having theirs.

As long as you have dependent children you are responsible for being a parent, whether you want to be responsible or not. And you don't get to opt out of your responsibility because your lover needs a place to stay or you need the school clothes money to make the payment on your Corvette. And you don't get to snort cocaine on your posh leather sofa or smoke crack on your tattered vinyl recliner because you've had a hard day. Sorry. So grow up.

In Loco Parentis

Over the last three decades, high school guidance counselors have seen their jobs change from helping students pick a college or a job (simple and basic) to trying to help children survive the fallout from a society that stretches the ethics of infertility treatment to help people desperate to make babies, at the same time as it marginalizes the importance of parents and trivializes the values necessary to raise these children to become decent human beings.

Andy Whelahan, a guidance counselor from Wellesley High School, said in the *Boston Globe* (May 17, 1999), "Kids are dealing with a lot of issues they never used to have to deal with, like broken families, abuses of all kinds, eating disorders, violence in the home, drug abuse, and suicidal thoughts. It used to be that they would communicate their concerns over the dinner table. But there is no dinner table time anymore; there's just not a lot of family time at all. So, we are here to be the shoulder and the guide that Mom and Dad used to be."

Now, as competent and caring as school guidance counselors can be, they are school employees with lives and families of their own. They can pay attention to a young person only for the time allotted to an appointment squeezed in between classes. Their necessarily limited attention can't possibly substitute for the loving investment of time, attention, warmth, and joy that a mom and dad are supposed to be there to provide.

Just Plain "Loco"

But even guidance counselors are probably irrelevant, according to *The Nurture Assumption*—a book about adolescence by Judith Rich Harris, full of bizarre opinion masquerading as research that argues that parenting doesn't matter. Nothing that mothers and fathers do will have any long-term effect on their children. Genes and peer-group pressures are the real formative factors.

Despite the fact that leading child development experts, such as Harvard's Jerome Kagan and T. Berry Brazelton, discredited the thesis as nonsense, the media gave this book extraordinary attention. Why?

As John Leo of *U.S. News & World Report* points out in an article about the book, "Many anxious parents want reassurance that their child-rearing habits haven't hurt their children. And self-absorbed parents with a track record of putting their own desires ahead of their children's needs want absolution, now available in book form for only $26."

This garbage is all part of the swill of books and articles arguing that divorce doesn't hurt children, quality time is superior to quantity time, fathers don't matter, day care is superior to mothering, and all that matters to children is that their parents' lives are fulfilling.

Jacqueline Kennedy Onassis said it best: "If you bungle raising your children, I don't think whatever else you do well matters very much."

Yet it is the "whatever else" that our society is obsessively focused on. In the same way Margaret Mead studied so-called uncivilized cultures, several anthropologists are evidently studying the families in California's Silicon Valley, according to *USA*

Today (May 26, 1999). Evidently, they have unusual customs, too.

Lisa McNally from Oklahoma City wrote me about the article. *These are two-income families who use e-mail and pagers to communicate with each other.*

They don't grocery shop (lists are e-mailed to grocers who deliver). They don't take their kids to extracurricular activities (companies are hired to transport them), and it seems they rarely see their children.

It is as if they treat their children as animals. The parents are so busy with their lifestyles that they have to hire someone to let their children out—such as letting a dog out of the house so he won't mess on the carpet.

The whole article is appalling and unbelievable, but the most unbelievable part about it is that this way of life is acceptable to those who live there. What organized people they must be to be able to have it all—kids involved in activities and wonderful jobs—without ever skipping a beat. I believe the "families" have skipped the biggest beat of all—the beat of one's heart when they hold their spouse or their child just because.

Now I must go because it is time to put my two oldest boys to bed—being on the computer writing you for the last five minutes has already taken enough time from them.

Some of the most horrifying books ever written were horrifying specifically because they presented a Brave New World where some government force depersonalized life with technology. Human bonds and intimacy were virtually eliminated, and the children were institutionalized and trained by the state. I can hardly believe that what was once considered inhuman and oppressive is now being intentionally chosen. What was once considered a horror is now being embraced.

And not only embraced but celebrated! Renee, a listener, sent me a copy of an article about the ultimate working "so-called" mother published in the *Toledo Blade* (May 2, 1999) touting her accomplishment as Owen-Corning's first million-dollar bonus employee. Evidently this career success was not without its price: "I was only in town fourteen business days last year," she said. "It was a year of sacrifice. It took a lot of time and energy. My dogs are mad at me, and even my kids are a little mad at me."

Mind you, she has two teenage children, is divorced, and is planning a wedding sometime in June 2000. Her kids don't have an intact home, saw their mother sometime in the two weeks she was around, but she had time for a love life. This gets a congratulatory article in a major metropolitan newspaper, with no nasty adjectives, no judgmental commentary, no critical quotes from colleagues or child development experts.

You have to be blind not to see the conspiracy to weaken what has been one of the most important institutions over thousands of years of human existence—the family as protector of the children. I receive thousands of stories, articles, and letters with examples of attempts by business, government, professional associations, and media to eliminate the *Ozzie and Harriet* ideal of home. *The Donna Reed Show*, *Father Knows Best*, and *Leave It to Beaver* images of the traditional family are feared because they emphasize the sacrifices necessary to guarantee a cohesive family that many don't want to make. So the next best thing to improving performance, I guess, is to lower the bar—in this case, to the floor! Whatever happened to the notion of rising to the challenge?

This conspiracy is designed to undermine families and marginalize children in favor of a life devoid of a moral framework and to assuage the guilt of the intentionally inadequate and the blatantly selfish or deviant.

The Institute for American Values released a report in 1997 called "Closed Hearts, Closed Minds: The Textbook Story of Marriage." It was an evaluation of the nation's twenty leading college-level textbooks on marriage and family life. Its findings include the following dismal facts:

➤ Family textbooks are almost twice as likely to devote space to the topic of "swinging" as to the relationship between family structure and juvenile crime.

➤ Family textbooks display remarkably little interest in the effects of marital disruption or single parenting on children, devoting an average of only 3.5 pages to this topic.

➤ Just 24 of 338 total chapters in these textbooks deal with family effects on children. Three times as much space is devoted to adult relations, without regard to how they affect children.

➤ Current textbooks convey a pessimistic view of marriage. The potential costs of marriage to adults receive exaggerated treatment, while the benefits of marriage, both to individuals and to society, are downplayed or ignored.

➤ Current textbooks are riddled with glaring errors, distortions of research, omissions of important data, and incorrect attributions of scholarship.

The author of the study, Professor Norval D. Glenn, a professor of the University of Texas at Austin, is a former editor of both the *Journal of Family Issues* and *Contemporary Sociology*, and a board member of the *Journal of Marriage and the Family* since 1979. He commented, "Often what is presented in these books as an 'expert consensus' is sharply at odds with much of the weight of social science evidence. The result is a one-sided story of marriage that seriously downplays the importance of marriage in benefiting adults and protecting children."

Who Benefits?

How is it that so many supposedly educated and professional folks would mislead, exaggerate, distort, and outright lie about such important issues as marriage and family? What is the underlying agenda?

As detectives determined to find the perpetrator always ask in homicide cases, who stands to benefit the most from the "expert consensus"? Not children—they end up with unsafe, insecure situations in which they are neglected. Not adults—all research indicates psychological, emotional, economic, and physical well-being is increased within families. So who *does* benefit from discounting these truths?

Is it those who wish to justify their inadequacies or tortured family histories? Denying the value of commitment and sacrifice for family and children might be the way in which some professional "experts" deal with their own childhood loss and pain, caused by parental neglect and inadequacy.

Is it those who wish to justify their challenges and choices? The agenda of homosexual activists has moved past the demand for tolerance and respect to demanding acceptance of homosexuality as healthy, normal, and equivalent in every way to heterosexuality. Necessary to advancing this agenda is undermining the significance of the traditional definition of family as husband, wife, and children. Once that is accomplished, any combination of partners becomes automatically acceptable or valid. Homosexual marriage, adoption, and childbearing are seen only in the context of satisfying the desires of the adult individual and not in the broader context of the best interest of children or society. Many of those who disparage men for telling their pregnant lady friend to abort, or for abandoning their families, are the same people who support two lesbians having a child without a father at all.

Perhaps those who benefit from distorting the facts about families and children are people who wish to eliminate G-d and the Ten Commandments from earthly life. It is astonishing how much disdain there is in the mainstream media and among the cultural elite for belief in a Higher Power and in a universal morality. Although this country was originally conceived as a land promising "inalienable rights" given by G-d, there is no respect for religion as a factor in national life.

The First Amendment has been distorted from freedom *of* religion to an insistence on freedom *from* religion. The result is a secular mentality that anoints feeling and desires as divine— idol worship at its most destructive. We become our own gods, marching to our own version of a new commandment—if it feels good, do it! Contrast this with G-d's Commandments, which require us to be righteous in spite of our desires.

Are the beneficiaries of the "big lie" to be found among the feminists? The lesbian feminist activists at Barnard College in New York were successful last year in "cleansing" the recruitment brochure sent to parents of marriage statistics for Barnard graduates. The statistics had to be removed to calm the nerves of lesbians who claimed it was insulting for the college to attempt to assure parents that Barnard graduates *do* get married.

F. Carolyn Graglia, author of *Domestic Tranquility: A Brief Against Feminism*, wrote in the *Wall Street Journal* on August 7, 1998:

> Feminism isn't anti-sex. It's only anti-family. The founding principle of NOW [National Organization for Women] was that women should abandon homemaking and child rearing and enter the workplace, so as to become economically and politically independent from men. Childcare, in the words of one critic of the domestic role, is "boring, tedious and lonely" and the greatest impediment to her career success. Being financially dependent on a husband is "irksome and humiliating."
>
> Do those who worship "freedom" heedlessly and irrationally stand to benefit from the destruction of the family? The American Library Association (ALA) Bill of Rights proclaims that libraries should not discriminate against access to information by *age*. Thus, children have a right to access anything they want on the Internet, including pornography. It is the ALA's

position that the responsibility for protecting children should rest with the parents, even though parents cannot always be present when their children are in the library, and computer screens are highly visible, unlike the contents of books.

It's time we take our civilization back from the moral and social chaos it has devolved into. Is this hopeless? While I often despair, I am not without hope, especially after receiving the following essay from a sixth-grade student, sent by her teacher, Marla Schlatter, in 1997. The assignment was to describe what it would be like to be your own parent.

LOVE WITHOUT ENDING

As a parent I must always think of my children before myself. If there is something that I want, but there is something my child needs, I have to get that thing for my child. I must be totally unselfish. Being a parent means that I've got to put other people's needs in front of my own, no matter what. Being a parent is hard work, but I will love it.

We must acknowledge that we've gone wrong. Syndicated author Kathleen Parker may have started the ball rolling in her May 1999 column entitled "We Owe the Children an Apology": "I'm sorry. That we adults have shirked our duties to rear, nurture and protect you. That we've convinced ourselves that you don't need two parents—a mother and a father—but that any sex-neutral combo will do. I'm sorry. That even when you were nearly newborn, we handed you over to strangers, whom we trusted to care for you, but who, in our hearts, we knew couldn't love you as we would. I'm sorry."

I join Ms. Parker in apologizing for other such ostensibly well-meaning experiments:

➤ The early sexualization of children in schools through the introduction of sex education at the elementary level, the distribution of condoms on the premises, and on-site medical clinics where children can be counseled and treated, often without parental consent or notification.

➤ The widespread acceptance of abortion as another form of birth control, and easy access to clinics and doctors for teenagers who, in many places, do not need parental consent.

➤ Psychotropic medication to deal with a wide range of behaviors, from attention deficit disorder to depression, many of which would undoubtedly improve without medication with more time and attention from parents and caring adults.

➤ Giving children the power to challenge authority and disobey rules by legitimizing their rebellion with lawsuits and providing access to the courts to resolve problems that should have been solved by expulsion from school, grounding at home, or incarceration.

➤ Elimination of family rituals such as eating dinner together daily, vacationing together, practicing a religion and going to church, thereby robbing children's lives of reverence, significance, and stability.

➤ Modeling behavior that values acquisition, power, and selfishness through emphasis on career and materialism and neglect of children and family.

➤ Tolerating a mass-media environment of immorality, ignorance, violence, and vulgarity; worse, ignoring it by not monitoring what children listen to, watch, read, or play with.

Fourteen-year-old Amanda McAlpine had it right in her article about what is wrong with kids today published in the Springfield, Missouri, *News-Leader* (June 15, 1998). Her answer:

The adults of today. Parents used to help their children grow up. Now they just watch them grow up. Parents used to correct their kids. Now they just ignore them. Parents have traded their children for jobs, money and stuff—more stuff, bigger stuff, better stuff. No one is there for the kids at home. Teens need a mom at home for them, more so than a baby does.

Our computers, TV, radios are full of trash, murder, sex, blood, gore and guts. It makes me sick. Did a child put that trash on the airways? I don't think so. Well, who is responsible for it? Adults. If parents loved their kids they would put a stop to it.

People, wake up, take control, take your kids to church. Get out the book of instructions (the Bible) and use it. Be what you would like your kids to be—good, honest decent people. Love them. Listen to them. Be there for them. You will have a better life with love from your kids than with money, bigger stuff, newer cars and designer clothes.

Spend time with your kids, get to know them and about them. Use the word "no" and mean it. Moms need to be at home with a big hug ready like my mom.

And the children shall lead us.

More than 550 high school students in Annapolis, Maryland, responded to a survey asking them what they believed caused children to be violent. The results were published in the *Annapolis Capital* (May 5, 1999). Guess what the top two answers were? Number one—lack of parental attention and guidance. Number two—lack of discipline in the home and in school. Numbers three and four indicated what numbers one and two might save children from—peer pressure and guns.

Our society has abdicated its responsibility to support the traditional family, and the destructive results are all too evident. It is not an accident that the first commandment in Genesis is to go forth and multiply. Being a parent is a blessing from G-d and an obligation to G-d.

It is telling that *Nightline*'s Ted Koppel once wondered

aloud whether my radio signature "I Am My Kid's Mom" was meant to be provocative! No, Ted. It is a statement of my ultimate responsibility and my intense gratitude for what having my son has given me.

This book is my entreaty to parents to get more involved in their children's lives and to help their children to understand right from wrong. For many parents this may mean a radical change in lifestyle, behaviors, attitudes, choices, and feelings. This is likely to be an upsetting process, because there is little in society to support a family-focused life and because the "progressive" establishment will make things uncomfortable for you. This may be a time when you need the values and compassionate support of your religious community. You know, that religion you never had time for, or disagreed with, or outgrew.

1

The Death of the Family

Here, Dad. I'd like you to sign this form and have it notarized:

"*I, the undersigned Dad, attest that I have never parented before, and insofar as I have no experience in the job, I am liable for my mistakes and I agree to pay for any counseling in perpetuity Calvin may require as a result of my parental ineptitude.*"

I don't see how you're allowed to have a kid without signing one of those!

Calvin and Hobbes, by Bill Watterson, 1993

"The Family Must Go!"

"The nuclear family structure has to be abolished before women can be totally liberated was the opinion of 100 participants in the first statewide [Wisconsin] Women's Liberation Conference . . ." (*The Sentinel*, May 11, 1970). The article goes on to say that "Feminists at the conference believe a child shouldn't be limited to one mother or father. They say the child would benefit from being reared by a variety of individuals."

Mrs. Carl W. Thompson, then associated with the Center for Women's and Family Living at the University of Wisconsin, and wife of Senator Thompson, prophesied that "In twenty years there won't be the formal marriage as today. It's happening now. These [fluid, unmarried couplings] are meaningful relationships. They just don't want to get into the traditional thing."

While many feminists have decried marriage, parenthood, and child care as oppressive, degrading, and designed to enslave women, most folks yearn for the love, commitment, home, hearth, and attachments that marriage and families provide—however imperfectly.

Nonetheless, the paranoia and hyper-individualism projected by that conference did accurately portend the destruction of the family. Under the mantle of exaggerated freedom of expression and experience came a loosening of the ties that bind us. No-fault, no-stigma divorce; shacking up without shame; bearing children out of wedlock as a privilege; aborting babies for personal convenience; birth control for pregnancy-free promiscuity; tolerating single parenting and gay adoption as valid social experiments; and constant propaganda promoting child-free parenting through day care have all served to undermine the value and very existence of the family unit.

Family is what kids need and want. "Almost one-quarter (22 percent) of Generation X (ages eighteen to twenty-four) say that a lack of family structure and guidance are the most important issues it faces . . ." according to a poll reported in *USA Today* (October 30, 1995). These concerns take precedence over AIDS and illiteracy (each 15 percent), violence (14 percent), and drugs (9 percent). "'The collapse of many of our social institutions, like the family, has left its mark on them,' said Ross Goldstein of Generation Insights that tracks social trends."

There is no question that Generation X has been damaged by the coming to pass of Mrs. Thompson's greatest dream.

According to an article on the politics of Gen X in the August 1999 issue of the *Atlantic Monthly:*

> Gen Xers have internalized core beliefs and characteristics that bode ill for the future of American democracy. This generation is more likely to describe itself as having a negative attitude toward America, and as placing little importance on citizenship and national identity, than its predecessors. And Xers exhibit a more materialist and individualistic streak than did their parents at a similar age. Moreover, there is a general decline in social trust among the young, whether that is trust in their fellow citizens, in established institutions or in elected officials. These tendencies are, of course, related: heightened individualism and materialism, as Alexis de Tocqueville pointed out, tend to isolate people from one another, weakening the communal bonds that give meaning and force to notions of national identity and the common good.

The article minimizes the influence on Xer apathy of the breakdown of the traditional family where children learn about love, commitment, obligation, compassion, and duty. Instead, the analysis goes on at great length about the importance of the politics of the economy. Yet, later, the text offers that "There are numerous indications that Xers—many of whom grew up without a formal religion—are actively searching for a moral compass to guide their lives, and a recent poll suggests that the highest priority for the majority of young adults is building a strong and close-knit family."

No matter what, it always comes back to the family. It is within the family, and best in the context of a relationship with G-d, that children come to believe life in general, and their life in particular, is worth living and has meaning and ultimate purpose. Otherwise, children are left with only the most self centered survival mode—acquire and compete. I haven't read too many autobiographies of folks who described themselves as happy with only those two concepts to guide and comfort them. Have you?

In fact, one particular section of Senator John McCain's 1999 autobiography was heralded as "the rare passage in a political book parents will want to read aloud to their children" (*Los Angeles Times*, September 6, 1999). Noting that McCain spent five and one-half years as a prisoner of war in Vietnam, the reporter wrote, "In captivity, he demonstrated a personal fortitude that answers any questions about his capacity to handle the pressure of the White House. Yet the book's most powerful moment is his realization, in the darkest hours, that what allowed him to survive was not so much his *individual* strength as his communal allegiances—his religious conviction, love of country and faith in his fellow prisoners. The candidate writes, 'Glory . . . is not a decoration for valor . . . [It] belongs to the act of being constant to something greater than yourself, to a cause, to your principles, to the people on whom you rely, and who rely on you in return.'"

This is not what we are teaching our children. As we marginalize the value of traditional family allegiance and sacrifice, we are creating an "each for himself" mindset.

The Family Must Stay!

Edward, an attorney and listener, wrote of his experience standing up for the family.

We (myself, wife, and two girls, eleven and fifteen) listen to you regularly on WLS in Chicago. I just had an interesting conversation at a traffic light. The SUV in front of me had a license plate frame which read "LOVE MAKES A FAMILY."

Now, at first glance, that sounds romantic and correct, doesn't it? Not to Edward!

At the next stoplight, I pulled up alongside, rolled down my passenger-side window, and the following conversation occurred:

ME (EDWARD): *"Excuse me. I respectfully disagree with the statement on your license plate frame."*

SHE: *"Okay—I'll listen."*

ME: *"I presume you are married and have children?"*

SHE: *"Yes, that's correct."*

ME: *"Have you ever wanted to stick your husband's head in the toilet and flush it—or stick your kid's hand in the toaster, set for crisp?"*

SHE: *"Of course, haven't you?"*

ME: *"Yes, of course. But neither of us did. I'll bet you weren't feeling very loving at that moment."*

SHE: *"You got that right!"*

ME: *"While I admit love is very important, it appears that there must be something else involved too . . ."*

SHE: *(thoughtfully) "Hmmmm. What might that be?"*

ME: *"Commitment. Carbon-based creatures, shacking up, knocking out a kid—they say they love each other. Do they have a family? I don't think so. The difference between you and me and them is commitment."*

SHE: *(thoughtfully . . . long pause) "You know, I think I'll take that frame off. Thanks."*

Commitment is taught by the words and deeds of those who populate our children's most vulnerable and impressionable years. If these adults are rarely there or mostly hired help with high turnover; if their interaction and input are limited; if their focus is on their own harried work schedules or serial love lives, they are not mature and stable role models. Thus, the concept of commitment will never persist as a cultural standard.

I believe our job as parents, writes Susan, a listener, *is to civilize our young, and provide society with decent, moral citizens. If, along the way, parents are able to provide nice things, etc., that's nice. But the only things a parent "owes" a child are the parents' total concentration for about twenty years, their love and guidance (both physical and spiritual) and the requisite food, clothing, and shelter.*

From the *Atlantic Monthly* essay to Susan's letter, it is clear that the job done by the commitment of mother and father in the context of the family has not only personal ramifications for that child, but also social and political ramifications in the world. The universe is affected by the values honed (or not) within the family, because the products of each home—the adult children—go out into that world seeing themselves as either takers or givers, participants in something greater than themselves or the centers of their own universes.

On numerous occasions I have chastised a caller on the practical consequences of that concept. I often get calls from divorced or never-married parents who are planning a move to get on with their love life and leave their child behind. I always remind them that "Whatever you do that hurts your child— including the misplaced guilt, confusion, pain, and anger caused by your neglect and abandonment because your relationship with the other parent just didn't work out—creates a child with less patience, compassion, morals, and self-control.

"In other words," I continue, "when your kid is hurting, he or she is more likely to hurt some other kid—maybe mine. As a fellow citizen and human being, you owe me something. And part of what you owe me is not to launch a child irresponsibly into this world who is spoiling for a fight because you left him. It isn't, and can never be, just about you. You, as one person, are so important. Your actions have impact on the universe. Think about that while you're packing!"

"The family is not one of several alternative life-styles," writes James Q. Wilson for *Reader's Digest* (March 1996). "It is not an arena in which rights are negotiated; it is not an old-fashioned barrier to a promiscuous sex life; it is not a set of cost-benefit calculations. It is a commitment for which there is no feasible substitute. No child ought to be brought into a world where that commitment—from both parents—is absent.

"There is no way," Dr. Wilson continues, "to prepare for the commitment other than to make it. Living together is not a way of finding out how married life will be, because married life is shaped by the fact that the couple has made a solemn vow before their family and friends that this is for keeps and that any children will be their joint and permanent responsibility. It changes everything."

And So It Went . . .

"New Study Finds Traditional Families in Only 26% of Homes," shouted the headline in the *Los Angeles Times* (November 24, 1999), announcing the dramatic decline in the stable, two-parent, child-raising family unit in America.

Unbelievably, this development is seen by many in the media, social science professions, and liberal activist groups as a positive development. Indeed, there are many who advocate and/or directly profit from the decline of the traditional family, including homosexual activists, radical feminists, welfare advocates, and the child care industry. Clearly, the one group that doesn't benefit from the liberal, self-indulgent, creative variations on the theme of family is the children. I don't think anyone would argue that America's children are not in crisis.

The National Marriage Project at Rutgers University issued a report on July 4, 1999. It states quite bluntly:

> Nothing could be more anti-marriage than much of popular culture. As an institution marriage has lost much of its legal, religious and social meaning and authority. It has dwindled to a "couples relationship" mainly designed for the sexual and emotional gratification of each adult. With the growing plurality of intimate relationships, people now tend to speak inclusively about "relationships" and "intimate partners," burying marriage within a general category. Moreover, some elites seem to believe that support for marriage is synonymous with far-right political or religious views, discrimination against single parents, and tolerance of domestic violence.
>
> These attitudes prevail despite consistent documentation that

marriage is healthy for adults and critical to the development of children. This fact is being denied, challenged, lied about, distorted, or ignored by people and movements that seek to replace this time-honored social and sacred contract with "do your own thing," which changes rapidly and unpredictably.

Oh, Give Me a Home . . . Where My Family Can Roam

The facts in the *Los Angeles Times* story referred to above are extremely disturbing. Not only is the traditional family represented in only 26 percent of American homes, but the University of Chicago researchers who did the study say that "Americans are becoming more accepting of these changes."

While June Cleaver might not approve, Americans seem to be accepting what Tom W. Smith, director of the survey conducted annually by the university's National Opinion Research Center, calls the "modern family." For example, 67 percent of people surveyed disagreed with the statement that parents ought to stay together just because they have children.

"The single earner families with young children still present in the household have become the exception rather than the rule," said Smith.

Other findings include: 56 percent of adults were married (barely half), compared with 75 percent in 1972, the first year of the survey; 51 percent of children lived in a household with their two parents (73 percent in 1972); the percentage of children living with single parents rose to 18 percent, versus about 4.5 percent in 1972.

Marital instability and nonmarriage have become dominant characteristics of our era. This destructive and dangerous downward slide has numerous causes:

➤ The exodus of families to urban centers from small, close-knit homogenous communities where family values were esteemed, and social pressure was a deterrent to divorce and out-of-wedlock births.

➤ The ready access to birth control and abortion that loosened the spiritual and practical connection between sexuality and marriage, resulting in a marked increase in out-of-wedlock births.

➤ The feminist movement's obsession with independent financial power, leading women to value personal success over marital and family obligations and making single parenting, no-fault divorce, and full-time day care noble rights rather than last resorts.

➤ The abdication of values with respect to sexual behavior, leading to an increased societal acceptance of abortion as "family planning" (ironic term, isn't it?), and single parenting as equivalent to a nuclear family.

➤ The increasing concentration of liberal psychological "experts" whose research is tainted by advocacy positions, resulting in distortions and misinformation about childbearing, child rearing, child care, marriage, divorce, stepfamilies, shacking up, same-sex marriage and parenting, which confuses and intimidates naïve civilians about the importance of the traditional family as the ideal setting for raising children.

➤ The media that glamorize so-called freedom with respect to sexual behavior and child rearing, while marginalizing and demeaning commitment, sacrifice, and values.

➤ The growing cultural materialism that values money, power, and possessions over sacrifice and commitment to family.

➤ The welfare fiasco that undermines family structure by protecting and rewarding reproductive "rights" over reproductive responsibility.

➤ The movement to destigmatize behaviors once thought to be immoral and destructive for the sake of self-esteem, political correctness, and New Age dogma that *condemns* judgment.

➤ The growing disregard for the religious foundation of healthy sexuality and family obligations.

In general, when compared with children in two-parent families, children in single-parent homes have lower measures of academic achievement. They also have increased levels of stress, depression, anxiety, and aggression; more sexual experience, mental illness, substance abuse, juvenile delinquency, and membership in gangs, as well as other physical, emotional, and behavioral problems. Additionally, the one-parent family is correlated with an increased risk of poverty; infant mortality; child abuse and neglect; violence; and less parental attention, affection, and supervision.

"Something is seriously and deeply wrong with a society that has lost its ability to foster stable environments—especially two-parent families with married biological parents—within which children are loved and protected. The barometer of this failing is a vicious one: the increasing abuse of children and the related increase in violent crime" (The Heritage Foundation: "Child Abuse Crisis," June 3, 1997).

The plain, commonsense truth about families is that kids want 'em and need 'em. Period.

School Days . . . School Daze

In a survey for *Investors Business Daily* by the Technometrica Institute of Policy and Politics, more than two hundred CEOs and CFOs from the nation's fastest growing publicly held companies were asked their opinions on the state of education in America. What makes this survey significant is that these executives inherit the product of America's educational system as employees. Their answers reflect their experiences in training, hiring, and firing young, hopeful workers.

Ostensibly, this poll was intended to condemn or congratulate America's public educational system. While most executives believed that schools need to adopt a traditional back-to-basics educational program including phonics, basic math, reading comprehension, spelling, and vocabulary, the headline on the article was "Are Parents Behind Ed Crisis? Top CEOs Think So, Citing Empty Homes as Problem" (October 27, 1997)!

"More business leaders fault parents for the system's failure than they do teachers, teachers' unions or the government," says the article. "'I think the problem is 90 percent parents, 10 percent teachers,' said Reid Bechtle, CEO of Computer Learning Centers Inc.

"Not having parents in the home is a serious problem," the executives reported. "A full 78 percent of them say parents should take the *lead* role in improving their kids' education. The more that parents are working or away from the home, the less they're supervising their kids' studies and getting involved in their schools."

USA Today (September 8, 1997) published a survey from the Educational Communications department of Who's Who Among America's Teachers. The headline was "Teachers Flunk Parents." They asked veteran teachers a number of questions about parents and how their parenting behaviors have changed during their teaching careers:

➤ 73 percent said parents were less willing/able to give their kids time.

➤ 69 percent said parents were less ethical/moral.

➤ 63 percent said parents were less involved in kids' school lives.

➤ 53 percent said parents were more self-centered.

Ouch.

Family life with children requires more emphasis on children than Power Bar breakfasts and kissing them off to school or day care, shuttles from after-school day care to extracurricular activities, wolfing down fast-food takeout, unsupervised evening activities, and weekend teen mall roaming. Frankly, children's very existence needs to be the central focus of the family. This must include attention to their need for love, nurturing, support, tutoring, coaching, supervision, discipline, values instruction, family meal rituals, and just plain silly "goofing off" time. Or else? Or else the children don't just do poorly in school; they do poorly in life, as well.

Deborah, one of my listeners, wrote an impassioned letter to me after the 1999 tragedy at Columbine High School in Colorado.

I am a former PTA president, tutor and mother of three. I am very active in educational issues as I have a child at each educational level: high, middle and elementary school. I'm what you might call a professional volunteer. I have made some personal observations over the past several years and would like to share them.

Schools, instead of being basic institutions of learning, have become more and more the centers for all kinds of services to benefit families. They offer parenting classes, free health clinics, adult literacy programs, behavioral classes, health curriculums, drug education. The list goes on and on. Now they are being called upon to handle peace and security. We have more support for families today outside the home than ever before. Yet, are our families more successful, productive and loving than before?

1. The divorce rate is continuing to grow. I can't think of a better way to bring chaos and instability into a child's life.

2. *Elementary children are warehoused in huge after school programs, sometimes not picked up until 6 P.M. or later. Middle and high school students are on their own, unsupervised.*

3. *Many families spend much too little time even eating together during the week. One of my daughter's friends asked, "Do you do this every night?" when invited to dinner at our house.*

4. *Poor homework and study habits are one of the major character flaws I have noticed. Many parents do not see the value in making their children do assigned schoolwork. Why? Because it takes effort on the parents' part to sit down and help them.*

5. *Many children are not eager to learn, have poor behavior skills and little if any manners.*

6. *Adults are not setting examples for children on appropriate entertainment choices. A friend recently found an old copy of* Seventeen *magazine from the '70s that had been her mother's in high school. The girls looked like girls, not sexualized women. The articles were on health and beauty, not sexual practices and techniques. Where are parental supervision and complaints?*

7. *Children today have less respect for authority figures. When parents abdicate their parental responsibility for overseeing and enforcing limits on behavior and recreational practices of their children, then children get the message that they are in charge.*

Children are in charge only because adults are egocentrically focused on their personal gratification, careers, and love and/or sex lives.

Even those parents who maintain that desperate economic demands require sacrificing time and attention their children need probably could do it differently *and* better. I have spoken with innumerable people who, once convinced they were completely constrained by forces outside their control, came to realize that was often more perception than reality. Once they adopted the determined attitude of a NASA executive who said (on learning Apollo 13 astronauts might never return from the moon due to a power failure), "Failure is not an option!" they began to explore alternative income-generating solutions that didn't shortchange their children.

Ideas range from at-home businesses, spouses working split shifts or evenings, to moving to a less expensive place and seriously budgeting for a different lifestyle. Remarkable in their letters to me is the pride, rather than regret, over what others might consider substantial losses in freedom, status, and privileges.

There just isn't much value placed these days on self-sacrifice and obligation. These values have been replaced by self-centered ideals of acquisition and (preferably instant) gratification, with no opportunity left unexplored, no whim, desire, or want left unfulfilled. Amazingly, our society seems surprised when our inexperienced, immature, valueless, and undisciplined children behave in *exactly the same way*, and the results are promiscuity, violence, addictions, deviancy, and death.

There is much parents have to teach their children to prepare them for life, love, work, friendship, loss, and death. There is no "quality time" that can be set aside for sacred and significant communications. It is a continual process of opportunities and surprises, and those memorable moments show up when least expected within a *quantity* of time spent together. For any of this to work out right, the "time" must be the ongoing present. That means parents have to be available, aware, and alert. Are you ready to hear that?

The following young graduate of the Philadelphia College of Textiles and Science isn't. "What's wrong with wanting to work crazy hours to become a millionaire by the time you're thirty? I see what he [the commencement speaker] is saying about personal and moral responsibility. But I really think that you can work hard and still raise kids who won't shoot up their schools" (*Philadelphia Inquirer*, May 17, 1999).

This graduate, who requested that his or her heartfelt philosophy be quoted without attribution (do we hide things we believe are right or good?), was responding to a graduation speech given by Stephen L. Carter, a professor of law at Yale University. Carter told the students that whatever they choose to become—doctors, lawyers, entrepreneurs, or engineers—they need to start ranking *family* over work, children over bosses. "The tragedy of our workplace today is that it is not set up to honor commitment to family . . . Our young people are in a spiritual crisis, crying out at us for a clear sense of what is right and what is wrong," he said. "And often, we are too busy doing something else to stop and listen."

It's My Life, Isn't It?

Leslie Maxon, Ph.D., is a licensed clinical psychologist in private practice in Glendale, California, according to the mini-bio following her advice column in *L.A. Parent* magazine (October 1994). In this column, a married lawyer, complete with housekeeper, is struggling with the decision to work full-time so she can become a partner in the law firm. She writes, "I can't decide what's best for me *and* my kids."

Here comes Maxon's answer! "The important thing to remember is that there is not a right or wrong solution to this problem—the decision has to feel right to *you* . . . the tradeoff, of course, is you do not have the satisfaction of extra time with your kids. Tough choice!"

She then ruminates about how families should make this decision together to "help mom as well as kids develop their potential. Happy responsive mothers tend to be the ones who have meaningful projects—whether paid or volunteer—in addition to their mothering."

I completely *plotzed* reading this. No "right or wrong"? "Has to *feel* right"? "*You* do not have the satisfaction of extra time with your kids." "Meaningful projects"—a full-time lawyer's job is simply a "meaningful project"?

I contend that psychologists are the last people on earth who should be giving advice. First of all, they are trained to deal with psychopathology or mental disorder. Second, the liberal philosophy that dominates the psychological community today makes personal adult satisfaction paramount. Third, they are also trained to eschew morality as it is so variable, subjective, judgmental, and personal. The irony is that psychology is *deceptive* when it asserts it takes no moral position. Saying there is no wrong answer or action is a moral conclusion. Saying that decisions should be made on personal feelings is a moral conclusion.

Furthermore, the mother's question clearly asks about what is best for her children. Anyone with basic common sense knows that having parents around, involved, and interested in *them* is what is important to kids. Maxon leaves that issue alone because the liberal feminist mantra—child care, marriage, and men are oppressive—precludes any discussion of obligation and sacrifice for family. This is not the kind of reinforcement our families and our children need to "*develop their potential.*"

Sadly, Americans are sinking to the occasion. Americans would rather curl up with a good book or lounge in front of the television than spend time with their families, according to a survey released July 8, 1998, by the Harris Poll. This poll of Americans' leisure activities showed that 30 percent of those surveyed chose reading and 21 percent chose watching television as their favorite pastime, compared to 13 percent who chose spending time with family.

"Gone are the days when every American family seemed to include four kids, a dog, and a station wagon . . ." writes Bella English (*Boston Globe*, August 12, 1999). "According to the U.S. Census Bureau, one-third of American families started today will have only one child. Three-person families have grown from ten million in 1972 to more than fifteen million. Experts cite various reasons for the downsizing: two working parents under a time crunch, better-educated women who know what they can realistically juggle, the increasing costs of raising children . . ."

I doubt that this will lead to more so-called quality time for those lone remaining receptacles of all good wishes and expectations. As Thomas J. Saccenti, the executive director of Community Counseling Services, Inc., in Bucyrus, Ohio, wrote: "Quality is built with small details over time. If we made cars like we make kids, with quality time, the Mercedes-Benz could have great door panels and head rests, but the engine could fall out. Quality is not chunks of greatness."

An editorial cartoon in the *Indianapolis Star* (June 20, 1999) handled the time issue so well in response to school shootings. It depicts a politician blaming the school; Hollywood blaming the gun makers; churches blaming Hollywood . . . and parents were *not available* for comment.

Even that great role model for family values, President Bill Clinton, is quoted as saying, "'Americans are suffering because they are spending far less time with their families than a generation ago. And,' he warned, 'unless we act now, that problem will get worse'" (*Los Angeles Times*, May 24, 1999). This rhetoric was part of his plan at the time to promote federally financed family leave for parents after a birth or adoption. All well and good, but this does very little for ongoing family life.

Nah, Kids Don't Really Care About Family Time!

This afternoon, as I was having an early dinner with my daughter at a local restaurant, I heard something on the radio that shocked me beyond belief, writes Ella, a listener.

The radio host made the following announcement: "All you parents out there that are concerned about not spending enough time with your kids, listen up! You gotta go out and get the new issue of Newsweek *magazine. There is an article in there you have to read."*

I hope you are sitting down, Dr. Laura! This article reports that, based on a SURVEY, it was concluded that kids these days DO NOT want more time with their parents. Despite how parents worry about juggling work, meetings, and housework, kids do not feel they need their parents around. The radio personality made it seem like he was delivering GOOD NEWS!?

Tell me, Dr. Laura, are there really parents out there who believe this garbage? Are there parents who, after breathing a sigh of relief, will decide that starting tomorrow morning the kids CAN stay at daycare longer?—After all, they are being backed up by garbage surveys and articles!

Ella was referring to a survey by the New York–based Families and Work Institute of one thousand children, grades three through twelve, across the country to hear what they had to say about working parents. In an article published in that same *Newsweek* (August 30, 1999), Ellen Galinsky, president of the institute, reported that 56 percent of parents assume that their children would wish for more time together and less parental time at work. But only 10 percent of children surveyed wish that their mothers would spend more time with them, and 15.5 percent say the same thing about their dads. Although the data are not presented in the article, Galinsky writes that "children with employed mothers and those with mothers at home do not differ on whether they feel they have too little time with Mom."

Asking children their opinion is interesting in the first place. Why not also ask them about more time in school or church or with ill or elderly relatives? How about asking them if they should have more time doing community service or odd jobs for spending money, instead of an easy allowance?

As Kathleen Parker wrote in her syndicated column of September 20, 1999, "America has become a nightmarish Never Never Land, where no one wants to grow up and parents just wanna be friends. In such a culture, it is perhaps inevitable— though no less scary—that we would abandon adult wisdom and seek solace from the commentary of kids. . . . But when adults rely on children to make them feel all better, we're in trouble."

A letter to the *Newsweek* editor from Jennifer Moeller, a stay-at-home mom and a listener, points out:

The fact that most children do not wish for more time with their parents does not necessarily mean that they are getting all of the attention they need. What it means is that our children, forced to make do with less and less, have finally accepted their plight. Adults will continue to force their children to be convenient, to move over and make more room for careers. Parents will continue to pay strangers to raise their children for them. And the children, who have never known anything else, will tell us it's just fine. Researchers and authors will chime in, telling us that denying our kids the care of their own parents is a valid choice. Our society will continue to under-value, even denigrate stay-at-home parents. So much effort is being put toward trying to prove that dual-career families do not shortchange children. Who are the proponents trying to convince, us or themselves?

Jennifer is correct in pointing out the undermining of the family's responsibility to children and the needs of children by the "so-called" psychological professionals. For example, Dr. Morris Green, who heads the behavioral and developmental pediatrics division at Indiana University's School of Medicine, said that "parents shouldn't feel guilty about their child-care choices. There's really no reason for it. They should just make sure to spend some individual time with their children. . . . Give them the gift of time" (*Los Angeles Times*, September 5, 1999).

The GIFT! I thought it was a developmental necessity and a moral obligation of a parent. No reason for guilt? Really?

Curiously, while the main thrust of the publicity hype about the Families and Work Institute survey was relieving parents of any guilt for not spending time with their children, a very important paragraph in Galinsky's *Newsweek* article appears to have been largely ignored by both media and psy-chologizers.

> We found that the quantity of time with mothers and fathers does matter a great deal. Children who spend more time with their mothers and fathers on workdays and non workdays see their parents more positively, feel that their parents are more successful at managing work and family responsibilities, and see their parents as putting their families first. "I think that if the parents spend more time with their children, they will become better people in life," says a twelve-year-old boy, whose father works part-time while his mom stays home.

How does the study's author reconcile this information with the conclusion that kids are fine with whatever is happening? She doesn't. How do the media reconcile their anti-parent hype with this finding? They don't.

So many of you already know that kids value family time. Jerri, a listener, surely does.

I would like to share a story reinforcing how much even teens appreciate the security of family. Due to shutdowns and layoffs, we needed to relocate. My husband found a job in a city eighty miles away. He commuted for nine months. During the summer he and our sixteen-year-old son moved into a small rented house. We enrolled our son in high school at the new location and I remained behind with our other two children. However, we were together on the weekends at one location or the other. On a Monday in November, I went to the refrigerator to begin breakfast. When opening a carton of eggs I found a letter placed there by our oldest son. The gist of the letter was that he hated coming home to an empty house after school and missed not living together.

After I regained my composure, I called my husband and shared the letter with him. We decided to move regardless of the sale of the house—which eventually sold for a loss. We probably did not make the best financial decisions. I can honestly say that all of our needs have been supplied. The love we share and our emotional well being over-rode our poor financial decisions.

A friend of my teenage son made a comment that paid our family a wonderful compliment. She has known us for several years and refers to us as her second family. Her comment was "You all work together in your family owned business, live together, and play together. The incredible thing is you all get along and enjoy being together. I just do not understand this."

My reply was, "Isn't that how it's supposed to be?"
Yes.

The Evil Scientists . . .

The Families and Work Institute study is just one of hundreds of social science research projects in the last decade that purport to demonstrate that traditional values negatively affect self-fulfillment—the new Holy Grail. Pandering to the general cultural ethos of self-centeredness, self-gratification, and self-indulgence, the so-called experts provide "scientific" justification for weakening the traditional family. And the media, with its love affair with surveys, percentages, charts, and graphs, compounds the problem by jumping on the conclusions (often overstating them), then disseminating them far and wide.

Joe Woodard wrote in the *Calgary Sun* that the law of nature backs traditional families and parent care. "But for the last two generations the social sciences have been trying to scuttle the home-truths of human common sense, largely due to ideological ambitions. Feminism, careerism and just plain me-ism have been eager to consign our little tykes to baby-farms. And like a shyster lawyer, part of the social science community has squirmed and turned to rationalize that project" (July 16, 1995).

What underlies support for those "ideological ambitions"? It's dangerous to tell the truth—but here goes. A significant and powerful segment of the social scientists has been co-opted in the campaign to deconstruct the family and distort the needs of children by certain groups of adults who endorse social and/or political agendas. These include:

➤ Homosexuals, both male and female, who want to have legally sanctioned marriages and access to child raising through legal adoptions and biotechnology.

➤ Feminist activists who believe that all the ills of the world for women are due to relationships with men and the oppression of patriarchy. They want to have children without fathers and want to be married without personal obligation to home and children.

➤ Ideologues who believe that parents at home are inadequate and inappropriate for the proper raising of children. There are innumerable efforts by government and professional organizations to establish mandatory preschool and to abandon the requirement for parental knowledge or consent for a wide range of services to their children, including health clinics and specific types of sex education in the public schools. The American Academy of Pediatrics does not support mandatory reporting to parents of their child's decision to have an abortion.

➤ The day care industry, which has become a lucrative enterprise.

➤ Those baby-boomer types and their adult offspring who treat the world as a candy store and see responsibility to children and family as an impediment to gratification.

➤ The sexual liberation lobby that claims irresponsible sex is a "right" and anything goes in the sexual arena, including pornography, incest, and pedophilia (redefined, of course).

➤ The "politically correct" who support any choice, including having children out of wedlock, since this is yet another aspect of "choice" and a woman's "reproductive right" (even if she's had innumerable children, or is drug- or alcohol-addicted).

➤ Liberated men who have been taught that masculinity is no longer defined by a man's ability to protect, nurture, and support a family. They seek self-gratification like teenagers, frivolously divorce, and demand their ex-wives put the children in day care and get back to work, so they don't have to pay much in alimony and child support.

My indictment of some in the social sciences includes much of the media that perpetuates myths based on specious research without independent analysis. Worse still, publications misrepresent published research in their competitive rush for "news."

A glaring example of this unholy alliance of social science and media is a widely publicized article by Elizabeth Harvey in the academic journal *Developmental Psychology* (March 1999). This journal is published by the American Psychological Association (APA), which came under serious scrutiny in 1999 for publishing a scientifically questionable analysis of research in an attempt to influence public policy regarding child molestation.

Dr. Harvey said she found no difference in the development of children whose mothers were employed vs. children whose mothers were not employed during the first three years of life. "Flashing her agenda," writes Don Feder in the *Boston Globe* (March 8, 1999), "Harvey admits: 'Working mothers have a lot of guilt. I hope this study will alleviate some of that guilt.'"

The media jumped in to help her! The *CBS Evening News*: "Well, if you're a mom getting ready to leave the house for work, listen to this. A new study shows children of women who work outside the home do just as well as those with stay-at-home moms" The *Atlanta Journal and Constitution* headlined: "Working Moms Not Shortchanging Kids, Study Suggests." Another headline, in the *Boston Herald*, was "Working Moms Don't Spoil the Child with Day Care." Another magazine trumpeted, "Working Moms Don't Hurt Kids—Give Up the Guilt." Relieving guilt was the consistent thread.

The media's enthusiasm for this "study" was ill-spent for a number of significant reasons:

1. The individuals studied were not a cross-section of the population. According to a report by the independent Statistical Assessment Service (STATS) in March 1999, "The sample was heavily skewed towards mothers who were young, poor, ill-educated and largely members of minority groups (58 percent). Between 33 and 45 percent of the mothers, depending on age category, were unmarried at the time of the child's birth, compared to 27 percent of the general population. Finally, the mothers studied were relatively young and they scored substantially below average on an intelligence test." The median IQ of the tested mothers was in the low seventies; the median IQ in America is one hundred.

2. It also mixed mothers who returned to work four weeks after birth with those returning up to three years after birth.

3. This study did not examine the type of care children actually did receive in their mothers' absence. Therefore, as STATS points out, "We can't gauge whether the lack of negative effects [of working moms] might be a product of care provided by fathers or other family members, as an alternative to institutional daycare."

   Dr. Harvey cites another current study on nonmaternal care as finding no difference between children raised in maternal and nonmaternal care. This is not true. That study from the National Institute on Child Health and Human

Development (NICHD), 1996–1997, includes fathers as "nonmaternal." Thus they equate dad care with day care. This completely confuses the analysis because the children who are at home with their fathers are very likely to have higher (more positive) scores than children in nonparental day care. The result is to minimize the difference in scores between the nonmaternal and maternal care groups.

4. The study changed the standard of what is a "significant negative effect" from that used by six prior analyses of exactly the same data. This means that previously observed differences automatically became less significant. "The research," STATS writes, "was designed to make negative differences that would be considered 'statistically significant' harder to detect."

5. The study did not consider where the maternal employment was located. There is a tremendous increase of mothers working out of their homes, and those children are likely to have a very different experience than those whose parents work elsewhere.

6. "Finally," states STATS, "it is not clear how closely psychological tests can capture such important but intangible features of a child's life as loneliness or the emptiness of lost love. The whole history of human development attests that there is no more important bond than that between mother and child."

There was, in this study, no analysis of what happens to mother-child bonding when children are actually placed in day care; nor were teachers consulted about behavior problems in the classroom. No test can gauge how much a child loses when he loses that daily, ongoing interaction with both of his parents. Nor can any institution or other person ever re-create that consistent, loving, and personal parental presence.

Basically, this study's true conclusion is very limited. For low-income, low IQ, mostly minority, young, unmarried mothers, the more hours their children spend in a quality day care situation, the more they benefit. The value of this study for the general welfare of families and children is negligible. Carol White, a college professor, wrote in response to this research, "Higher-income professionals, having a choice of whether a mother works, should not feel vindicated. Lower-income parents might take issue with the idea that their family environment is so poor that kids are better off if mom is working."

Is the solution better day care institutions? No. The solution is a return to respect for and commitment to family and parenting.

Neglect Is Abuse

According to an article in the *Los Angeles Daily News* (April 27, 1997), a 1993 study found that the most frequent type of child abuse was neglect (46 percent), followed by physical abuse (25 percent), and sexual abuse (15 percent). Yet, in all the media frenzy about guilt-free and child-free parenting, the truth about psychological and emotional neglect as the number one form of abuse goes unmentioned.

"If you asked me to take a six-month-old and choose between breaking every bone in its body or emotionally ignoring it for two months, I'd say the baby would be better off if you broke every bone in its body," said Dr. Bruce Perry, chief of psychiatry at Texas Children's Hospital in Houston (*Detroit Free Press*, March 20, 1999). "Bone tissue is different from brain tissue. Bones can heal. But if an infant misses out on two months of crucial brain stimulation, you will forever have a disorganized brain"!

The article estimates that more than half of the three million children who come to the attention of child protective services each year have been neglected in some way.

"Some child psychologists who have studied the problem

estimate that as many as one in three children live in homes where they are not given adequate emotional nurturing.

"A 1998 University of Michigan study of 2,394 families across the nation found that fewer than half of parents said they found time for an adequate number of everyday activities with their children, such as looking at books, working on homework, talking, playing games, or preparing food . . . When parents can't find the time to hug, encourage and develop relationships with their children . . . the damage can be enormous, affecting everything from brain development to future relations with spouses or children."

Basically speaking, when parents have overwhelmed themselves with demanding jobs, divorces, love affairs, serial marriages, chaotic stepfamilies and/or single parenthood, they are often emotionally neglectful of their children. Thinking that structured activities like school, day care, or organized sports make up for one-on-one parent-child family experiences is plain wrong.

Children need attention. Human beings are complex creatures, and unlike the behaviors of most lower animals, almost nothing is instinctual. That means that children must be taught to love, trust, bond, and develop relationships. This learning experience comes directly from family life.

"Without such interactions children become withdrawn, antisocial and insecure, and have difficulty making friends and maintaining relationships. They also tend to do significantly worse at school—from elementary through high school—than children who were physically or sexually abused" (*Detroit Free Press*, March 20, 1999).

Kathleen, a listener, was appalled at a WANTED poster placed in her mailbox. She sent it to me. It says "WANTED In-Your-Home Daytime Babysitter; 7:45 A.M.—5:15 P.M. Weekdays." Underneath are the photos of Beth (seventeen months) and Olivia (fourteen weeks), who are described like puppies up for adoption. Beth "Enjoys Barney & playing outside. Healthy, eats table food, good disposition." Olivia is "healthy, bottle fed formula, good disposition."

Kathleen wrote:

I think it is a very sad commentary on today's lifestyles. Also, I recently had a three-year-old over during the day when my son was home from school. This child is raised by sitters and the mom takes over at night. Anyway, the little girl kept asking me if I was the day mommy *for my son. I repeatedly told her that I was the only* mommy. *The poor child could not grasp this concept. All I could do was give her a hug and feel sorry for her. I, of course, confronted the mother—but she laughed it off.*

But It's My Job!

Eight-year-old Nicolas suffered from terrible migraine headaches, lasting for months, and doctors couldn't figure out what was wrong. Curiously, when his dad transferred to a navy base at home, Nicolas's headaches went away. "The doctors said Nicolas' headaches were due to stress—from his dad's long absences" (*Los Angeles Times*, February 15, 1999). Nicolas's dad had missed his son's first steps, his daughter's softball games, both of their birthday parties, and even Christmas Day.

"'It's my job,' he said. 'It's what I do. It's what I signed up to do. I love what I do, and I have to provide for my family.'"

All the realities and rationalizations don't change what children truly need and want.

"'This is not a family-friendly place to work,' says John Feehery, spokesman for House Speaker Dennis Hastert, R-Ill. 'If you want to have a normal family life, don't be a member of Congress. It's a tough, tough place to work.'

"'If the schedule [House and Senate sessions] discourages young people with families from running for office, you're going to have less representation and feel for the problems facing American families today,' says Rep. Tim Roemer, D-Ind., who has young children but notes that top House leaders don't" (*USA Today*, September 27, 1999).

Imagine. Fitting in family around job and career instead of the other way around!

"Traveling Parents Need Not Pack Guilt," says the headline in the nineties family section of the *Los Angeles Times* (July 20, 1994). Relieving that guilt is Susan Ginsberg, an educational consultant in New York who edits the monthly *Work and Family Life* newsletter. Writing about a Gallup survey of 563 parents who also belong to frequent flier clubs, she noted that 60 percent said they had missed a child's birthday or special event, such as a school play or athletic event. They may feel bad, but if they *had* to go, they don't have to feel guilt, according to Ginsberg, who wrote, "They can say, 'Can I get somebody else to go to this event? Can I get somebody to take a picture for me?'"

I see, we are indispensable to employers and corporations, but easily replaceable in our children's lives and hearts.

"With one parent gone there may be increased insecurities, increased anger or scary feelings," said Dr. Stanley I. Greenspan, a clinical professor at the George Washington University Medical School in Washington, D.C., in the same *Los Angeles Times* story. But, never mind. I guess they'll get over it. Especially if you let them emote and bring them lots of stuff from your trip.

That's what an ad in British Airways' *In-Flight* magazine offered. The ad shows an angry adolescent girl, arms folded, with the caption: "How *could* you forget my birthday?" The text reads as follows:

"Oh-oh. Someone's in deep water. What with everything else on your mind during this trip, you've completely forgotten it's your daughter's birthday. Don't worry. It's not too late. You're sure to find something to bring a smile back to her face in the brand new *Shopping the World* brochure in your seatback pocket. Open it up and you'll find an entirely new range of top quality tax-free gifts and little luxuries."

Victoria, the traveler who sent me this ad, wrote: "It's no longer necessary to be home with them on their birthdays—or any days for that matter. So nice to know that we can get out of 'deep water' with our children by simply buying them something."

Children may be robbed of the necessities of family life and parental attention and involvement, but they will sure learn about capitalism!

"I am childless at thirty-three," writes Rebecca, a listener, "but observe my siblings' parenting skills. Short tempers caused mostly by over-booked schedules (work, church, friends, etc.) cause my brothers and sisters-in-law to lash out for unreasonable (?) actions of their children. Yes, a lot of the children's mistakes are inconvenient, but how many were truly done out of spite or vengeance? I only hope God will teach me patience when it is time for me to be my kids' mom. Parental lack of patience, so evident in today's world, really scares the living daylights out of me!"

Well, there is just so much time and energy. And, when you've spent it all at the office . . .

Sophia writes, "What happened to parents? Today was my sons' first day of school. It was hectic! Everybody running to their classes. Parents rushing to the office. At the end of making sure the children were in their classrooms, there was a place for parents to mingle and drink coffee. I came across a woman who was complaining about how, after all of this commotion, she would have to now take her two-year-old to the pediatrician for his shots and how relieved she would be when she went back to work in a few hours!! This person did not sound like a parent but a frustrated chauffeur! I am happy that I don't share her point of view. I was really sad to hear that her mommy duties were written off as a bother and not a blessing."

What Kid?

Hey, at least she remembered to "bother." One father forgot that he still had his twenty-month-old daughter in the van when he arrived at work. He left her in the van in a parking garage for five and one-half hours. Did he remember during those five and one-half hours? Nope. The toddler was discovered by a passerby who called police.

"Basically I was distracted," he said, "and I thought I had dropped my daughter off. I did not realize that she was in the car. She was sound asleep. It was a typical morning, and I thought I had completed my routine" (*Washington Post*, March 27, 1999).

This father was cited for leaving a child unattended in a motor vehicle, which carries a $500 fine and thirty days in jail. What was most disturbing was his description of the response of others, which was not the shock, horror, and recrimination one might have expected in earlier times. "Basically, everybody has been very understanding and saying, 'My God, it could have happened to me.'"

It *has* happened to a number of parents and day care workers during 1999. Many children died in the heat of the cars. Many others felt the fear of being neglected . . . misplaced . . . forgotten, like gloves or a lunch box.

Unbelievably, Christine, one of my listeners, wrote to me of a conversation she had with two woman acquaintances about another "forgotten baby" case I discussed on-air.

I am only nineteen years old, married, no kids yet. I work with an eighteen-year-old girl who has no children, but baby-sits, and also a twenty-eight-year-old mother of four children. We all heard your comments on the college professor father who forgot his baby in the car while he went off to work, and it died. I was shocked and cannot understand how you forget a child. But the other two women had a different view. They think that it was just a mistake. The older woman says that because I'm not a mother, I can't possibly understand how busy and distracted parents can be. Especially with a sleeping baby in the back seat. But I disagree. My mother never forgot me; my sister and brother-in-law have never forgotten their toddlers. I have worked as a nanny and plan on being my kid's stay-at-home mom, and I just don't get it. I agree at times it may be busy and distracting, but when something tiny and alive comes out of you, or your wife, how do you forget about it?

It's very simple—you just have other compelling, competing, important issues on your mind. An October 1999 *Good Housekeeping* cartoon says it all. Two toddlers are shown running to the front door to greet their returning, exhausted, attaché-case-clutching mother, who says, "Oh my God, I forgot I have children."

Scary, huh?

Technology to the Rescue . . .

"In this day of so many two-worker households, no one has time to prepare for the holidays. So people are turning to personal shoppers and pre-made foods. Others are skipping the fuss altogether," writes Lynn Smith in the *Los Angeles Times* (December 10, 1997). "The holidays have changed. As modern home life adjusts to working women, an uneven economy, a relaxation-averse culture, split, blended and re-mixed families, and relatives scattered around the globe, the holiday rituals that many remember with wistful longing are now being delegated, diluted or, in some cases, dropped altogether," she continues.

The answer? Hire someone to research and buy presents for family and friends, get handymen to select and deliver trees, forget holiday card writing, get the grocer to prepare a holiday feast or don't have one.

And forget, therefore, any nurturing or family-building activities . . . and memories for the children. There's just no time. The children should understand. They won't mind. It doesn't matter. Some psychologists tell us that the test scores of these children are the same as those of children who are attended to, loved, nurtured, supervised, and such. And as we all love to believe, test scores are everything in the realm of healthy human development.

More truthfully, this is all about putting children and home life last. "Just how absent is the busy, high achieving '90s parent?" asks Mary Eberstadt in the *Wall Street Journal* (May 2, 1995). "Absent enough, to judge by a pamphlet put out by MCI Telecommunications, to seek technological fixes—sending messages by fax, tape-recording bedtime stories, videotaping events that take place (for example, 'the soccer championship') while parents are away. Even the parent too busy to record his own bedtime stories can rely on the information age to ease the parental conscience. A prerecorded storytelling-by-phone service called Let's Imagine! is available now for eighty-five cents a minute."

The time it takes to feed, bathe, and get a kid to sleep is also an area for creativity, according to Lori Bergman, who writes a column in the *Indianapolis Star* (April 12, 1999).

> There is only so much a woman can take before she reaches the boiling point. . . . I happened across a piece on how to expedite a child's bedtime routine. The article suggested you combine dinnertime, bath time and bed time by doing the following: Give your child a bath and put a cheeseburger on a float toy, which you set sail alongside junior in the tub. While the child is bathing and eating (and no doubt grabbing at ship wrecked pickles), read him a bedtime story. Dry the child and dress him in the clothes you want him to wear the next day so that when you pull him out of bed in the morning, he'll be all ready to go.

I pray she's kidding!

The very rituals we are rushing through or eliminating altogether are the ones that keep us connected as families and nur-

tured as individuals, give us purpose in life as parents, and ultimately nourish our souls. Look at the blessings we are intentionally running away from. How foolish and blind can we be?

One syndicated cartoon by Dan Foote (March 1999)
depicted a teenage boy arriving at his home after school to a
note pinned on the outside of the front door: "Honey, Dad and
I have to work late again . . . If you need us . . . go to our web-
site at www.2busy.com. Love, Mom."

Technology does not replace a loving, attentive, available
parent. And a busy parent is NOT a source of solace and pride
to children as we have been browbeaten by some family demo-
lition experts to believe. According to Ms. Eberstadt in the
Wall Street Journal article referred to above, the American
Academy of Pediatrics handbook, *Caring for Your Young
Baby and Child*, actually says: "As a mother who successfully
manages both an outside job and parenthood, you provide an
excellent role model for your child. He will be proud of your
achievements and feel motivated to become more independent,
responsible, and achievement-oriented himself."

Well, there you have it. Parents are to work full-time away
from home to make their children proud and to make their
children (first among all goals) achievement-oriented. I guess
that means that children raised by their at-home parents are at
great risk of disdaining their parents and eschewing accomplishment and goal orientation. I wonder, then, how these
folks explain the personal and professional success and compe-
tency of those children of the Depression and the few decades
afterward when family nurturing was a primary goal?

It's crucial that each generation teach the next what is really
important. This generation wants to teach children that self-
fulfillment, competition, acquisition, power, money, and career
are more important than marriage, children, love, G-d, family,
and community. *The Buckets*, a syndicated cartoon (April 23,
1999), "got it." It shows a father busy at work at his computer. His child comes over to entice him to play catch with a

football. The father says, "Not now, Eddie. I have important stuff to do." As he works away for a while, he wonders to himself, "Important stuff?!?" In the last frame he is playing catch with his son.

Two Busy Parents = Too Awful Kids

"A 1997 survey of 2000 adults showed that two-thirds thought teenagers were 'rude,' 'irresponsible,' 'wild,' and 'spoiled.' More than half of the respondents thought these failings applied even to children ages five to twelve, when kids used to be considered 'adorable.' Many also say they know what the problem is—parents," wrote John Dorschner in the *Miami Herald* (January 25, 1998).

The article quotes pastors, parents, and child development experts, pointing out that "I've never seen a generation so parentless. Parents may love their kids, but they're busy with work, with their own activities."

"Kids who spend more time with their parents do better."

"When teens have a problem they want to talk about it when they're thinking of it. It won't save up until 7:30 when mom or dad gets home. Teens appreciate quality time, but it can't replace availability."

The result of this neglect is articulated brilliantly by Ed, one of my listeners, a father of four and a clinical social worker in rural Utah.

Today on a radio program the comment was made that children don't respect their parents, care that their parents will think bad of them, or even fear their parents—because parents have not respected the emotional and spiritual needs of the children. Instead of investing time, which children equate with love, parents put their children way down the priority list. This communicates a fundamental disrespect to children that the parents end up paying for later.

The parental disrespect of their child's needs is basically self-

ishness. It is putting the parent's needs (desires?) ahead of their children. The children grow up modeling this "disrespect" by doing whatever they feel and whatever fulfills their needs (desires?) even though it may hurt others at times. After all, why shouldn't they treat others the way they have been treated and devalued? They are modeling those that supposedly love them.

Unfortunately, these same children are likely to repeat the pattern of parental neglect and disrespect with their own children. So the question is are we communicating value and respect to our children by spending time with them? If not, can we expect them to care if they do something wrong that would cause parents not to think highly of them?

On the other hand, if we are spending time with them, thus communicating love and respect, perhaps our children will honor the relationship more readily and would be more careful about displeasing the parents. We are not taking the time to communicate love and values to our children, and we wonder why they don't seem to feel guilt about doing something wrong. After all, they were looking out for number one just as they were so dutifully taught in the home.

Neal Reynolds, a father who has been managing his son's softball team for seven years, has firsthand experience with the lack of time too many fathers spend with their sons. In a small local newspaper in Atlanta (June 2, 1999), he wrote about taking his son hunting and fishing for many years: "I have seen many boys with their dads on these trips, but I have never seen one with an earring, a tattoo, or a skinned head. I have seen many in camouflage coats, but never in a trench coat. Why? Is it that boys with earrings and tattoos don't want to be seen with their dads, or is it that boys with dads don't need earrings and tattoos?"

It's easy to blame guns; the Internet; violent videos, movies, and games for children's violence. And, though I agree that these insidious influences undermine the core morality of our society, most of these influences would be virtually powerless in the face of involved, intact family units with parents praying, eating, talking, playing, hanging out with their children.

Instead, we get the excuses, like "It's the economy, stupid," or "It's the nineties and adults are entitled to their freedom from marriage and child care."

The *Morning Call*, a newspaper serving Bethlehem, Pennsylvania, ran an article with the headline: "Juvenile Crime Indicates Need for Day Care—State United Way Leader Says Youth Incidents in Allentown Are Higher During the Week Than on Weekends." The president of United Way of Pennsylvania was quoted as saying, "It is very clear prime time for juvenile crime is really that time when their parents aren't around" (April 24, 1999).

Astonishingly, the emphasis was on the shortage of quality day care space—not a call for parents to rearrange their schedules, lifestyles, and budgets to be more available as the parental supervisors and role models that children so desperately need.

Parents—Go Home

"'It kept coming back to families . . . in addressing the needs of kids after school,' explained the Rev. Matt McDermott to church volunteers and school officials in Palo Alto, California, working together to launch a new after-school homework center at Jordan Middle School.

"Along with tutoring, the center at Jordan Middle School would give kids a chance to connect with adults and build confidence in themselves" (*San Jose Mercury News*, May 18, 1999).

Let me repeat the reverend's opening sentence. "It kept coming back to families." So you organize strangers to volunteer? Diane, who wrote me about this affluent city's dilemma, shares my incredulity. "This means that kids are not 'connecting' with their parents . . . It is the parents' job to connect, love, respect, discipline, pay attention to, and nourish their kids. This is not the job of volunteers. These parents are dropping the ball. My husband and I bought a home in a less affluent area so that we would require ONE modest salary to meet expenses. I would love to live in a more expensive area, but not at the expense of my (future) kids."

According to the *Rocky Mountain News* (March 2, 1997), the Colorado Psychiatric Society came up with an essay topic for a statewide contest for high school students: "Teen-agers today continue to be the victims of psychiatric crises—suicide, depression, eating disorders, drug addiction to name a few. What are the issues behind this that adults need to understand in order to be more help." I don't think the Psychiatric Society got the answers it expected. Instead of concerns ranging from the economy to peer pressure and global warming, the consistent, practically universal answer was: Parents should be there for their children "to listen to us"; "so my dad would have more time to play with my brothers and me"; "Just talk to me . . . make time in your busy schedule to learn more about me."

The *New York Observer* (March 31, 1997) reported that "New York City parents consider themselves world champions of child rearing. They find the best preschool, best nanny, the latest dance classes, baby gymnastics—no expense is spared from turning Junior into a Renaissance tyke."

The *Observer* referred to a story in the *New York Daily News* about high school students who received national recognition as Westinghouse Science Talent Winners. According to these students, "the biggest factor [in their success] seemed to be parental commitment: actually taking the kids around the city, rather than dumping them at an after-school program."

It is amazing how we want to reframe or outright ignore this self-evident truth. In *Childbirth Instructor Magazine* (May/June 1999), there are two news briefs side by side that emphasize our desire to ignore the obvious. The first shows Mom and Dad snuggling their newborn—"By six months of age, babies understand the meaning of the words 'mama' and 'dada' . . . Previously, scientists believed that infants that young could not attach meaning to sounds."

This touching "revelation" was next to a picture of a woman carrying her infant like a grocery bag around the middle. The child is facing away, as she, suited up for work, marches toward the day care center. This photo is explained with the following text. "Based on a study that began in 1979, researchers at the University of Massachusetts at Amherst found no difference between children of working moms and those whose mothers stayed at home."

Oh, please. One only has to look at the expressions of the two children. The first is raptly focused on Mom's eyes. The second stares blankly into the universe. You've got to be kidding yourself to believe there's no difference in these two sentient beings. Worse, you've got to be lying to yourself.

Feed Me!

"This is mealtime '99, and kids are cooking—or, at least, heating and eating. Call it the convergence of time crunch and convenience. In an era of microwave magic, dual-earner homes and single-parent family surveys show an increasing number of children and teenagers fixing meals not only for themselves but also for their families. People spend less time these days eating together. . . . Among children ages nine to seventeen, almost half regularly prepare meals for themselves, up from 15 percent in 1988, according to the Connecticut-based Yankelovich Partners" (*Boston Globe*, August 13, 1999).

Reading this article made me—and should make everyone—very sad for the growing mentality that discounts the fulfillment of the most important human needs—for nurture and bonding. Watch Discovery Channel any night and see the behavior of all other primates as they groom, touch, play, communicate, share mealtime, snuggle, jockey for position, and just generally hang together. Watch your local television and see humans solitary in traffic, frantic at work, separated from their children, grabbing fast food on the run, giving their kids nutrition bars or doughnuts as they rush off to day care. And we are the *pinnacle* of primate development?

While results vary with the above survey (and numbers are based on the assumption that people admit the truth—yeah, right), we are not giving our kids what we got. A survey by CBS News/*New York Times* (November 1990) reported that while 85 percent of respondents usually had family dinners together when they were about the age of their children, only 67 percent reported eating five to seven evenings of the past week with their own families. And this was a decade ago!

I thought each generation wanted more for their offspring— or did we get off track somewhere and think "more" meant only tangible objects, success, and importance?

"A survey of 527 rural teens, ages twelve to eighteen, found that those who showed signs of good adjustment (measured by use of cigarettes, alcohol or illicit drugs, school motivation and hopefulness about the future) ate a meal with an adult in their family an average of about five days a week. This compared with three days for teens who didn't show such good adjustment," reported the *Washington Post* (August 16, 1997).

What the Heck Are Parents for, Anyway?

"Americans spend more than thirty minutes *daily* managing the deluge of messages they receive, based on a study by Casio PhoneMate, compared with the roughly forty minutes they say they spend *(weekly)* in meaningful conversation with their children" (*USA Today*, March 2, 1999).

During the summer of 1999, I spoke at a dinner for a major retail chain. During the question and answer period that followed, one rather belligerent woman stood up in the back of the room and angrily challenged my position that a parent actually needs to be physically present to parent adequately. I wondered aloud how she could be considered a good employee if she rarely showed up at work. "If one is not actually *there* doing the job, as parent or painter, how does one qualify as *doing* the job, much less as being good at it?"

This logic seems obvious, but it raises the hackles of those who want something for nothing, which is the false notion you have to buy if you want to pretend you can have and do have it all simultaneously.

Nonetheless, the facts are indisputable, backed up by common sense. "Researchers find consensus between campus and home that making [school] policy is best left to professionals, and that good child-rearing is parents' most important contribution. . . . Raising polite, disciplined, respectful children who want to learn and work hard . . . is the most fundamental and indispensable job for parents . . . there is a realization that schools can't do their jobs if parents aren't taking care of business at home" (*Los Angeles Times*, March 24, 1999).

There it is: for the educational system to be of value to your children, you have to teach your children respect, hard work, and good values, in a milieu of love, affection, and discipline.

How can you do that if you aren't there or are too tired, frazzled, stressed, and busy? Hmmm?

Immunizing Children Against Disasters

"I hope you have not missed the discovery of the Century!" wrote Harry, a retired physician and listener. "Headline in my morning paper: 'Parents Really Do Matter.' This unbelievable discovery was made by a University of Maryland study which found that children living in Baltimore public-housing projects who felt their parents set limits and talked with them about their concerns were far less likely to use alcohol and marijuana, sell drugs or have unprotected sex.

"Research consistently reveals that the steady presence of

even one caring adult can alter a teenager's life for the better. But a Temple University study of 20,000 high school students found that about 30% of parents were significantly uninvolved in their kids' lives. . . . Psychologist Lawrence Steinberg, who conducted the survey several years ago, calls this 'frightening'" (*Los Angeles Times*, July 18, 1999).

"Feeling Loved Helps Young People Avoid Risky Behavior," was the headline in the *Kansas City Star* (September 10, 1997) about a study published in the *Journal of the American Medical Association*. No kidding!

In response to my www.drlaura.com Web site question, "What do you believe were the worst behaviors or actions of your parents that caused you difficulty or pain?" the most frequent answer was being ignored, feeling alone and isolated.

"My parents inadvertently (more or less) ignored me. They both worked, and got home about 6 P.M. From age 11 on, I was home alone in the afternoons. There was little communication or 'parenting' on their part," wrote Joe.

As long as I wasn't "in trouble," they left me alone. They failed to give me healthy doses of encouragement and praise, as well as CONSTRUCTIVE criticism to correct my wrongs. The consequence of their behavior was that I had very low self-esteem and few friends. I was underdeveloped socially and could not develop strong friendships. I became withdrawn and developed clinical depression.

My mom was a mental-health professional who worked with adolescents on a daily basis, but did not care to notice her own son's problems. I am just now, at 28, beginning to dig myself out of the hole I fell into as a young child with little or no guidance. They should have talked to me on a daily basis about how I was doing. Praised me more. Given me encouragement. It is the job of the parent to make a kid feel confident and strong.

Sandy's answer is also representative.

My parents focused more on each other and themselves than on our family. Both worked. My mom was an elementary school principal and my father was a traveling salesman. They both worked lots of hours to achieve the American Dream. My parents were too busy with their own lives to be concerned about my adolescent difficulties. I felt very alone, isolated and distant from my parents throughout all of my teen years.

I became involved with the wrong group of kids. My parents did not try to do anything other than to prohibit me from seeing them. This caused further rebellion and disrespect. I ran away from home, became involved with drugs and sexually promiscuous.

I don't think my mom working was a terrible thing, but I think the constant feeling that I was not as important as her job was a bad message to send. I think we should have done more things as a family. I truly wish that people would realize that children are a gift, but a gift with responsibility and that it is the most important job in the world to prepare them to be good human beings. My husband saved me and taught me what the real meaning of love, commitment and family is. I know that God intervened here and found something lovable about me and has a deeper purpose for me than I knew. Our family is small, but our two children have the full commitment of both parents so I hope they will both grow up to be wonderful human beings.

Terry, one of my listeners, was selected to sit on a jury in an attempted murder case involving a young Hispanic gang member who shot and severely wounded another gang member. Eleven of the twelve jurors were, according to Terry's letter, middle-aged, white, middle-class people. There was a young Hispanic man also on the jury.

During deliberations we found out that he had lived all his life in the same neighborhood and gone to the same high school. He was a few years older and therefore did not know any of the actual persons involved. He was able to give us much needed information of the gang lifestyle, the environment of hatred and abuse that exists and the fear that most people of that area live in daily. Without him we never would have understood the gang mentality or how the young man could really be a cold-blooded gangbanger. He also had no problems in voting the first time around for a guilty verdict and also the stiffest penalty available to us. In his words, "It has to stop somewhere, my family is never safe."

I was so impressed that after we were all finished, I asked the question that everyone had on their minds, "How did the same environment that produced so many criminals produce you?"

He said one word: "PARENTS." When we asked how they were different he said that his father worked a small repair business and his mother cleaned houses. When his mother could not be at home when he and his sisters came from school, his father would pick them up and take them to the repair shop. They would do their homework at his desk. When they were finished to his satisfaction they did chores around the shop to keep them busy. You could see the pride in his face when he spoke of his parents . . . with an "S" on the end.

I get thousands of such stories. One thirty-two-year-old listener, Henry, wrote that he grew up in Seattle, with both parents working, and was basically on his own from the age of six. Being starved for attention, he quickly learned that even negative attention was better than none at all, but his parents even began ignoring that. By fourteen he was using drugs and alcohol to numb the feelings.

After undergoing therapy to put closure to his painful past with his parents, he went to visit and talk to them about his personal journey. "In talking with them about growing up, their first comment to me was, 'Why didn't you tell us?' and I was very direct in saying that they were never there to talk with.

Many tears were shed over that weekend. At the end of our five-hour talk, my mom said to me, 'If I could do this over again I would have been at home to be there for you.' I accepted her apology."

Jamie, a seventeen-year-old boy, wrote to me in response to a call he heard on my show from a woman wondering why her older children from a former marriage weren't accepting her new child. "My mom just had a new baby last Thursday. Even though, because of the baby, my whole family forgot my birthday the following Sunday, neither I nor my brothers and sister are jealous of him. I think the reason we're not jealous is that my mom has always stayed home with us and given us her time and attention. My dad, too, always spent time with us. They show us that we're the most important part of their lives. More family members only mean that there are that many more people for you to love and to love you back."

Success at Last

I have listened to you for almost two years, writes Annie. We had a wonderful happening with our 17-year-old daughter last week—and I want to share this with you. Angela had become troubled and slightly withdrawn for a day or so and knowing she would eventually talk to me, I patiently waited. Sure enough, she did.

Her dear friend had confided to her that she had had sex for the first time with a boy she had known one month and realized, after the fact, that she had made a major mistake and was in deep agony. This rocked my daughter's foundation with her friend, and it challenged her own values. We talked about many issues including our own religious values, integrity, character, courage, pregnancy, venereal disease, etc. Since she has just begun dating, it was a timely discussion.

Two days later when she came home from her summer job, she asked if she could tell me something. "Sure," I said. (Here is one of the moments that re-confirmed that my life as a stay-at-home mother is worth every sacrifice.) With a calm, serious look on her face she said, "Mom, I just want you to know that you and dad did a good job of raising me." Her dad had just walked in the door from work and I said, "I think it would be nice if you told him that too." She did and with tears in our eyes, we hugged and thanked God for the gift of a wonderful child.

Compare that spontaneous reaction from a child to the one in *The Wizard of Id*, a syndicated cartoon by Parker (September 27, 1999). The furious little boy walks up to the judge and says "I'd like to sue my grandparents."

"For what?" asks the judge.

"Having my parents," says the boy.

Like the Smith Barney television commercial that proclaims, "We make money the old-fashioned way; we *earn* it," people who wish to be successful at life, at marriage, and at parenting have to *earn* that success by hard work and commitment.

You can't become a success at family life just by having a family!

2

Don't Have Them If
You Won't Raise Them

> Dr. Laura: I saw a personalized license plate yesterday that made me immediately think of you. It read "MOMS2BZ." This was on a Cadillac, and I don't know if I was more ashamed of the woman driving or sadder for her children. Do you think her kids gave her this for maybe a Mother's Day gift, or she ordered it for herself?
>
> Chris

> Dr. Laura: In response to your remark yesterday about the license plate which read "MOMS2BZ," I went to pick up the little girl I work with and saw a license plate reading, "2BMOM" . . . so, they do exist!!!
>
> Jenna, nineteen

Parents magazine has a column called "I Can't Believe I Did That." The following astonishing admission appeared in the April 1999 edition:

"As a new mom, I was very nervous the first morning I left my six-week-old daughter to return to work. My mother knew the couple who was caring for her, so I trusted them, but I still spent quite a while telling them how to feed her, diaper her, etc. When I came to pick her up at the end of the day, though, I realized I'd forgotten one important bit of information. 'You never told us your daughter's name,' said the caregiver, 'so we decided to call her Dolly.' That's one way to get a nickname!"

I was sickened by reading this. I wondered about the times we live in when a woman would cheerfully admit that she handed over her nearly newborn to strangers for some eight to twelve hours without even the personal touch of a first name. That this woman is not embarrassed to share this with thousands of readers is the shame of it all.

Kim, one of my listeners, sent me the following classified ad from her local newspaper in Nevada: "PLEASE HELP US. Our mommy is so busy and we need a really nice, mature lady, who will enjoy taking care of us until our mommy comes home from work. We would like it if you could cook us yummy dinners and be our friend. We are eight and ten, and you need a dependable car to tote us around."

Busy Mommy is not even going to be home for dinner? Busy Mommy expects that somebody can be paid to be a friend? At least there is some acknowledgment that the children *need* a mommy.

Lynn, another listener, sent this ad from her metro Denver paper, writing, "It looked like a standard ad until I read the last sentence. Makes you wonder why she even bothered to have kids: 'NANNY NEEDED. Mature woman to care for my children ages three and twelve in my home. Forty hours and four-day week, paid vacation. Duties will include meal prep, light housekeeping, as well as mothering my children. Leave Message.'"

Yet another woman expects to hire a stranger to love, adore, bond, treasure, nurture, protect, reassure, and commit to her children for money, while she's willing to forgo the experience for money? And does the "leave message" suggest she's rarely around even now for a conversation with a potential "surrogate mother"?

There was a time when hiring employees to take care of children was the choice of either the elite, who didn't want to be bothered because of social and other self-indulgent activities, or the struggling parent, who needed the support to survive. No more. The desire for freedom from our children to do our own thing, be fulfilled, and not be burdened with their needs and demanding presence has become more of an entitlement.

"In fact, for those who can pay up to $50,000 a year, a new cadre of highly educated, professional nannies is transforming childcare," according to an article in the *Los Angeles Times* (July 25, 1999) that describes the training of high-priced nannies who can help with homework, model good nutrition, plan trips to the museum, and maybe teach children a second language. Sadly, the article ends with: "those investments buy an upper-class working mother a huge luxury: a companion for her children who looks like her in terms of education and social values, and who has time to rollerblade to the park, read a story and play in the sandbox." And love? And hug? And snuggle? And talk about the unimportant on the way to the profound?

Ironically, the title of this piece is "Giving Mary Poppins a Run for Her Money." The editors, the writer, and the parents seem to forget who Mary Poppins was. Angela, one of my listeners, wrote:

I'm sick and tired of poor Mary Poppins being misrepresented. Mary Poppins was the perfect nanny. However, not for the reasons most think. Yes, Mary took unruly kids, loved them, disciplined them, kept them clothed and fed. The children were taught to be well-mannered and respectful. She enriched their little lives and encouraged their imaginations with flights of fancy.

But Mary Poppins understood that only the parents could give their children what they longed for most—attention, appreciation, love and acceptance from their parents. This was Mary Poppins' true goal; not to be the perfect companion to the Banks children, but rather to help the parents see how self-centered, self-involved, and materialistic they were.

Mary Poppins set about to get Mr. Banks fired from his job and turn the parents' world upside down so that they would see what is truly important in life—family, not money and success.

If only the nannies in this article were truly Mary Poppins, they would be worth far more than the $50,000. They would be priceless and no longer needed.

And in the final words of Mary Poppins, "That is the way it should be."

I Am Woman—Watch Me Roar

In contrast is an all too typical modern lifestyle of virtually abandoning children to success, which is rarely publicly challenged or criticized. The *Milwaukee Journal Sentinel* did an article on moms who stay at home (March 29, 1998). But the article also included working women under the heading, "For Others, Career Track Is Still a Clear Road."

"Not everyone is abandoning the boardroom for the nursery," the section begins. The article continued with a description of the life of Nancy Sennett, an attorney with three children. They describe her as having been on the front lines of the working mothers' movement for nineteen years.

"When her daughter, Amy, was born . . . Sennett barely skipped a beat. . . . Her full-time nanny tended to the baby while Sennett continued working well into the evening and on weekends.

"Sennett, now forty-six, and her husband had two more children. 'We had a wonderful nanny who actually held two of my kids before I did,' she says.

"'I recognize that I'm missing out on some things. . . . This is the life that I have chosen. I'm not physically there with them. I'm not there when they come running in from the bus. But I'm there for them in other ways.'"

She's missing out on some things? The children have completely missed out on a mother!

In what possible ways does she think she's "been there for her children"? Get a load of this thinking: "Sennett sees her children greatly benefiting from her pursuing her career. 'They are more organized and independent than they would be if I were at home all day,' she says." And listen to this last rationalization: "'I am an interesting person . . .'"

The July 1999 issue of *Marie Claire* magazine profiled five women from different countries who became millionaires by the age of twenty-five. One of them said it best: "My big luxury is my three nannies, who provide my two-year-old daughter with twenty-four-hour care. I also have another baby on the way. It's very important to me that I have the freedom to leave without guilt, and that I know my child will be with people she knows and loves."

I'm sure when her daughter grows up, having learned that love and nurturance can be surrogated, she won't think twice about putting her aged momma in a home, instead of bringing her to live with her family. Momma is teaching her money can buy you freedom from family, bonding, and wasted time with kids.

"Sequencing" is the new term given to the practice of frequently going in and out of the workforce after having children, according to a May 19, 1999, story in the *Wall Street Journal*.

> The off-work episodes are in response to the needs of the children as they experience and provide challenges based upon their level of development. As children sprout teeth, learn to walk, start school, struggle with puberty and go in and out of being a mystery or a challenge, many parents are experiencing problems with maintaining their careers while balancing

raising a family firsthand. This is because this post-modern work era is defined by a rapid pace of change in technology, products, people and trends. In this high-paced, rapidly growing and changing world, time out often means seriously falling out of step.

This reality often makes people forgo parenting to stay "with it" within their careers. Others, like Carol Nelson, a software marketer described in the *WSJ* article, make quite a different quality of choice. She has been home for one and a half years. She had planned to stay out only a year, but her first summer at home with the children out of school and day care was so pleasant, she's eagerly anticipating the second year and has decided to delay plans to start a consulting business.

"'I really struggled with the decision, which meant altering retirement plans,' she says. After she weighed 'taking one or two years off my retirement and enjoying myself now, versus taking time off when I'm sixty-five and the kids aren't around anymore,' she opted for the time now. Seeing her children's delight in her presence, she says, "I know I did the right thing.'"

Mary Poppins would be proud.

What Mothers and Fathers Really Want

In January 1998, the president and his wife announced a historic initiative: $20 billion in increased federal spending for child care over the next five years. This, they said, would address a "silent child-care crisis" afflicting the nation. I, for one, had a fit. Ignoring partisan politics and rhetoric as I always do in searching simply for the "right thing," I am intensely suspicious and frightened of initiatives that purport to speak for family welfare, but so obviously undermine the foundation of all families—the bonded relationship between children and parents. There is a difference between the concept of welfare rescuing families in dire need, and promoting a

lifestyle that common sense tells anyone is not in the best interests of children, unless of course their parents are destructive,
dysfunctional, in prison, or dead.

Contrast President Clinton's determination to focus on institutionalized day care with the perspective of a Canadian Par-
liamentary Committee Report (June 1999) rejecting the government's assumption that couples who choose to have one
parent stay at home to raise their kids do so because they are
rich enough to afford it. It said families who decide to forgo
one income to care for their children make a significant financial sacrifice. "The issue of single-earner versus dual-earner
families is not one of rich versus poor or middle income versus
upper income. It is very much an issue about the choices parents face and make in what they think is the best interest of
their families," the report said. The committee suggested a new
refundable tax credit under the Canadian Child Tax Benefit for
stay-at-home parents in "recognition of the value to society of
child rearing."

It would seem that most Americans appreciate this Canadian
committee's point of view over their own government's. Wirthlin
Worldwide conducted a nationwide poll during December 1997.
Surveying 1,004 adults in the United States, the poll asked
respondents to rate which kind of child care they believed was
the most desirable.

Across the board, regardless of race, age, political party
affiliation, or income level, Americans rated child care by a
child's own mother as the single most desirable kind of care for
children. Commercial and government centers were rated the
least desirable. Perhaps the message people are sending the
government is less that they have a desire to spiff up institutionalized day care centers, and more that the government
should provide tax relief, not just to families who pay for day
care, but to all families with pre-school-aged children.

In May 1997, the Pew Research Center conducted a poll of
1,101 women and found that 25 percent of the women employed

full-time preferred to stay home with their children. Another 44 percent of women with children under eighteen wanted to work part-time rather than full-time.

In 1996, the Independent Women's Forum commissioned a poll that found that 64 percent of women desired to be at home (full-time 31 percent, part-time 33 percent).

A poll of 18,000 women in *Parents* magazine in May 1996 found that 61 percent of the women wanted work flexibility in order to work part-time and have more time for their children. An additional 29 percent wanted to be at home with their children full-time. Only 4 percent of the women who responded would choose full-time employment if they could do whatever they wished.

A *Los Angeles Times* poll (June 20, 1999) discovered that four to one, respondents backed a tax break for families in which one parent stays at home to care for children under the age of five. And in another *Los Angeles Times* poll (June 13, 1999), 69 percent of California parents, men and women alike, agreed that "It is much better for a family if the father works outside the home and the mother takes care of the children."

You would think that with responses like these, in poll after poll, that almost all American families would have a stay-at-home parent. But that is not the case. In 1994 the U.S. Census Bureau issued a report called "Who's Minding Our Pre-Schoolers?" It found that of the nearly twenty million children under the age of five in America, fewer than 48 percent were cared for by their own mothers at home, with another 9.5 percent cared for by their fathers.

Show Me the Money

Please don't whine, complain, and holler at me that the economy makes it impossible for one parent to stay home. The *Sunday Capital* in Annapolis, Maryland, profiled two families of four on

September 5, 1999. One showed the family and the nanny. The other showed the mom interacting with her two kids, while the dad was away at work. The first family is described with all the accoutrements of success. The second family is described as having made sacrifices. "'We never thought of this as sacrifice,' the father said. 'We think of it as living within our means.'

"The Escobarosas, who could easily have afforded more house than the modest fixer-upper with the backyard pool, didn't want more house. They wanted more time—'time for life beyond their jobs.'"

In her book *How to Get What You Want in Life with the Money You Already Have*, Carole Keeffe writes, "Over and over again I hear couples say, 'I wish one of us could be home with our children, but we both have to work, just to get by.' Most often, this is a myth rather than a fact. Years ago I read that the first $10,000 earned by the second working parent goes to pay child care, transportation, work clothes, higher food bills (expensive package meals, convenience foods and eating out more), and higher medical bills due to increased stress. Too often we think we're bringing in more money, when in fact, we're creating more bills."

Money is not the problem it appears to be for most working parents. Many seem to believe that having a parent at home has become the exclusive province of the rich. But the facts are quite different.

According to the U.S. Census Bureau, Current Population Survey, 1998, the median income of families in which the wife is not in the paid labor force is $37,161 compared with the median of $63,751 for dual-income families. It appears that those most generous with time for their children have more modest financial means.

What is there about money and things that distracts people from core values? I remember reading with disgust the following conclusions of a *Los Angeles Times* poll on child rearing (June 13, 1999). "More affluent women—those with household incomes of more than $60,000 annually—were more prone than their less affluent counterparts to say that children interfere with a career; that working mothers face discrimination, and that working mothers are better mothers than stay-at-home moms." Really? Not being around or being totally stressed when you *are* provides exactly *what* toward being a good mother?

The self-centered, myopic perception of affluent parents was further demonstrated in the difference in attitude toward self and child with respect to who suffers more in the work/family balancing act. Among those Californians with household incomes of less than $20,000 annually, 46 percent said their personal needs suffer and more than a third (37 percent) agreed their children suffer. Among those in households making more than $60,000, a whopping 66 percent said they personally suffer and only 11 percent believe their children bear the brunt.

I believe women work because, increasingly, the identification between occupational success and self-worth is as strong for women as for men. Action and money add up to a sense of independence, power, and the ability to have a lot of things.

The Fido-ization of America's Kids

Melinda Ledden Sidak offered a suggestion I have made to my radio audience many times during the quarter of a century I've been broadcasting. She wrote in the spring 1998 issue of *The Women's Quarterly*:

> You've heard of couples who treat their dogs as surrogate children? Welcome to the late 20th century, where couples treat their children as surrogate pets. The typical parents of the child-as-pet are employed full-time in demanding jobs and spend the bulk of their time at work. In the evenings and sometimes on the weekends, there are a few brief hours to eat, sleep, do chores, and occasionally, to consume leisure. During those all-too-brief periods available for enjoyment, these parents spend "quality

time" playing with and caring for their children just as pet owners will toss the ball for Fido or take him for a run.

This appropriate tirade was in response to an article in the *New York Times Magazine*, which had featured a story about the unique problems faced by busy working mothers. Among others, it profiled a wife and mother of two who commutes every week from her suburban Chicago home to her company's headquarters in Norwalk, Connecticut. Stories like these are always told from the woman's perspective: her guilt, her feelings, her needs.

In her *Women's Quarterly* piece, Sidak quotes a column written by Kathleen Parker in response to the same *Times* story. Ms. Parker observed, "Spare us the statements of angst filled moms like this woman, who laments that there is nothing worse than sitting on a runway, realizing you won't be home in time for your child's play at school.

"Yes there is," writes Ms. Parker. "Worse is being a child who knows his mother can't make it to his school play."

"As for all those would-be professional working women out there, all I can say is please, please visit your local animal shelter. There's a cuddly puppy or kitty waiting just for you," concludes Ms. Sidak.

"Lies Parents Tell Themselves About Why They Work"

This is exactly the title of a May 12, 1997, cover story in *U.S. News & World Report* about how much parents work and why: "it is often hard to disentangle rationalization from self-awareness, self-deception from reality. Listen to most men and women discussing work and family and one thing becomes clear: People are lying—to others, or to themselves."

The following are the "five lies" exposed in the *U.S. News & World Report* article.

Lie #1: "We need the extra money." Yet better-off Americans are nearly as likely to say they work for "basic necessities" as those who live near the poverty line. Many families have, in effect, defined "necessity" upward. In a November 10, 1999, story in the *Los Angeles Times* about the cost of living in California, a chart showed that a family of four with one earner had $31,356 in taxes and expenses, while the same family with two incomes had $44,880 in expenses. A lot of that "extra" money goes to higher taxes and day care costs.

Lie #2: "Day care is perfectly good." The most recent comprehensive study conducted by researchers at four universities found that while 15 percent of day care facilities were excellent, 70 percent were "barely adequate," and 15 percent were abysmal. Parents overlook problems in their day care setup as a defense against the ideal notion of children being raised by their parents.

Lie #3: "Inflexible companies are the key problem." On paper, most companies are flexible. Most parents don't take advantage of the flexibility because they don't want to limit their careers, and others actually "want to spend more time at the office than at home, with its incessant demands from noisy children, endless piles of laundry, few tangible rewards and little time to relax."

Lie #4: "Dads would gladly stay home." Men may say they are willing to stay home and be the house-husband, but when given the chance, only about two million actually do. In spite of egalitarian notions about men and women, both still define masculinity in terms of financial success. In addition, many women would rather leave their children with a stranger than deal with the jealousy they feel toward husbands who have the primary relationship with the children. This is an attitude I've encountered often on my radio program.

Lie #5: "High taxes force both of us to work." While many women are locked unhappily in full-time jobs only for the sake of health benefits their self-employed husband doesn't provide, most women who work full-time do not do so because they absolutely have to or because they've been taxed out of their home. The total tax bite on the average family has changed little in twenty years.

To make the point, on April 15, 1997, the following appeared in the *Wall Street Journal:* "It's April 15th—was it worth it? Two-worker families suffer. University of Southern California tax-law professor Edward McCaffery, in a new book, calculates that a married, working parent earning $30,000 last year took home half that after taxes if the other spouse made $60,000. The family would net more, if the $60,000 parent got a $4,000 raise, and the lower earner stayed home, all thanks to lower tax costs and savings in child care expenses."

"Working entails tradeoffs," a *Newsweek* (May 12, 1997) story concludes, "and it would be easier not to have to face them. That's why parents cling to false explanations that have an end of discussion quality. . . . Self-deceptions make it harder to devise solutions. . . . If the assumption is that daycare is fine, then there is no need to forgo buying a new car or to push business and government to improve it."

"Major surveys conclude that 48 percent of top executives claim their lives are empty or meaningless," states *Hemisphere Magazine* (November 1997). "Teen suicides, adolescent drug abuse, and high school dropout rates are rising. And although the country's Gross Domestic Product has risen steadily for the past twenty-five years, the American Index of Social Health (a figure compiled from sixteen measurable social indicators) is 52 percent lower than it was in 1973. These are not favorable signs that the chase of the paycheck or the buildup of dual-income families is bearing the fruits we desire."

Oh, Happy Day Care

Patrick Garry wrote in the *Chicago Tribune* (January 6, 1997):

Adequate day care is the great equalizer, representing everything parents must have to offset the unfair advantage enjoyed by their childless colleagues. Adequate day care also marks the last front in the battle for sexual fulfillment. It is the final liberator of the libido; the one missing component in the drive for safe sex . . . adequate day care is the ultimate precaution. While the birth control movement sought to ensure everyone an enjoyment of sex without fear of pregnancy, day care goes one step further. For those who used faulty contraception, or for those who accidentally forgot to suit up, adequate day care is a back-up prophylactic—a precaution against the unwanted consequences of sex, and insurance that parenthood will not be imposed without vacation benefits and time off for good behavior. It is the safety net of sex—a safeguard against having to bear the sole burden for any children that arrive.

As evidence of this growing mentality, I recently took a call on my radio program from a twenty-five-year-old woman who wanted to know if she should give up her career prospects to marry her fiancé. He is in the military, and she'd have to give up her job and the perks and promotions that seemed to be imminent, to move on base with him. "Well," I asked, "what are your future plans with respect to family, children, and all that?"

"I guess I'd like to have kids someday," she answered laconically.

"You didn't sound very enthusiastic about that. It sounded more like just another thing to do, and not something you're particularly thrilled about," I reflected.

"Oh, I don't know."

"Who or how do you plan to take care of your child?"

"Day care, of course," was her confident answer.

"How old will the child be when you put him or her in day care?"

"Oh, I don't know. Maybe six months or less."

"You are going to give over your tiny baby to a stranger in

an institutionalized day care center to love, nurture, and raise?" I shot back.

"Well," came back the answer with more than obvious disdain, "I'm not really interested in being a *mother.*"

"Then, please stay right where you are, get on with your career, tie your tubes, don't get married, and don't get pregnant. Please. Women with your attitude shouldn't make babies. Too many children suffer for it."

It's so interesting how especially cavalier many young women are about day care. I remember an appearance on the now-defunct Phil Donahue show in 1994, where I was presenting my first book, *Ten Stupid Things Women Do to Mess Up Their Lives.* As I faced an audience of largely younger women hostile to my ideas, the conversation got to day care. I was attacked for my oppressive notions about mothering when I turned the tables.

"If you were going to wake up tomorrow morning as an infant, would you choose to be raised by a day care center, nanny, or baby-sitter rather than by your mother?" I challenged. "If so, stand up now!"

The camera panned the audience. Nobody got up. Nobody even spoke. It was a telling silence.

Nonetheless, people lie about day care. They lie to themselves. They lie to others.

Day Care as a Symptom of Feminist Paranoia

The benefits of a mother's time, attention, and bonds with her children are written off by feminists as dangerous, prevailing myths. Much so-called research is actually produced by politically correct pop psychologists and used to bolster the incredible notion that developing human beings are unaffected by the loss of a constant, loving, involved mommy and daddy.

"So I decided to look into it [day care]. And, in fact, there have been decades of studies that show being a good mother has nothing to do with whether you work. . . . That is because working in and of itself doesn't affect how you treat your child. . . . In the end, not surprisingly, a child does best if her mother is happy," writes Susan Chira in *BabyCenter* (August 1999).

My one simple question here is, how can you be proficient at anything, much less mothering, if you are not actually physically there to do it? Would we really be able to say Michelangelo was a great sculptor if he did a little scraping on marble some nights and weekends after shopping, errands, and R&R, but never spent all day, day after day, on the *Pietà*? I don't think so.

Chira wonders, with day care "proven" not to be bad and maybe even positive for children, why these pesky myths prevail? She writes, "Where do these myths come from? I think women are being scared back into the home by people who find it frightening to have women working. Working means that women are independent and powerful, and some people—for ideological and political reasons—are threatened by women having power."

She then admits that the world out there is menacing; that a lot of scary things can and do happen to kids, and that it is hard to find someone you trust to take care of them. "As a result," she complains, "many women believe that it's better for their children if they stay home.

"In effect, then, working women are being blamed for social problems that are putting large numbers of children at risk. Our society doesn't do enough for children. . . . It is because our society doesn't really put children first, and because people would rather sacrifice mothers than think about how to better take care of children."

Can you believe this? Society (not parents) is responsible for meeting children's needs and for causing the guilt parents feel for not parenting their kids. It's hard to believe, but this distorted view of reality is prevalent among too many women.

Stacie, one of my callers, wrote that her mother raised her to be a feminist. She earned her BFA in advertising and worked briefly until getting pregnant. She told her boss, "Not to worry. I'm not one of *those* women. I would be back as soon as my maternity leave was over."

After a year off, she returned to work at a different agency. When she picked up her son from his first day in one of the best day care centers in her area, he slapped her in the face. After nine months and too many visits to doctors and hospitals with ailments he contracted from the other children, she quit her job to stay home permanently.

I waited three months to tell my mother. Why? Because I knew she would be disappointed in me. When I finally told her, the only thing she said was, "What about your needs?" At that moment, twenty-eight years of depression and loneliness, and three years of therapy suddenly made sense. For their needs I had been sacrificed.

I'm horribly torn by the way I was raised and the pain I know it would bring my children to leave them in day care. This is what being raised as a feminist has done for me. You tell me how far this conspiracy has gone.

Evidently, the *Lansing State Journal* (April 26, 1999) published a series of articles devoted to caring, child-centered parenting and rearing. According to columnist Mary Cunningham in the same publication (May 14, 1999), "The only children who were left out of the picture were the children who are consistently and lovingly reared by their parents, full-time, in the home. . . . As part of the sexual revolution and prominent role of the National Organization for Women of the 1970s, we women were told we were too valuable to do menial work like child rearing, and that child rearing was best left to the professionals."

For three decades feminists have produced a flood of literature challenging and criticizing every aspect of a woman's role in society, the marketplace, and the home. They have attacked femininity, child rearing, the role of wife, and the very institution of marriage. They have touted promiscuity as sexually liberating and lesbianism as politically liberating from patriarchal oppression. They have defended women's reproductive rights— whether promoting abortion as contraception or protecting the right of drug-addicted single women to have innumerable children whose lives are forever marked by neurological damage or neglect.

"It is curious," writes F. Carolyn Graglia in her book *Domestic Tranquility: A Brief Against Feminism* (October 1998), "that with the exception of Betty Friedan, who found taking care of her family mindless, the great feminist revolutionaries and theoreticians were, by choice, childless. And either by their own admission (Gloria Steinem) or the revelations in recent biographies (Simone de Beauvoir), we now know they were textbook examples of emotional damage whose relations with men were often so pathetic as to make a healthy reader cringe." This quote appeared in an article by Lisa Schiffren in the *Wall Street Journal*, March 19, 1998.

These feminist activists, instead of supporting increased choice for women, were totalitarian in their aim to push women, regardless of inclination or need, into the paid labor force. It would seem obvious that these activists rationalize their personal problems by projecting a patriarchal conspiracy.

The disdain these women have for men, marriage, and babies is blatant. Ms. Graglia's book documents how the feminist high command set about denigrating marriage and child rearing and marginalizing any woman who chose them over making money. For Betty Friedan, housewives were mindless, infantile parasites. Simone de Beauvoir stated that a woman should not have the choice to stay home to raise her children, "precisely because if there is such a choice, too many women will make that one."

Our current societal norms have made marriage optional and unstable. Illegitimacy and abortion are rampant, and mothers of babies are denigrated if they sacrifice their careers for the challenges of raising their own children.

Please Don't Have Children If You Don't Want to Raise Them

It all comes down to values and priorities. Our society does not value children; therefore, they are not a priority. In July 1999 alone, the news swelled with stories of parents whose children literally poached in the backs of their cars, sweltering in the summer heat for more than seven hours, while the parents worked, gambled, or partied. Believe it or not, there was little societal outcry, and, to the best of my knowledge, most of the parents were given probation rather than jailed.

This is part of the morning-after-pill, abortion, day care continuum. As children become less the point of our lives, less central to our daily doings and delegated to others for attention and maintenance, we become less and less aware of their very existence. Otherwise, how could a university professor father "forget" he had one more child to drop off at day care?

Children deserve to be put first. They shouldn't be worked around a mommy's or a daddy's more important schedule.

I'm sick of ads and commercials that pander to the frantic life most families lead. One print ad for a breakfast cereal bar has as text: "First thing in the morning. That's my time to herd everyone in the car. So the bucket seats? Those are our dining room chairs. And the armrests? You guessed it . . . Our table. And breakfast? That's gotta be something that won't spill, drip or stick to upholstery. Buy yourself some time. The only bars that are an excellent source of calcium, and put the goodness of a bowl of cereal in the palm of your hand."

Happy smiling faces show from the car windows. Let's make it easier and easier to erode family time and the parent-child bond. As long as they get their calcium—it doesn't matter if they miss special, unhurried, focused time with Mommy.

The *Rose Is Rose* syndicated cartoon strip summarized my feelings about this issue on May 20, 1998. Rose says to her child, "I'm rushed this morning, Pasquale! I have only a few minutes to fix breakfast . . ."

"Are scrambled eggs okay?" asks her daughter.

"Let's have apples and minutes," says Pasquale.

Mom stops and looks at them both.

In the last scene, Mom and Pasquale are eating apples out on the front porch, enjoying the lovely morning. "I guess there's more than one kind of healthy breakfast!" says Mom.

"I like my minutes sunnyside up!" replies Pasquale, happily. Amen.

The cavalier manner in which our society treats child care, not as a matter of intimacy and love, but as a matter of convenience and economics, is deeply destructive to our children's sense of attachment, identity, and importance.

I have said over and again for years, if you won't or can't offer your child your being and time, don't make a baby—get a parakeet. You can always throw a towel over the cage and quiet it when you're busy or just not interested.

Children Need and Deserve Mommies and Daddies

"Raising young children is a profoundly intimate and physical undertaking. And private too. I would as soon hire a nanny to have sex with my husband as to raise my children," wrote Deborah Maes in the *Toronto Globe and Mail* (July 9, 1998).

As a young mother, Ms. Maes observes that she is surrounded by a world almost surreally devoid of mothers. This world is largely populated by a flock of lost and vulnerable little ones surrounded by "primary caretakers" (Orwell himself couldn't have come up with a better example of Newspeak) who view the children not as the apple of their eye, but as a job.

These children have been taught that anyone can take care of them and their feelings are (at best) of secondary importance, whereas I want my children to know that they mean the world to me.

The act of raising children—like all important human relationships—is a profoundly intimate one.

Having vulnerable, dependent, developing babies in the hands of basically unknown adults reveals an unbelievably alienating world where parents ignore their children's emotional, psychological, and spiritual needs, but assiduously tend to their own.

Few political, cultural, or religious leaders have spoken out against this growing practice of abandoning infants to paid strangers. To do so is to invite vicious critical attacks for being anti-women, anti-diversity, anti-capitalism, and definitely a right-wing moral zealot. Ideological ambitions have derailed what would seem like a basic law of nature.

"I'm totally convinced that nobody can do the job family can. Nobody. I know, there are family situations that are disastrous. . . . But setting all that aside, in *general,* parents do a considerably better job," said Burton White, Ph.D., a renowned expert on children, in *American Baby* (April 1998).

When asked by *American Baby*, "But what about couples that we all know of, where both parents have to work?" Dr. White responded, "I know it's difficult. The family has all these needs. But no matter what the parental situation is, you have to bring the needs of the child into the equation."

Governmental officials, generally, and the Clintons, specifically, are constantly talking about a child care crisis. Their solution is to *redefine* family and child care, bolstered by the "serpentine juggling of statistics perpetrated in the name of 'proving' that 'anything goes,'" laments Linda Burton in *Family Circle* magazine (June 7, 1994). "No matter how convenient or soothing an idea it may be," she writes, "child-rearing cannot be redefined as the responsibility of daycare workers and the schools. If we now find ourselves economically forced into the position of farming America's children out to daycare institutions, we need to stop and ask what's gone wrong and how we can fix it. Kids need their parents. They should be able to have them."

It is no mystery what small human beings need. "Experts say

that many of the most important elements in children's lives—
regular routines and domestic rituals, consistency, the sense
that their parents know and care about them—are exactly
what's jettisoned when quality time substitutes for quantity
time" (*Newsweek*, May 12, 1997).

And the kids are showing the scars. "These kids [of busy,
working parents] don't have the self-esteem that comes from
knowing your parents are really interested in you, really
behind you," says Ronald Levant, a psychologist at Harvard
Medical School.

And the kids are showing their rage. "White, middle-class violent gang members are far more likely to be diagnosed and be
treated for their depression than African-American and Latino
violent offenders whose behavior is seen more as emanating from
a lower-class criminal and gang culture," writes Dr. Armando
Morales in the *Denver Post* (May 16, 1999). "Historically poor,
broken homes were seen as risk factors related to gang membership; this is still a major contributing factor. In the 1980s and
1990s, however, an increase of middle-class white gang members
has been observed. No longer were poverty or broken homes a
factor, rather emotional neglect caused by economic necessity
requiring both parents to work two or more jobs in order to support two or three cars, a hefty mortgage, several large color TVs,
VCRs, computers, private school and college tuition."

The kids know what they need. Two sophomore composi-
tion classes at Annapolis High School in Maryland developed
a survey to ask students, in the wake of a rash of school violence around the country, what they believed caused kids to be
violent. More than 550 students put "lack of parental attention and guidance" number one. "Parents just aren't giving
kids the attention they need," said one student. "I take care of
myself after school. I think it's more people not spending time
with their kids," said another student.

Some parents are listening. The *Charlotte Observer* (February 7, 1999) profiled four parents who cut their work hours to

get more family time. One mother said, "My kids' rare memories were not with their mom and dad, but with their nanny. Most of us think that as our kids get older, they need us less. But I found the opposite is true."

Here's the blunt truth. "'It's become clear that if you have a family with two parents working ... they're not doing very much parenting,' said Mary Dean Lee, associate professor of organizational behavior and human resource management at Montreal's McGill University.

"One parent drafted a proposal for a thirty-hour week, working 7 A.M. to 1 P.M., with no lunch. She reports, 'It's only been one month, but I feel like I have the best of both worlds. I can stay in the loop at work, and keep my skills fresh, but still be at home with my kids.'"

How can they afford it? They budget accordingly. They give their children their due.

Test Yourself, If You Dare . . .

1. Add up all the time during this past week that you actually spent with your child, focused and involved (reading with or to him, giving a bath, taking a walk, talking about something important to your child).

2. When you and your child get back together after school, work, or play, do you demonstrate interest in hearing about her time, thoughts, and experiences? Or do you just ask, "Have a good time?"

3. When your child comes to you with some creation (sculpture, essay, picture, project), do you actually spend the time to look, listen, and ask questions?

4. How often do you blow your child off because you have a headache, stomachache, backache, or are just too pooped?

5. How frequently do you yell at your kid to "be quiet" or "go away and play somewhere else"?

6. How many times do you turn your kid down when he asks to play or talk?

7. How many hours does your kid spend at the computer or watching television while you are relieved she's not "bugging you"?

8. When was the last time your family planned a family adventure or outing?

9. When was the last time your kid came to you with his worries or problems?

10. When was the last time you tucked your kid into bed?

11. When was the last time you praised your child for a righteous action or display of good character?

12. When was the last time you hunkered down and dealt with heavy family issues as a family?

These dozen questions are taken from the *Detroit Free Press* (March 20, 1999). If reading them makes you uncomfortable, don't tell me that it's the twenty-first century so it doesn't matter. You know better. Or maybe you're only willing to accept the truth if it pertains to baby rats.

Canadian Press reported, "In his studies of the brain development of baby rats, Michael Meaney, a psychiatrist and neurosurgeon, found that frequent licking and grooming from their mothers stimulated the production of brain chemicals, helping them deal with stress effectively. He said that because a rat's central nervous system is not that different from a human's, the same need for nurturing physical contact in infancy is likely true for babies" (October 23, 1997).

What was horrifying about the rest of the report on Dr. Meaney's study was the blaming of "society" for "seriously compromising the ability of parents to care for the children properly." The final blow was: "if they (parents) have no choice, the hugging the child gets at a daycare center is just as good."

"No choice"? "Society" is us. And, absent extenuating tragic circumstances, each of us can freely choose to sacrifice, accommodate, budget, and modify our lives to focus on what's most important. While it's true that there is tremendous pressure in American society to achieve and aggregate power, there are millions who willingly suffer the taunts of others and give up material rewards to give their families what they most need—their physical presence, their time, their attention, and their love.

Alice, ironically a child's psychotherapist in a private psychiatric hospital, said it all in a letter sent to me with a copy of a picture she found on her kitchen table after coming home from a full day of work on a Saturday. It was drawn by her son, age twelve, while she and his dad were away at their prestigious, important, high-paying jobs.

I'm looking at it right now and it makes me cry. It shows a huge round table, with a boy at one end holding his hands over his crying eyes. Above him is a broken heart. The rest of the page is filled with "I hate it" written some two hundred times below the headline, "I hate being alone!"

When I spoke to my son about it, he tried to make light of it by telling me that he understood that I needed to work, that we needed the money, and that he was just feeling bad at the time he was drawing the picture. I told him that I was very proud of him for being so sweet and understanding, but that it was my job to worry about money, that we would be fine without my job, and that on Monday I was going to let my boss know that I was quitting.

I am now in a non-paid internship for my clinical psych

Ph.D. My work hours are during his school time. We don't eat out so much any more, and we rent movies instead of going to the theater. Our vacations consist of throwing water balloons at each other in the backyard, with a CD of Hawaiian music for atmosphere.

I don't know how it is that during my nine months working at the hospital I disregarded my own advice to parents who were financially strapped and worried about what their kids were missing out on. I said to them, "The best memories from childhood are never about how much money the grown-ups spent on you. They are about how they laughed at your jokes and read stories, made cookies, rode bikes and cried together over It's a Wonderful Life. *The best memories of childhood are memories of the heart."*

I finally listened to myself. I want my son's heart to be full.

Dr. Stanley Greenspan, clinical professor of psychiatry and pediatrics at George Washington University (and one of my personal heroes), has written, "We need to gradually bring about social arrangements which maximize at home care of young infants by their parents" (*Washington Post*, October 19, 1997). In his book *The Growth of the Mind and the Endangered Origins of Intelligence* (Addison Wesley, 1997), he says:

> For the first time in history, there is a growing trend for more and more middle- and upper-middle-class parents to farm out the needs of their babies to others, often in settings not conducive to meeting the children's irreducible needs.
>
> Impersonal childcare may be only the most obvious symptom of a society that is moving toward impersonal modes of communication, education, and health and mental health care. Major societal changes are clearly necessary. Unfortunately, the consequences of not making changes may not be immediately obvious. The impact will likely be slow and insidious. People may gradually become more self-centered and less concerned with others. Thinking may become more polarized, all or nothing,

rather than subtle and reflective. Impulsive behavior, helplessness, and depression may increase. The ability for self-awareness and problem-solving may decrease, as will our capacity to live together and govern ourselves in cohesive communities.

"What children need is the touching, holding, cooing, rocking, and stimulation that come traditionally from a mother. . . . Attention is the greatest gift that parents can bestow," writes Mortimer Zuckerman in *U.S. News & World Report* (August 18, 1997). I would add it's what they most want and need, but it's the one thing parents don't want to give.

A *Los Angeles Times* editorial about the dramatic surge in Prozac prescriptions for children pointed out, "Studies suggest that some time-crunched parents . . . might find it easier to medicate children than to talk to them long enough to explore potential sources of their troubles. But adults . . . should remember that children's problems are often rooted not only in their brains but in their lives"—the lives that too many parents view as by-products of their own selfish lifestyles.

The Purpose of Life Is to Make the Adults Happy

I have been enormously impressed with the Herculean efforts made by the media, business, and technology to keep parents feeling good about *themselves*. "From child-care experts to general-interest books and magazines, the cultural authorities to whom better-off parents turn for advice have become increasingly less solicitous of children and increasingly more solicitous of parents," writes Mary Eberstadt (*Wall Street Journal*, May 2, 1995).

In fact, a study underwritten by the National Institute for Mental Health found, according to Jon Marcus, a reporter for the Associated Press, "that two-career couples with children are under greater stress by being made to feel they are not doing a good job raising their families." The article quoted some researchers as saying that "families will suffer undue stress if they try to follow the advice of religious and political conservatives who urge mothers to spend more time with their children" (June 11, 1996).

I get it. Newborns should be sent home from the hospital with a tattoo on their behinds: "Warning! At-home care of this infant is injurious to your mental, emotional, physical, financial, and social well-being."

In line with this "protect the parents" mentality, here's a potpourri of concepts already in place to help *parents feel better* about their dual-career lifestyle choice:

"Digital Day-Care . . . Web video technology lets parents who drop kids off at daycare make virtual visits via computer throughout the day . . . 'This way I feel better that Mommy can go and do her job and give her best to her job, but I'm not ignoring my child . . . '" (*San Jose Mercury News*, May 7, 1999).

Really? How does the child know he/she is not being ignored?

I feel sad, writes Kristin, *for the children whose parents take advantage of such tools to further ease their conscience and make their daily abandonment of their children easier and more convenient. Please continue to tell your listeners that no matter what they do to ease their sense of guilt for leaving their children to be raised by another, their children still suffer, and so does our society.*

By the way—did you see the *New Yorker* cartoon that shows a little boy going to bed at night? He's looking up at the video camera on the wall and saying, "Good night, Mommy. Good night, Daddy."

"AirTouch Phones: AirTouch 411 Connect is the perfect tool for the information age. It's quick, convenient and safe because it connects you automatically to numbers in your home service area. And makes your AirTouch phone more useful than ever. Need to tell daycare you're running late? Now you can, even if you don't have the number handy. Want to order a pizza? Find a mechanic? Call a tow truck?"

Notice what they list first? writes a listener. *Daycare—and running late. The world today.*

"The media are full of promotions for one of this year's hottest toys: Microsoft Actimate's Interactive Barney," writes Carol Ratelle Leach, in a letter to the *Minneapolis Star Tribune* (November 27, 1997). "For a mere $99—plus another $150 or so for accessories—The Purple One will 'play' with your child or sit by his or her side to watch TV or work on the computer. According to the ad, Interactive Barney will use his 'thousands of words' to verbally guide, encourage, and compliment your child." If you can't think of anything better to do with your money, donate it . . . What our children need by their sides is interactive parents."

The ad began with a mother and father discussing what to do with their sick child while they went to work. Apparently this particular day was not convenient for either of them to miss work, and their regular daycare center wouldn't allow a sick child, writes Denita, a listener. *What happened next stunned me. . . . An announcer came on to extoll the virtues of the new "Nannies-to-Go" service which, in his opinion, is "the next best thing to family." Apparently with no more effort on the parents' part than what it takes to order a pizza, a uniformed nanny (a complete stranger) will come to your home and tend to your sick, miserable, and needy child.*

"Employers hail the new Get Well Center (a sick-child center) as a solution to the problem of employee absenteeism" (*The Tennessean,* April 18, 1999). "We're not diagnosing or treating," said the director of the center. "This is daycare not health care." The Broadway center has six separate rooms, to divide children by age and illness. One room, with its own heating, cooling and ventilation system, will be dedicated to children with potentially contagious illnesses."

As if healthy child day-care were not bad enough!!! writes Amy, one of my listeners. *What possesses so many to work so hard to make sure our future generation has an institution to* go to when they are ill and actually need their parents the most? I thank God every day that I cannot imagine or understand this ... for that would make me unworthy of the truly wondrous blessing that my boys are.

And now—for the last and most obvious step: ROBOMOM and ROBODAD. This is the brainchild of Rondi, one of my listeners.

Moms and dads who put career before their kids can breathe a sigh of relief. Worried about what might happen to your kids at day care? Feeling guilty because you spend minimal time with your children each day? Relax. The amazing world of robotics brings you ROBOMOM and ROBODAD. They look, speak and, yes, even feel like Mom or Dad to the touch. Our vinyl skin is so lifelike, your infant or toddler will never guess it's a robot that's holding, rocking, singing or comforting your precious ones. Many folks asks us "Won't our kids be confused when we finally come home and there are two moms or dads who look exactly alike?" Glad you asked. As you approach the house, simply activate the Robocare remote control stored in your overhead visor along with your garage door opener. One easy push of the button and ROBOMOM/DAD walks itself directly into its own storage case, allowing you to take over. After the kids are in bed, simply reactivate the robot and go out on the town. Your kids will be off to dreamland, feeling loved, happy, contented, and will be none the wiser. **Please note that children over the age of 12 may not be fooled.

Nonetheless . . .

Just when I thought it was hopeless for our children, the following came across my desk.

➤ According to the March 1996 report from the Bureau of Labor Statistics, the fastest-growing occupations include:

number one, computer scientists, and number two (brace yourself), HOMEMAKERS!

➤ The *New York Times Magazine*, November 15, 1998: "Eight-year-olds are deeply conservative. . . . And when it comes to their mothers, they are steadfastly retrograde, shunning the new, self-fulfilled model. Especially now, when 70 percent of mothers work, a stay-at-home mom has become the ultimate trophy, reflecting prosperity and proving to the children that they are, in fact, the center of the universe. . . . Indeed, a recent survey of six- to seventeen-year-olds by the Whirlpool Foundation revealed that out of 15 possible characteristics of the 'ideal' mother, having an important job was ranked 14th."

➤ "Generation X women prioritize kids over careers and view the women ahead of them on the career ladder who made huge sacrifices for their careers as role models to avoid, not emulate. Although they 'grew up with the idea of sexual equality,' these women 'do not question women's traditional role as caretakers.' Many fantasize about being mothers as boomer women fantasized about being CEOs . . ." (*USA Today,* May 1999).

➤ "A small church-run daycare center in the Albany, NY, area closed because the church people decided that it is against their beliefs to have a child raised away from the parents. It is willing to lose the money it earned because of this belief. The local newspaper and many of the people writing to the local newspaper thought that the church's action was terrible for the children and the parents. The following week the paper ran a large article in the family section detailing the suffering of toddlers who had been separated from their playmates and other ramifications and inconveniences to parents. Nowhere in either of these articles did it mention how a child might feel being separated from its parents in a day care center. I thought that you would be happy to hear that a whole congregation put their beliefs ahead of any monetary gain," wrote Mike, a listener.

➤ "Among humans and other advanced primates, the sex that does more of the child-rearing tends to live longer," according to a study in the June 1998 issue of the *Proceedings of the National Academy of Sciences*. "And the greater the difference in child-care responsibilities between the sexes, the greater the difference in longevity" (Reuters News Service, June 9, 1998).

➤ "Finnish researchers find that mothers who transfer saliva, via shared spoon and kisses, to their infants before teething help build up the children's antibodies to bacteria that initiate cavities" (*Los Angeles Times*, August 9, 1994). Yeah, I know, now I'm getting silly.

Common sense, compassion, and natural sensibilities should lead us to recognize that children are best cared for by available, attentive, sensitive, loving parents. Other-than-parent care ought to be reserved for desperate situations, such as disturbed or dangerous parents, times of financial desperation, or the death or abandonment of a spouse—and in even the last situation, day care can be temporary, if family members pool their resources. Other-than-parent care ought not to be falsely rationalized as best for either children or parents for political or financial reasons.

I have received thousands of letters from people who have budgeted, moved to more modest homes, changed jobs, worked split shifts with their spouse, have night-time, home-based businesses, and so forth. What is missing is not the *means*. What is missing is largely the *will*. And government, social sciences, business, and the innate selfishness of mankind all conspire to weaken that will.

Even though a federal research report issued in July 1999

(*American Journal of Public Health*) determined that nine out of every ten infant day care centers in the United States fail to meet minimum recommended quality standards, with significant negative effects on children's development, the thrust seems to be to change policies and enforce practices of day care centers, rather than reevaluate the entire sociopolitical movement of institutionalizing children.

The bottom line is this: There is just no way that any public or private facility can, for payment of any amount, provide for each individual, unique, developing human being, the relationship bonding, love, touch, care, concern, that a mommy or a daddy can for free! That parenting is sometimes difficult, challenging—even heartbreaking—is true. That it sometimes feels the worst of all worlds is also true. That it is the best of all worlds is equally true for the child, for the parent, and for society.

So Much Work, So Little Time

"Forty-five percent of business executives surveyed," announced a trade paper for travel agents in 1997, "said they would be willing to miss Christmas, a wedding anniversary, a funeral or caring for a sick spouse to make a business trip," referring to a poll of five hundred executives conducted by Hyatt Hotels. "Four in five executives with children under age 18 said they would be willing to travel during a child's birthday."

Work is obviously where the laurels lie.

A nurse wrote me about a story in her hospital's newsletter praising another nurse, who put in 140 hours one pay period, despite the fact that she has a son at home. "Thank goodness Nancy Jo Gillis' teenage son knows his way around the kitchen," begins the *Enloe Medical Center Newsletter* (March 1999), "because his mother can't recall the last time she fixed her son a relaxing, home cooked meal."

Doesn't it scare you as a potential patient to know that medical personnel are working seventy-hour weeks? And doesn't it sadden you that child neglect is praiseworthy?

But this is not an isolated public huzzah for work as first, child as leftover. The president and CEO of Charming Shoppes, Inc., Dorrit J. Bern, is forty-seven and, according to an October 8, 1998, *Wall Street Journal* article "one of a growing number of female executives whose spectacularly complex lifestyles entail leaving family members behind during the week for high-powered jobs in other places. Long-distance commuting demands deft juggling, a supportive employer and an empathetic spouse— especially when the family has school-age children. But Bern's experience suggests that this unusual living arrangement can work well for women with plenty of money and power."

Oh, REALLY? Listen to these quotes from or about the "mother":

➤ "'No motherhood guilt kicks in around 7 or 8 P.M.,' she said, referring to the advantage of living thousands of miles away from her children during the week. 'You have an individual who thinks about nothing else but work on weekdays.'"

➤ "The Bern boys also need to adjust. They were accustomed to their mother's frequent backaches and headaches, business trips and dinnertime absences during the years she worked at Sears (closer to home). But it was 'nice, seeing her every night and knowing she was there,' said Collier Bern, age fifteen."

➤ "Bern's odd schedule created awkward moments when her son entered middle school and made new friends. 'She would come home on the weekends and our friends would ask who she was,' he recalls. A few thought his parents were divorced."

The last line of the article was just pathetic: "Later that evening, Bern grabbed Tyler and Collier on their way upstairs to bed. 'Hold on, guys. Give me a kiss,' she said. 'I won't see you in the morning.'"

I guess we're supposed to feel sympathy for *her loss* when we're told that a business meeting "forced her" to miss a sports banquet honoring her son as his football team's most valuable player. "'That hurt,' she said."

We are also told she battles sporadic loneliness by poring over the company's latest financial results or having dinner with a son who is now in college. My heart bleeds for her pain. What about the loss for her children and husband? And for what?

"I wish many of your listeners could follow me through a week in my shoes," writes Peg, a middle school counselor for over thirty years.

The biggest problem I deal with is LACK OF PARENT-ING. While I realize that many parents do not have a choice and have to work, they always have the option to parent. Too many times in my workshops in anger management and/or conflict resolution, the acting out of the youngster is the direct result of lack of time with the parents. If the parents only would realize that it is not the material things their youngsters want (which seems to be the trade off for guilt of working), but someone to listen, with no distractions.

I hear all too often, "They don't care what I do," but the students want and will tell me they wish they had more rules, more family structure and sometimes act out just to see if the parent cares enough to follow through with consequences.

Kids have not changed as much as we think. It is the lack of supervision and parental time denied them that causes them to react in destructive ways. It is a sad commentary to me that I know many of these young people, their hurts, fears, friends and goals better than their parents. I feel sorry for those parents who have missed in their children what I have gained— and their children have lost.

Face up to it. Our kids get in trouble because they've been

abandoned to the elements. "Tykes gallop and cavort merrily along their destructive ways as parents beam with pride. Kiddies are pumped full of Prozac and Ritalin as a proxy for discipline. Children commit bizarre, callous acts because the adults in their lives treat them callously, in warehouses . . . Children are part of a frantic 'to do' list. Parents provide for their children. [They] have pictures of their children at work, kiss them good night and even prohibit sugary snacks. All the motions say, 'I care,' but they are encased in a 'Just don't cramp my style,'" writes Marianne Moody Jennings in the *Arizona Republic* (October 3, 1999).

The *Dallas Morning News* had a very interesting story on August 19, 1999. "Last year, Americans worked an average of 43.1 hours a week, according to the U.S. Department of Labor. Our hours spent at work have steadily and slowly increased during the past two decades.

"From 1976 to 1993, the average work hours for men increased three percent, and work hours for women increased 15 percent. . . . In the last twenty years, working time has increased by 15 percent, and leisure time has decreased by 33 percent."

The article goes on to talk about the real problem: a lack of balance (health, family, financial, intellectual, social, professional, and spiritual). "A typical person twenty-five years of age finds himself in divorce court at forty-five," says Dr. Donald E. Wetmore, author of *Beat the Clock*, a book about time management. "That person gives up 50 percent of everything they have ever worked for. Ninety-five percent of all divorces are caused by a lack of communication."

In another article—this one in the *Washington Post* (May 25, 1999)—we learn that "the time married women with children spend working outside the home for pay has almost doubled in the past three decades," to an average of 1,200 hours per year. This leaves them much less time for other things, including caring for their children, according to the Council of

Economic Advisers (CEA). "'The increase in time mothers spend in paid work, combined with the shift toward single-parent families, has resulted in families, on average, experiencing a decrease of twenty-two hours per week . . . that parents could spend with children,' CEA Chairman Janet L. Yellen said at a news conference."

Yet women are whining that they're just too stressed. They are dismayed that their children don't really seem to be able to get with the program. "For Employed Moms, the Pinnacle of Stress Comes After Work," reads a June 3, 1999, headline in the *New York Times*. The article states, "'Children hold together until their parents pick them up from day care, and then they fall apart,' according to Carol A. Seefeldt, a professor of human development at the Institute for Child Study at the University of Maryland at College Park. They fall apart for several reasons, according to Seefeldt, but fatigue may be the biggest problem. 'Parents keep their children up late at night so they can spend time with them,' she said."

Dr. Alice D. Domar, the director of the Mind/Body Center for Women's Health at Beth Israel Deaconess Medical Center, is also quoted in this article. Her research has shown that "unrelenting stress is more than just an irritation. It can take a physical toll on a woman's body, weakening her immune system, threatening her cardiovascular system and contributing to headaches, backaches, gastrointestinal distress and insomnia."

But what about the children? "According to Dr. Bryan Robinson, professor at the University of North Carolina, nationally known therapist for the treatment of workaholism, and author of *Work Addiction* (Health Communications, Inc.), 'workaholics often earn comfortable incomes; their families appear to have everything. But when a workaholic's kids reach adulthood their emotional framework often collapses like so many matchsticks.

"'Adult children of workaholics often end up in therapy with

failing marriages, depression or a sense of anger they can't identify.' At the heart of their troubles, Robinson believes, was a well-
meaning but absent parent who unconsciously taught them that
you are judged by what you do, not who you are" (*Charlotte
Observer*, January 16, 1997).

And what you have also taught them is that being an available parent is not an adequate identity option. This perspective
also translates into seeing children and family as unimportant.
So much for boosting a child's self-esteem by boosting your
own through work. That's one form of "trickle-down theory"
that doesn't flow.

That reality was underscored in a *Pepper . . . and Salt* syndicated cartoon in the *Wall Street Journal* (April 20, 1999).
Mom and Dad are leaving for work. The baby-sitter is standing behind the toddler daughter. Dad is patting the girl on the
head and saying, "Sweetie, when we leave you every day with
Sarah, we're doing it for you. That way we can have successful
careers and you can be proud of us."

I prefer the attitude of listener Sam Noble, a Dallas health-
care analyst, who wrote that he "assigns high importance to
my time when I pick an employer. More important [than more
money] is a relaxed work style and the time to be with my children and family, on my terms."

He works for Value Management Group, which evidently
has the following motto: "Make sure you get the job done, and
done well. Then, take what time you need and don't abuse it."

"A very significant group, roughly a third of the labor force,
is working more hours than they want. . . . They are feeling
high levels of time pressure and stress. They feel their job inter-
feres with their family life" (*New York Times*, September 5,
1999).

So, you folks better do something about this, because your
sanity, health, marriage, family life, emotionally needy children, and society are depending on you to do the right thing!
In spite of all this information and your own personal reality,

some of you are a tough sell until the fates conspire to slap you with the truth.

I have been meaning to write you and say thank you. I am a mother of four children and have, for the past year and a half, been an at-home mom, writes Ann, a listener. *I started my own company about seven years ago because I wanted to have the choice of spending more time with my children. But, instead, I was drawn into playing boss, office manager, purchasing manager, etc.*

I listened to you daily and scoffed at what I referred to as you "spouting" about the harm we were doing our children by allowing someone else to raise them while we raised empires. After all, I had spared no expense on a nanny. And, besides, statistics stated that our children were gaining a better sense of their own identity by spending time away from us.

About two years ago, I injured my knee and was forced to spend nine months at home, off my feet. I was surprised that our kids actually battled daily over who was getting the major portion of my attention. As time passed, although my knee became stable enough to return to work full time, I continued to spend my time at home with the kids. I set up a home office so I could work at home and be with the kids.

One day I asked them if they had liked having a nanny in the past. They said that they had not said anything, because they did not want to make me feel bad, but that they had missed me terribly when I was gone. They said now they were very proud (when all the other kids were talking about their parents being away at work) to say that their Mom was always there, at home with them.

This taught me a very valuable lesson. No matter what statistics say, ask your children. Thank you, Dr. Laura, for continuing to spout.

Finally, this is a copy of an e-mail sent to more than 20,000 agents and employees of State Farm Insurance in November 1997: "We are deeply saddened to inform you of the passing of

Dorothy Jackson, age eighty-eight. Dorothy was the mother of Agent Wendell Jackson. Wendell has requested that in lieu of flowers, please go home early sometime this week or next. Take your spouse home some flowers, gather the family and spend some time with them . . . love them to pieces."

3

Dads Need Not Apply

I thought you would be interested in this story in the Washington Times *(about single women who go to clinics for sperm insemination from perfect strangers because it's safer than bar-hopping for potential fathers for their children). How sad that women who "don't have the time to find a husband" want a baby—how could such a woman possibly "have time" to be both a father and a mother to that child?*

Helen Blackwell, July 30, 1999

People always told me that the world was too messed up to have more children. I always said that because this world IS so messed up, it NEEDS people like my children. I have remarkable kids.

Angela

Are there good and bad reasons for having children? Certainly. But people determined to "make a baby" can easily discount the negatives or inappropriateness of their decision because they simply "wanna" do what they "wanna" do.

Our society has elevated personal rights and desires above responsibility and traditional values. The obvious result of this pervasive selfishness is social chaos: illegitimacy; divorce; indiscriminate sex without commitment; materialism; socially sanctioned child neglect; graphic sex and sadistic violence on radio and TV, in print and films; and the denigration of spirituality by an influential secular minority.

This selfishness is nowhere more in evidence than in the production of new human life. Some of these selfish motivations are as old as the existence of humanity. Although many bad reasons for having children are not necessarily new, their growing acceptance *is,* as society moves more and more toward an "anything goes" mentality.

I recently asked my Web site visitors (www.drlaura.com) to list the stupidest and smartest reasons to have children. Here are the results.

The Stupidest Reasons to Have Children

1. "I just want somebody to love me."

2. "Now everybody will see that I'm a MAN."

3. As a cure for loneliness or unhappiness.

4. As a way out of the parents' home into subsidized housing.

5. "To get him to marry me."

6. To fix a bad, failing, or faltering marriage—"Maybe he'll stay around and stop cheating on me."

7. "Because my biological clock is ticking loudly."

8. "In-laws are pressuring us so that they can become grand-parents."

9. So you can prove you can have children *and* a career. No modern-day ensemble (high-paying career, SUV, country home, dog, husband, highlighted hair, British nanny, and acrylic nails) is complete without a kid (in daycare).

10. Because all your friends are having kids.

11. To have someone to take care of you when you're older.

12. "I'll have a tax write-off."

13. "To show my boyfriend I really love him."

14. "This child will do in life all that I failed to do."

15. Something to remember the relationship by.

16. "I need someone to need me."

17. Babies are cute and cuddly and fun to dress up.

18. To try to change your mate into a better person.

19. "To prove I'm not too old to do it."

20. To get attention.

21. An unmarried "oops."

What is frightening, and sometimes demoralizing to me, is that I hear folks every week on my radio program fumbling through these excuses in their attempt to explain why their children were conceived without a healthy nest to welcome them. Sometimes they will even deny that the birth was inten-tional. In fact, many national surveys indicate that about one-half of all births are "unintentional." I don't buy that. I have never found one caller who didn't know that intercourse is the way human beings procreate. What is true is that most folks growing up in the era of contraceptives, abortions, and celebrated illegitimacy all too blithely ignore the correlation between sex and pregnancy, or are entirely willing to take the risk in immature denial of the consequences to another helpless, innocent human life.

The Smartest Reasons to Have Children

The most sensitive and complete answer to this question came from a father named Eli:

Because G-d commanded us to "be fruitful and multiply." The purpose of man is to live up to ". . . let us make man in our image . . ." The way to do this is to emulate G-d's attributes of kindness, mercy, forgiveness, being slow to anger, quick to forgive. The way in which a man can acquire these traits is to become married and have children—in other words, to become responsible for others, to learn patience, to learn to place the importance of others' needs ahead of his own. The best vehicle for this is marriage and parenthood. Ultimately, this is the purpose of mankind.

To pass along one's heritage. It says in Jewish writings that when G-d gave the Torah to the Jewish People at Sinai he asked Moses, "Who will guarantee the Torah?"

Moses offered many options, including the elders, the Prophets and the Forefathers (Abraham, Jacob, and Isaac), all of which were rejected by G-d. When Moses suggested the children as guarantors, G-d accepted and then proceeded to give the Torah at Sinai.

To make the world better by having an influence on future generations. To bring new young people into the world and to raise them with proper values. To counter-balance the craziness in society. Someone has to raise good, nice, moral human beings; or else we may as well throw in the towel.

To repay our parents for the love and caring and giving and sacrifice by doing the same for our children.

What I appreciated most about this analysis is that it clearly places each of us in the eternal and gives each and every one of us the ability and the responsibility to affect the future of humanity. It is true that parenting presents the opportunity to fill yourself up with joy, celebration, and love. More important, though, is seeing your children and your family as an opportunity to contribute to the goodness of the world and the hope for mankind for innumerable generations. That point of view will help you persevere through the heartbreaks, difficult challenges, disappointments, fear, and pain that are an integral part of parenting.

Deborah wrote, "So obviously the best reason to have a child is from a sense of mission; an awareness that you can change the world with your legacy to the future and a commitment to making sure that legacy is a worthy one. Come to think of it, I don't know any other good reason."

This perspective requires a maturity and selflessness not readily taught or reinforced in a society perpetually championing and defending individual rights with little consideration of the consequences to a child or society. Underscoring this distortion is the politically correct pandering that many sociological and psychological professionals do in studies, obfuscating the destructive aspects of illegitimacy and institutional child care, oversimplified and overstateed in the sensation-hungry media.

Licensing Parents

One frustrated Canadian, Jerry Steinberg, wrote an interesting Letter to the Editor in the *Vancouver Sun* (June 27, 1998), in which he said that people should have a license before they were allowed to make babies.

> We require education and testing for a license to drive a car, shoot a gun, fly a plane, catch a fish or operate a ham

radio. Yet, most people give very little forethought to parenthood and are given very little, if any, training for life's most demanding and most important job.

Even though, in a democracy, we can't prevent people from making babies irresponsibly, such courses . . . might even convince a few people that parenthood wasn't right for them and save society from the catastrophic consequences of poor parenting. Parenting should be seen as a privilege, not a right. It shouldn't be automatic or accidental, and it should certainly not be taken lightly.

I don't think this idea will ever blossom. There are parenting classes available from adult education programs, but they are usually attended by folks who are already having family problems. The reason education about parenting in advance of actually making babies is not wildly popular is the same reason most folks avoid premarital therapy—they just don't want to know what they don't know (but desperately need to!). Most people prefer ignorance, filling that void with fantasies, thereby avoiding uncomplimentary truths about themselves and the need to deal with conflicts and differences of opinion with their mates.

Don't Make Babies

The truth is that some people simply ought not to make babies—some people, never; others, just not right now.

One of my listeners, Cassandra, recognized that truth.

As my husband and I approach our second anniversary, we feel that we are not emotionally, financially, and relationship ready for a child. Therefore, we put aside our selfish yearnings for a child and are simply NOT getting pregnant. I think one of the stupidest things parents do to their children is have them before they are ready, because they simply cannot meet the CHILDREN'S needs. Just imagine if everyone had to be as ready to have children as they are to drive a car. The lack of poverty-stricken, abused and neglected children would lessen. Hmmmm, and what is more important? Driving a car or rais-ing a child?

When talking with a female caller who didn't bother to marry to make a family with a loving, available father, I often say, "You know, a bird has the good sense not to lay eggs until she's got a nest. And birds have very small brains. Why is it that so many women don't have that much good sense?"

A syndicated cartoon called *Murray's Law* (April 5, 1999) took that idea one step further. The male bird is looking into a nest with two eggs. The female bird says, "I realize we're endan-gered, Randolph, but I can't lay any more than that and still have a career."

Although I am worried about those two eggs, it looks as if only the birds are thinking, yet again.

Don't Worry—Be Sexy—The Contraceptive Will Save Us

In spite of the technological advances in contraception, a sur-prising number of adults still use the "oops, the pill/condom didn't work" bad reason for getting pregnant. According to *Family Planning Perspectives* (March/April 1999), "About three million pregnancies in the United States (48%) were unin-tended in 1994 (last date of complete data). Some 53% of those occurred among women who were using contraceptives." There are two reasons for the failure rate—the limited effec-tiveness of contraception and pilot error and irresponsibility. According to *Perspectives*:

> When contraceptive methods are ranked by effectiveness over the first twelve months of use (corrected for abortion underreporting), the implant and injectables have the lowest failure rates (2–3%), followed by the pill (8%), the diaphragm and the cervical cap (12%), the male condom (14%), periodic abstinence (21%), withdrawal (24%), and spermicides (26%).

> In general, failure rates are highest among cohabiting and
> other unmarried women. Women under twenty who are not mar-
> ried but cohabiting experience a failure rate of about 31% in their
> first year of contraceptive use, while the twelve-month failure rate
> among married women aged thirty and older is only 7%.

In spite of the liberating cry of the sixties that sex and reproduction have been safely separated, sexually active women still
risk conceiving children. *Perspectives* says, "The typical woman
who uses reversible methods of contraception continuously . . .
will experience 1.8 contraceptive failures."

On my program I ask women to think what they will do
with a possible baby before having illicit sex. Will they terminate it; give birth, then abandon it to full-time institutionalized
day care; give it up for adoption by a married, heterosexual
couple; or make the sacrifice to marry the father and give the
child an intact home? Unfortunately, too many of them haven't
given it a thought.

Infinite Possibilities

One of the main problems facing basically decent people,
struggling today with the challenges of marriage and children,
is the loss of societal focus and commitment to ideals, obligations, and self-sacrifice. This is not a first in human history.
Will Durant wrote in *The Life of Greece* (Simon and Schuster,
1939), "Athens had ruined itself by carrying to excess the principles of liberty and equality, by training the citizens in such
fashion that they looked upon insolence as democracy, lawless-
ness as liberty, impudence of speech as equality, and license to
do what they pleased as happiness."

Our society has virtually redefined the term "rights" to include
almost any desire by any individual regardless of common sense,
propriety, morality, legality, or the price paid by other individuals, families, or civilization. Any attempt to decry such chaos is

met with hostility and name-calling, including such terms as "hateful," "intolerant," "judgmental," "retro," "fundamentalist," "discriminatory," "dangerous," "arrogant," and "mean."

The subtle (and not-so-subtle) undermining of the traditional family is widespread. My radio listeners are alert to signs of it everywhere—in business and the media, in government, and among many professionals.

Brian and Nuka wrote about their experiences in a well-known toy store chain.

We registered for our baby shower. While filling out the forms, I was appalled to see the first line say "Mother's Name" and the second line say "Additional Name." It did not say "Father's Name" or even another ambiguous title I have had to deal with, "Partner's Name."

You've said it before, Dr. Laura, "What is this world coming to" when family toy stores go so far out of their way to make the "non-married" mother comfortable even to the extent of disregarding responsible fathers? When they printed out the registry my "Additional Name" wasn't even listed, and I was told that the nationwide registry could only be looked up by the mother's name. When I asked the representative to please add my name to the registry she snidely told me, "There is no space. It is not set up for a Father's name."

No "space" for fathers—not in their computer, not in the store, not at the hospital, not in this world of "political correctness." Throughout the pregnancy, my wife has always been called the mother, and I have been no more than a nameless sperm contributor. In the end of this heated debate, with a couple of simple key strokes on the computer, I put my own name on the registry.

That's business.

Fern wrote about her experience with one of the many television shows that describe the new ideal family: *Grace Under Fire*.

We had put my daughter to bed and were flipping channels and stopped for a few moments on Grace Under Fire. *We laughed at a couple of the jokes, but the laughter changed to disgust quickly. The scene moved upstairs where her two kids were in bed talking. The little girl told her brother that she had a friend whose mother was married to another woman. Her friend had two mommies. Her brother was disbelieving, to which the little girl replies, "At least we're normal. We have one parent like everybody else." I looked at my husband during the canned laughter and asked, "Was that supposed to be funny?" My husband and I are our little girl's parents and intend to stay that way. I guess we will be "abnormal" and give her two parents. I wish more parents did the same.*

That's media.

Sue wrote about an announcement she'd recently received about a new OB/GYN practice in her neighborhood. The bio of one of the new female doctors was academically impressive. The critical part was the listing of the woman's *hobbies*: "Her personal interests include: gardening, outdoor activities, *parenting*, and reading detective novels."

I felt sick to my stomach. I am astonished that someone can actually rank parenting along with gardening and detective novels. What's even worse, she listed parenting third on a list of four hobbies. She must think that what Miracle Gro does for plants, daycare does for children. Perhaps if she put parenting first before everything—even her job, she would notice that although plants don't wither from a lack of hugs and a parent's time, children do.

That's professionalism.

Last Mother's Day was excessive in terms of the typical promotions touting the benevolence, kindness, sweetness, importance, and love-ability of mothers. The *Wall Street Journal* (April 29, 1999) reported that "Mother's Day cards aim for a bigger market with sisterhood themes. Hallmark Cards, Inc., says its new cards for girlfriends, sisters and daughters, not just Mom and Grandma, celebrate 'women's empowerment.' A sample verse: 'Those who follow their own choices, think for themselves, and don't accept limitations are those who really help others most.'"

It should be noted that the woman who helped to found Mother's Day never married or had children. She did this to honor her mother, not to honor herself. But we are in the era of marketing to the "self." To do that, it would seem, we have to dilute the significance of traditional sacrifices women make for husbands, children, and family.

Indeed, Hallmark's exploitation of our social chaos was highlighted in an editorial cartoon in the *Arkansas Democrat Gazette* (May 9, 1999). A small child is looking for a traditional Mother's Day card among a sea of single mother, stepmom, surrogate mother, egg donor, foster parent, au pair, and grandparent-as-mom cards. Instead of acknowledging the sad chaos, we are heralding the chaos as choice, reasonable options, and rights.

The conspiracy to minimize the value and importance of marriage and fathers to children was profoundly obvious when one examined the Mother's Day stories that ran in the lifestyles sections of many newspapers. The front page of the *San Francisco Examiner* (May 9, 1999) ran a glowing piece on a couple who had a baby out of wedlock. The bio-dad was going away to school.

"'I wish I could stay at home and not miss anything,' said the bio-dad. 'But Michelle's doing a pretty damned good job.'" This—from a guy who has another daughter he hasn't seen in years—is what is highlighted on Mother's Day, without any critical commentary. Score another one for the media!

In Sweden and Iceland, one out of every two children is born to a single mother. According to a report in the *Swiss American Review* (September 25, 1997), "While there may be many reasons why women opt for single motherhood, the most obvious appears to be the amount of child assistance benefits appropriated to mothers who raise their children without a father, divorced and widowed mothers included. Where women can count on generous government subsidies the mood for marriage seems to decline rapidly." That's just not in Sweden, either.

Then we have the American Psychological Association (APA) weighing in with the definitive analysis of what is indeed right, normal, and healthy for children. In the June 1999 issue of *The American Psychologist,* an article entitled "Deconstructing the Father" proudly takes aim at the old-fashioned notion that fathers and two-parent heterosexual marriages are necessary for the psychological health of children. "The authors argue that neither mothers nor fathers are essential to child development . . . and that responsible fathering can occur within a variety of family structures." This dangerous and irresponsible tripe is increasingly coming out of the APA—ideology masquerading as science, infecting public policy, and recasting behavioral norms.

Marriage, Mommies, and Daddies Do Matter

If marriage is not important, why does it matter at what age children start having sex? If sex is only about physical pleasure and emotional bonds, why begrudge a twelve-year-old these benefits? (Another outrageous so-called research project published by the APA in 1999 suggested that it doesn't *always* hurt them!)

Philip Lawler writes in the *Wall Street Journal* (March 4, 1999):

> Our society has already suffered profound damage because of an attitude that treats sexuality as a means of casual recreation detached from all responsibility. The sexual revolution—facilitated by the birth-control pill—has brought in its wake epidemics of teen pregnancy, venereal disease, abortion, divorce, child abuse, and illegitimacy.
>
> Parenthood, on the other hand, entails enormous responsibilities. Young mothers and fathers routinely sacrifice their own pleasures to ensure the security of their children. Parents look

beyond their own welfare, and take an interest in the sort of world their children—and perhaps even their grandchildren—will inhabit. Note the abundant demographic data that show married couples are more successful than their single neighbors (healthier, wealthier, more likely to vote, to save money, and to contribute to charities).

According to a report in *USA Today* (July 1, 1999), "The percentage of high school senior girls who say having a child while unmarried is a worthwhile lifestyle rose from 33 percent in 1976 to 53 percent in 1995." This is sick and sad. Several generations of adults have created an atmosphere of negativity and cynicism about love and commitment—the children pay the price.

I Don't Need Me a Man

Steve Breen's 1998 cartoon was published in the *Asbury Park Press* right around Father's Day. It depicts two small children reading a nostalgic epitaph for Robert Young. One child says, "What's 'Father Knows Best'?" The other child responds, "What's a father?"

It is absolutely horrifying that celebrities having babies without marriage, or even an involved bio-dad, are touted in the media as role models. Jodie Foster was so treated in *People* magazine. She was a high school valedictorian; a Yale magna cum laude graduate; an award-winning actress, director, and producer. What was left? Motherhood, to fulfill a need for yet another accomplishment. No mention of the father's presence or even existence. Foster is rich. She can give her child the best things. She may even be a good mommy. But she cannot substitute for a daddy.

Sinead O'Connor, thirty-two, voluntarily turned over custody of her three-year-old daughter to the father. O'Connor, who barely knew the man before agreeing to have his baby, will see her child on weekends and holidays. She is quoted as saying, "This is what happens when you go around having babies with total strangers."

Camryn Manheim said in *Parade* (May 9, 1999), "I want to have children, but right now I'm not in a relationship. I'd love to be a biological parent and I want my child to know its father. I have some friends whom I'm considering as co-parent. I'm thinking about entering into a negotiation with one of them. I plan on doing this soon. I haven't given up on being married, but I'm not going to wait for it. I don't want to wait for things I have no control over."

It's almost unbelievable that there are people who believe they are entitled to children and can "negotiate" a deal to have them. As Jack, a listener, wrote, "I have always thought that the contract you entered into to produce a child was a marriage contract and that contract came before conceiving a child. I can't accept the idea of contracting to produce a child as you would to add a room onto your house."

A Philadelphia anchorwoman actually thinks she is a great black, female role model for intentionally having an out-of-wedlock child using sperm from a bank. "I am a role model. The message I'm sending to young black women is to get as much education as you can and be able to support yourself before you have a baby" (*Philadelphia Inquirer*, May 11, 1998). Amazing. Does she really believe children of rich and successful mothers don't miss daddies?

As columnist Kathleen Parker so aptly put it, "What's appalling is our mindless celebration of single motherhood at a time when fatherlessness is a national crisis. On any given day in any American city, a fatherless boy is booked on murder or a girl barely pubescent gives birth to another fatherless infant. Like morons unable to connect the numbered dots, we continue to treat each celebrity announcement of single motherhood as a virgin event" (*Orlando Sentinel*, March 25, 1998).

And Baby Makes Two is a documentary about a group of single New York women eager to have children. It was partially financed by the Corporation for Public Broadcasting. Lawrence Van Gelder, in his *New York Times* review (June 25, 1999), describes the piece as a warmhearted group portrait of three articulate and independent women whose time and options are "running out." He does point out that the documentary pays only passing attention to the larger dimensions of the story it tells:

> But nowhere does the film deal with how a woman without a helpful group, in a small town, for example, might fare in choosing single motherhood. Nor does it seek out any similarly maternal unmarried women who bring children into poverty. And while some of the mothers here raise the question of rearing children in the absence of a full-time father, or any father at all, the brief documentary does not strive in any serious way to pursue the long-term psychological impact of such an upbringing.

The reason for that omission is simple. Children are being considered as merely one more acquisition. If you want to do something, first declare it "good." Somehow we believe that we have become like G-d in Genesis—if we deem it good, it just is.

Well, it isn't! As Sara McLanahan, a Princeton sociologist, sums up in an essay in *Lost Fathers* (St. Martin's Press, 1998):

> Even after controlling for factors such as race and socio-economic status, children who grow up apart from their biological fathers are disadvantaged across a broad array of outcomes. They are twice as likely to drop out of high school, 2.5 times as likely to become teen mothers, and 1.4 times as likely to be idle— out of school and out of work—as are children who grow up with both parents. Children in one-parent families also have lower grade-point averages, lower college aspirations and poorer attendance records. As adults, they have higher rates of divorce.

In that same book, even Judith Stacey, the Streisand Professor of Women's Studies at the University of Southern California, and a tireless advocate for family "diversity," begins her essay by conceding that "the predominate (but by no means universal) prevailing view among family scholars is that *all other things being equal*, two-parent families generally are preferable to one-parent families."

Single motherhood may be more acceptable to society, but it is not acceptable to children; nor is it in their best interest. Nonetheless, such national parenting magazines as *American Baby* (July 1999) give this advice to those who may be criticized for their solo flight into parenthood, "You have nothing to be ashamed of."

Then there is this insidious, self-serving commentary published in *Newsweek* (May 10, 1999), entitled "Since Motherhood Is a Joy, Not a Disaster . . . I Choose to Keep My Baby. I've Never Been Happier." The contributor, Carolyn Edy, continues, "To those who said I needed to think of my child, I responded with questions of my own. . . . As for depriving her of an in-house father, I asked: How many children are abandoned by their fathers later in life? How many have to deal with divorce?"

Though I applaud her decision to avoid abortion, I am disheartened by her disingenuous use of extreme situations and tragic circumstances as rationalizations for not being married when conceiving and not choosing adoption for this child.

Her parting shot makes me concerned about the influence she'll have on her daughter's attitude toward marriage when *she* considers it. "Whenever I do complain that single motherhood is hard, I've got my mom and grandmother to tell me I have it easy—I don't have a husband to take care of as well." Nor does she have a husband to take care of her. Nor a father to take care of his child!

How can you blame this woman when famous advice-givers like Dr. Joyce Brothers in her syndicated column (August 12, 1996) demonstrate that "the times" dictate the rightness or healthiness of such a decision. "Single parents can be excellent parents. Ideally, it's best for a child to have a relationship with both his father and mother, but the world is changing, and we have to redefine our concept of what family means."

Claptrap! Dr. Brothers has obviously decided to stay noncontroversial and politically correct. Nonetheless, what children need is universal. What people want or are willing to do changes with the wind.

The editor of the *Single Mother* newsletter shares her neurotic anxieties and hostilities toward men and marriage in the January/February 1999 issue: "There is a widespread fear that women are becoming single mothers because they have no need for fathers or men for that matter. Nothing could be further from the truth. Women simply don't want to be the property of men as they have been for centuries. Nor do they want their children to also be considered property." What confused propaganda! And what is she going to teach her son about his value and his place in society, in a family, in a marriage, and in his children's lives? What is his purpose in life—beyond posing a danger to women?

One seventeen-year-old listener sent me an ad from her local paper that said, "You: Want a pregnancy, but not a man around. Physically fit, emotionally and financially secure. Me: forty, lean, well-muscled genotype. Medium brown hair and eyes. Anglo/Polish ancestry. Calm disposition. High intelligence. Musical, multilingual, professional. V. fertile, several first-cycle impregnations. Smart, tough, cute kids, with good eyes and teeth. Aim: Progeny. No post-pregnancy contact."

Sounds like just the breeder for women who can't or won't handle their own insufficiencies, inadequacies, and fears about being an adult woman and interacting intimately in a committed relationship with a man. Isn't it horrifying that there are so many women who see childbearing on a par with animal husbandry? (No pun intended!)

Poor, Poor Single Moms

Being a single mom is hazardous to mental health. Canadian researchers have found single mothers suffer significantly more psychiatric problems than do mothers in two-parent families. "Single moms," says a study in the *Canadian Medical Association Journal*, "had a higher incidence of depression, anxiety disorders and substance abuse." Researchers found that most of the women surveyed were free of mental health problems until they became single parents—even when finances were not a problem.

What? Could a stable, committed, and sharing partner, loving husband, involved father, actually be healthy for women?

A *Parenting* magazine article "Combating Fatigue" (May 1998) elicited this letter to the editor: "You suggest that parents split the nighttime shifts. What are you supposed to do if you're a single parent? When my baby is born in three months, I'm going to be a single mother, and I don't have anyone to help with the stress, tiredness, or depression. I'd appreciate advice in your articles on how to handle problems when there's no one else around to turn to."

The title of that next article should be "Responsible Childbearing—Be Married, or Put the Child Up for Adoption to a Two-Parent Family Who Can Do the Job."

The most outrageous single-mom whining I've read to date was Francoise LaMour's in the *Dallas Morning News* (March 16, 1998), who "discovered" she was pregnant and wondered how on a yearly salary of $25,000 she was going to raise a child. "Making $25,000 per year and receiving no financial or emotional support from the father, I assumed there would be some government benefits that would help me support my child. But what the government doesn't consider is the cost of daycare, baby formula, diapers and other expenses that are incurred with a child. Where is justice for the middle class? Where do we fit into the American Dream?"

The American Dream used to involve married, intact, two-parent families, commitment, and acceptance of responsibility. In fact, the United States Census Bureau reports that the most effective program for lifting Americans out of poverty is *marriage*! According to the *Los Angeles Times* (October 6, 1997), "The poverty rate for all families today is about 17 percent higher than in 1976. Yet during the same intervening period, the poverty rate for married couples has remained almost unchanged." It's those pesky "I want to parent alone" types who are likely to sink below the poverty level.

Frankly, the most infuriating aspect of the epidemic of self-centered immaturity dictating individual behavior, and the social policy that supports it, is indifference to one's obligation to be responsible to society, especially to its most defenseless members. By defenseless, I don't mean the adults who make bad choices. I mean the children who are products of their irresponsibility. These adults are like teens who want the power and perks of maturity, but want to run back to Mommy and Daddy when they aren't really up to the task of taking on the responsibility.

This letter to the editor of *Stars & Stripes*, the military newspaper, is a classic:

> I am writing on behalf of all single or unwed mothers-to-be. I am one of them, and being five months pregnant, I am constantly being asked about "my husband." How closed-minded of them to automatically assume that because I am pregnant, I must be married.
>
> Wouldn't it be just as easy and more "user friendly" to say "the father"? That would apply in all cases. And it doesn't stop at supposedly friendly people asking questions.
>
> Nearly every form I had to fill out referred to the father as "husband." Come on, I hate to use a cliché, but it's the 1990s. I think we single mothers deserve recognition, too.

This is an example of our young womanhood in the armed services—and in lots of other occupations, too. Pride in disruption of the family and the social order. Pride in robbing a child of a father.

Oops, I Made a Mistake

A cartoon by Jim Borgman (King Features, November 1994) is devastating in its irony. It features a peek through an apartment window at a woman holding one baby, while another small boy is asking, "Mommy, where do Daddies come from?"

Another cartoon (*Stitches*, July/August 1997) shows a hippie-looking single mother pushing her child in a carriage, while a more traditional-looking woman sweetly peers at the baby. The hippie says, "I'm waiting until he's old enough to decide whether he wants to be legitimate."

Frankly, these cartoons are not as funny as *Dennis the Menace*, and they aren't meant to be. They are there to illuminate a painful truth about the loss of values in our society and the cost to our children. Those who worship any and all behavior as righteous lifestyle choices usually condemn these editorial jabs as "mean-spirited." The argument goes that since making such observations hurts the feelings of those who choose these "lifestyles," the *truth* should be changed. Never mind about the hurt to the feelings, psyches, and souls of the children condemned by adults acting out their own inadequacy, ignorance, and selfishness.

Some people do get it—and better late than never. Suzy wrote about her process of revelation:

> *I am a thirty-year-old single mother of a four-year-old daughter. I decided to become a single mother at twenty-six. I wasn't in a relationship and I didn't want to start having children in my thirties, and I had a great job and thought, "Hey, I can do this!" You know all the nineties woman bull ... So, some friends and I went to a nightclub one evening and I ran into a guy I knew from high school and told my friend, "There is the father of my child!" ... All it took was one time and I*

*was pregnant. We didn't end up dating long, and I was never
going to tell him . . . but the thing you are never told about
pregnancy is how that little life changes EVERYTHING you
think and feel. My whole moral structure did a 180 and the
consequences of my choice became clear. He is not the type of
man I would ever want, he drinks too much. He never contacted me again until after my daughter's first birthday. He
came by a couple of times when she was about two. He came
by drunk, told me he loved us, made promises, cried, then
skipped town. I located him and told him to stay out of our
lives and a few other choice things. But, I don't want my
daughter to resent me for telling him he couldn't come around.
Do I have a right to expect anything when I just decided for
him that he was to be a father? Should I keep trying? My little
girl wants her father.*

Boy, do I hate these kinds of letters and calls! It's wake-up
time, but not before there's a child in the world with no dad
and a frazzled, disillusioned, working mom. Reluctantly, I
always advise the custodial parent to keep the door open. Bar-
ring drunkenness and abuse, children want and need a mom
and a dad. *Hello!*

Nanette wrote me about a worst-case scenario.

*I wish I had known what I do today. As much as I love my
daughter and all that we have in common, I did her a great disservice by not providing that father figure from the beginning.
When I hear you advise these single women about adopting
out these babies, God bless you! I have come to realize that
when women think of having a child they only think of the
feelings they need filled in their lives. They don't ever think of
the future for that child—and don't acknowledge the long-
term responsibility. You see, my daughter has attempted suicide, started self-mutilating, ran away from home, has had to
deal with an eating disorder and went from a belief in God to
Witchcraft and Satan—all in a search for that special father
acceptance. I was there as much as working to support us*

would allow, and I tucked her in bed every night, reading to her when she was young. She was always the center of attention, all in an effort to compensate for the lack of the other parent. After much therapy and many hospitalizations, we have a wonderful relationship again. I just want other single mothers to know that having a child as an answer to all their problems is selfish and the most irresponsible thing a person could do to a child.

Finally, in response to an article in the *Los Angeles Times* (October 26, 1994) that asked the question "Does a Kid Need a Dad?" a reader responded:

Yes, a child does need a father, desperately needs him, and to deny a child a father is the worst thing these women could do. Women who choose to rob their baby of half its identity are selfish and have no idea of the life of questions and anguish they are condemning their children to. Twenty years ago I had a baby girl. I was unmarried; the father wanted no part of a baby. No problem. I had enough love for the both of us. All was well until the day my precious daughter started asking me questions about her dad. Questions I couldn't answer. Believe me, the teen years are traumatic enough without having to deal with this. Every time she looked at me, she only saw half of who she is. Someday these women will be facing a tearful, tortured young person demanding to know why half of who they are is missing and why was this done to them. What will they say? "Gee, I did the best I could. It seemed like a good idea at the time. I was lonely." Save it. It won't be enough.

I know the standard counterargument: "I raised my kids alone and they are just fine." Well, kids are often survivors. Academic accomplishment and financial independence are not the only parameters of a healthy outcome. How many of them ultimately wish to marry, feel optimistic about love and commitment, stay involved in relationships when the going gets difficult, or wish to make sacrifices for the needs of a spouse or children? That's where the devastation shows itself.

Three Dumb Arguments

Earlier in the chapter I listed dumb reasons to get pregnant. Here are three even dumber arguments for not marrying once a child is conceived:

➤ **You don't want to marry him "just because you're pregnant."** How does one explain to a child that he just wasn't an important enough reason to get married, even though his mother's lust was important enough to risk unprotected sex?

➤ **Marriage doesn't mean forever anyway.** It's true that the simple act of a marriage ceremony is not a guarantee you'll stay together, but at least you are starting out with that goal and a commitment to create a foundation for the child's growth and development.

➤ **I'm a good mother.** Your ability to be loving and attentive is only part of the description of a good mother. Good single mothers are rarely at home full-time raising their children because they're off earning a living. A better way to define a good mother is one who is actually physically there, doing the job in order to get the rating. Another definition of a good mother is one who provides the proper home for the baby's development, including marriage and a father. Don't believe me? Ask any child.

4

Brave New Baby

*I enclose a recent article on modern methods of
dealing with infertility, which you may or may
not have seen. I found the article, and especially
the list of ten ways to have a baby, to be particularly disturbing for its complete separation
between marriage and reproduction.*

Bruce McNair, 1999

The caller wondered aloud about whether it was a good idea
for her to give one of her eggs to a friend, so that she could get
pregnant. This caller was married with two small children of
her own.

"You may be underestimating the emotional price of watching someone else virtually give birth to and raise *your* child," I
offered. "You may also not recognize the complications to
your husband and children having someone of their *blood*
belonging to a neighborhood friend. I suggest you recommend
to your friend and her husband that they adopt."

"Oh no," said the caller, correcting my assumption. "My
friend isn't married. She's thirty-nine, doesn't really want to get

married, and has no one in her life anyway. She just really wants a baby."

"What?" I screamed into my microphone. "How can you, a wife and mother of two children in an intact home, justify giving up one of your potential babies to a woman who intends to rob that child of a father? How could you even think of that? She would be alone in providing for that child, who would have to be cared for by others. What in the world would make you even consider doing that to a child?"

"I didn't want to hurt her feelings," she replied weakly.

"How can you as a mother justify intentionally condemning a child to fatherlessness because you don't want to hurt your adult friend's feelings? How could you have become so cavalier about the life of a child when you have been blessed with two?"

"Oh," she said, finally, "I hadn't thought about it that way."

It would seem that not too many souls out there consider the best interest of a child when dazzled by the current extraordinary technology available to virtually create life where it can't be normally conceived.

Another caller wondered about accepting the invitation to be the godmother to her friend's baby. The friend, a single woman, has chosen to be impregnated with sperm from an anonymous donor. I asked the usual question about the value of a dad to a child and the caller replied, "I asked her about that, and she says kids don't need a dad."

"Does she hate men?" I asked.

"Yes, she does," came the answer.

"Can you imagine the sick and destructive influence she would be to a female child, much less to a male child? This is one of the last women on the face of the earth who should be fertile. I pray she's infertile," I responded.

"Oh, she's already three months pregnant," said the caller.

France has banned the sale of sperm to single women and the Italian parliament has approved a draft law on assisted fertility, which would ban single women from almost any fertility procedure, from artificial insemination to in-vitro fertilization (*New York Times*, May 28, 1999). Unlike the United States, most European countries are *at least debating* the morality, wisdom, and impact on children and society of supporting and assisting infertility treatments for single women.

At least three thousand fatherless babies are produced each year through artificial insemination, according to *U.S. News & World Report* (May 15, 1995). American discussions of ethical considerations concerning the welfare of the child under such conditions are virtually buried under the banner of "rights"— the rights of adults, not the rights or needs of children.

For decades, pundits have been decrying the negative impact on women, children, and society when fathers are absent and uninvolved. Even the radical feminists seem to have dropped that concern in their defense of the "right" of single lesbian and heterosexual women to have children. Of course, this means deconstructing and denigrating the family as we know it.

Look, Ma, No Parents!

"Orange Country Superior Court Judge Robert Monarch ruled in September, 1997, that little Jaycee has no legal parents. Period" (*Washington Post*, February 1998).

The story began when, in March 1995, an infertile couple hired a married woman to carry a child made of donated sperm and eggs to term for them. The genetics of this child are unrelated to the infertile couple as well as to the surrogate.

One month before the little girl was born, the infertile husband divorced the infertile wife and claimed he no longer had parental responsibility. The infertile wife wanted to be the mother, but wasn't related by genetics or birth. The surrogate mother didn't qualify because she had signed a contract relinquishing maternal rights. The egg and sperm donors didn't want to be parents either. This sure gets complicated as technology separates the intimacy and primacy of the man-woman committed relationship from the event of conception.

In June 1998 the California Supreme Court decided that the infertile couple, now divorced, were the legal parents. The panel cited a law that makes a husband who consents to his wife's artificial insemination responsible for the child. "Intent to become parents is more important than a biological relationship," said the court.

The infertile "father" has had no contact or relationship with the child, but is mandated by the court to pay about $380 each month until the girl is eighteen. He had been supporting the claim of the surrogate mother (who later dropped her claim), because he no longer wished to be in any way involved with the child for whom he originally "contracted."

So here is a child, virtually adopted from anonymous egg and sperm donors, gestated in yet another woman, abandoned by her nonbiological but legally ascribed "intentional" father, and raised by her intentional mother. What a family tree.

There has been growing activism by some adoptees demanding rights to the information about their bio-parents. Imagine the complexities in this instance as this curious young adult tries to piece together her heritage, her identity, her sense of belonging. I wonder if she will feel more important because of all the people, legal contracts, and medical technology involved in her creation—or less important because of all the people, legal contracts, and medical technology involved in her creation. And if she feels less important, will anyone care as long as the adults got what they wanted?

And Baby Makes . . . Seven

The caller was quite distressed. "My husband and I have fertility problems. The doctor said that with my husband's sperm and my egg combined in-vitro, we have a good chance of having babies. If we implant a number of embryos at least one should work."

"Well," I said, "what is the ethical or moral problem I could help you with today?"

"The doctor said that if too many of the embryos develop, I would have to do something called 'selective reduction.' Too many gestating babies are dangerous for the mother, and results in a greater risk for prematurity and disabilities for the babies. When he told me what the procedure entailed, I was just horrified. They go in and arbitrarily kill some of my babies. I don't see how I can be so happy about giving life when it simultaneously requires causing death."

"I am reminded," I responded, "of the movie *Sophie's Choice*. In this film, Meryl Streep plays a woman in a concentration camp with her children. As the commandant walks past the line of people, deciding who shall live and who shall die, he transfers the evil decision to her. She is left having to choose which of her two children survives and which one will be gassed. She makes a choice. They both die anyway, but you don't find this out until the end. The rest of the movie is about her tortured life, living with the memory of such an ugly, horrendous act. Your situation seems similar."

"Yes, it does, and I can't bear it—I can't do it," she cried. "How could I ever forgive myself for murdering some of my children in order to have the blessing of others? It doesn't seem right."

"You are obviously a moral, sensitive person," I offered. "And I agree, it isn't right. It is callous and treats babies more like commodities than human beings. With abortion a mainstay of women's reproductive 'health,' undesirable unborns are not considered human. I'm relieved that my audience is hearing you. Perhaps they will regain some humanity."

"What should I do?" she asked.

"My opinion is that you only implant, say, three at a time. There is a new law in Italy that physicians can only create three embryos at a time, which must be implanted within three months and cannot be frozen for later use. In England, Australia, and most of Europe, regulations require doctors to put no more than two or three embryos into a woman's uterus. The result is far fewer multiple pregnancies than in the United States, where it is not unheard of for some fertility doctors to implant ten embryos! Whereas the business, ego, and profit motive is alive and well here, most other countries are clearly leaning in the direction of protecting the dignity and divinity of human life over the expedience of treatment procedures and profits from desperate adults."

"Thank you." She sighed. "I feel much better and that's exactly what I'll do. I'd rather not have this work at all, than to live with the memory of killing some of my babies."

"Bless you for that," I answered.

When "selective reduction" can be considered a routine part of infertility treatment, it becomes clear that much of this Brave New World of biotechnology is not necessarily being done out of any love for children, as much as out of a desire to achieve adult goals and desires.

The proof of that pudding is that "selective reduction" is not only being employed in situations of life and death for mother or multiple fetuses, but for situations of choice and convenience. There is no bottom to how crass some baby-makers can get. Daniel, a surgical specialist and attorney, wrote to me about such a situation:

I had just finished attending a meeting at a local hospital when I saw an OB/GYN colleague I hadn't spoken with in quite some time. My colleague shared with me that it was too bad that he and his wife had to terminate two eighteen-week fetuses. It turns out that he and his wife specifically wanted a little girl. As a physician, he prescribed his wife fertility drugs, had his own sperm fractionated to obtain relatively high count female spermatozoa, and had artificial insemination. At eighteen weeks, the girls were seven to eight inches tall, had fully

*formed anatomy, were growing in size, and perhaps even start-
ing to suck their thumbs.*

*He then said that he and his wife made the decision that four
girls would be a huge inconvenience. Mom's life wasn't in danger. The girls had no known serious birth defects, and finances
were not a problem. Using imaging that allowed dad to see the
four little girls, two were selected for the termination. A long
needle entered mom's uterus and was guided sequentially into
two of the sisters' chest cavities, the small but functional hearts
being the specific targets. The potassium solution did the trick
and stopped their hearts. Two baby girls were terminated and
lost from mom's uterus a short time later. Even if the surviving
girls were unaware of the terror that invaded their "home,"
will Dad someday casually tell them about all the special
arrangements that had to be made for their arrival; and that it
was "too bad" he and mom had to eliminate their sisters?*

How chilling! Instead of accepting with grace the challenges
life and G-d afford us, too many folks are acting godlike, eliminating inconvenience, and being challenged only by their own
selfish desires. As one listener wrote in response to my reading
this letter on my radio program, "What kind of woman would
readily allow her husband to kill her children? What kind of
woman, after feeling the first tentative flutter of her children's
movements within her, would choose to end that life because it
would be inconvenient and overwhelming to raise more than
two children?"

Gimme My Baby

The history of infertility techniques is littered with tales of lost,
damaged, or misappropriated sperm, eggs, and embryos. For
example, the University of California at Irvine agreed to pay
nearly $20 million in damages to 107 infertile couples, includ-
ing dozens who had their eggs stolen.

"Two UCI physicians lost or pirated eggs and embryos from

scores of couples who went to one of their clinics to get pregnant. In some cases, eggs or embryos were given secretly to other patients or used for research. Some couples bore children conceived from the eggs of other women without the knowledge of the genetic parents" (*Los Angeles Times*, June 14, 1999).

I'm sure the lawyers for all parties were satisfied with their financial compensation, but what about the mislaid, mismatched children, and the parents who now imagine their neighbor with their babies? What about the possibilities of biological incest as innumerable families within a small geographical area have mix-'n'-match genetic offspring? What of the future conflicts when they run into a stranger's child who looks just like them? What about the psychological health of the families when they realize "their" children aren't their own?

Two particular families in New York are living with just that confusion. A white woman was implanted with her own in-vitro embryos. When Mom gave birth, surprise!—one of the twins was black. It seems that the physician's assistant had implanted some of a black couple's embryos into the white woman, along with her own, according to a story in the *New York Times*, April 17, 1999.

What ensued was a painful, frightening dispute about visitation. Although the white couple conceded that the black child belonged to the black couple, they sued to force the child's genetic parents to honor a visitation agreement that requires the black child to visit them in order to know his gestational twin. The fly in the ointment is that the deal is not reciprocal—the white child is not required to visit the black family for the same gestational sibling bonding.

Frankly, it is astonishing to me that any court would support the white family's position at all. Are these children really brothers? Is the gestational mom more of a legal or psychological mom than the genetic mom? What a twenty-first-century mess!

The only thing we can know for sure is that the fertility clinic will be royally sued.

We're always clear about the money.

Baby Trash

"If we have learned anything about technological advances in this century, it's that there is no stopping them, no matter their ethical or moral implications," wrote Marc Fisher in the *International Herald Tribune*, July 7, 1999.

Nowhere is this sentiment more horrifyingly apparent than in the options available for unused human embryos. Most of these embryos are in cold storage. The intent of some of the "parents" is possibly to use the embryos for future implantation. Others have in mind that should one of their current children need, for example, a bone marrow transplant from a perfect match, they would be able to produce another child for replacement parts.

Such a utilitarian perspective is demeaning to the significance of each human being, but right in line with our dangerous ambivalence about the value of human life. Some folks will pay and do anything to have a baby—ostensibly reflecting their sense of the immeasurable value of human life and children. Others selectively terminate the "extra" lives, maintain embryos for "spare parts," freeze extra embryos in a no-life-no-death suspended state, sell embryos like cars, fight over embryos as property in divorces or death, destroy them as useless debris, or turn them over to scientists for research, as though they were mere protozoans.

"All unclaimed specimens will be destroyed as of July 15th, '99," the ad warned. The notice, appearing in the *Arizona Republic* on June 27, may mark the first time that a fertility clinic in the United States has announced such plans. When the clinic first began freezing embryos in the mid-1980s, patients never even considered this dilemma. In 1997, an ethics panel of the

American Society for Reproductive Medicine concluded that the clinic could destroy embryos unclaimed after five years (*Washington Post*, July 12, 1999).

Although all fertility patients think of those embryos as their babies, it appears to be true only until one baby is born. Then the embryos left in storage are less babies than unwanted tissue. That's when arguments about the embryos come to the fore. It's always amazing to me that with this issue, as with abortion, people define things according to their own convenience. If you want it, it's a baby. If you don't, it's only "potential life," less worthy of our attention, respect, and responsibility.

Every Parent Can Be a Frankenstein

"A Presidential ethics panel has decided to recommend that the federal government begin funding some research on human embryos, saying that the moral cost of destroying embryos in the course of research is outweighed by the social good that could come from the work" (*Los Angeles Times*, May 23, 1999). The chairman of the Bioethics Commission is quoted as saying, "We have moral obligations to the future health and welfare of people, and we need to balance these with, at the very least, the symbolic moral obligation we have to the embryo."

This observation is not surprising from the commission chair, also the president of Princeton University, who defended the appointment of Peter Singer to the chair of ethics and human values at that prestigious college. Singer is the "ethicist" who suggests that parents be allowed to kill their newborns up to age twenty-eight days, if the children are ill or handicapped in any way that would diminish their own, or their family's, *happiness*!

Symbolic moral obligation?! Not *actual* moral obligation to the unique, potential life within each embryo? What if one of those embryos became the person with the brilliance to find cures for certain diseases without using embryos?

And here's that slippery slope in real life, reported by the *Washington Post* (June 14, 1999):

> A team of American researchers has quietly begun trying to create the world's first batches of cloned human embryos. Another team has resumed its controversial cloning of embryos that are part human and part cow. The Geron Corp. of Menlo Park, Calif., and Advanced Cell Therapeutics (ACT) of Worcester, Mass., are not trying to make full-grown human clones or human-cow hybrids. Rather, the goal is to use the newly cloned embryos as a source of embryonic stem cells, a recently discovered kind of cell that is thought to have the potential to treat a host of chronic ailments, including diabetes and Parkinson's disease.

According to this article, these are the first instances of scientists creating human embryos explicitly for the purpose of harvesting medically useful cells, which, while banned for federally funded researchers, is entirely legal in the private sector. The very next day, the *New York Times* reported that Geron Corporation denied the story.

Harvesting is also happening with excess embryos manufactured by the infertility industry. How much less valuable can human life be made? Are we to resort to such a class system where some people are made to function and others to provide the parts that repair them?

Nah . . . I Don't Want This One

An increasingly popular fertility treatment, ICSI (in which doctors inject a single sperm directly into a woman's egg in a laboratory dish) has already led to the birth of about twenty thousand babies worldwide. The procedure's safety was never assessed in animals before it became commercially available. According to the *Washington Post* (March 30, 1999), studies have found that human ICSI babies have three to five times the normal incidence of sex chromosome abnormalities, either due to the genetic information from the male, the procedure itself, or both. The concerns focus on mental retardation or developmental delays in children.

One researcher from Belgium said, "Parents should be told there is a small risk of chromosomal and developmental problems with the procedure. If they wish to, they can do prenatal testing and consider abortion if problems are apparent."

Oh, good, if it's broken, kill it. Then sue.

As reported in Focus on the Family's *Citizen Alert* (July 14, 1999), courts in recent years have seen a series of "wrongful birth lawsuits from parents who claim they were not informed of their children's birth defects in time to get abortions. Twenty-eight states currently permit such suits, which typically seek—and sometimes get—large monetary awards."

One Michigan court stands apart, "warning that the logic of wrongful birth suits could quickly slide into applied eugenics and the elimination of supposedly unfit human lives." On July 6, the Georgia Supreme Court reaffirmed a nine-year-old ruling holding that wrongful birth suits have no grounds in state law.

Many folks have filed suits claiming that their physicians did not do enough tests, do the right tests, interpret the tests correctly, or give them sufficient information about statistics for them to make an informed decision about abortion. With all the new technology and its limitations, it would seem we, as a society, will be more and more propelled into demanding perfection or death. Is this the mentality we wish to teach our children? Is this how we want to define our parental instincts? Is this what we wish to stand for with respect to the value of life? Is this responsible childbearing?

Is There Conception After Death?

Remember the joke about whether there was "sex after death"? Well, forget that. We're in the era of producing life after death. We've covered the impact of donated eggs and sperm, surrogate mothers, test tube manipulations, and other fertility technology. How about the situation wherein the child's parent or parents are corpses? Since we care nothing about children and everything about the feelings of adults, children are being born whose parents are cadavers long before their conception.

Tracey Veloff was a paid surrogate mother. The child she was carrying had been made from the egg of a woman who had been dead for a year and the sperm of an anonymous donor (*Washington Post*, February 8, 1998). The dead woman's parents had arranged the pregnancy, having inherited the embryos along with their daughter's furniture and other possessions. They said it was their prerogative to grow them into grandchildren.

The surrogate had no intention of raising the child; neither did the anonymous sperm donor nor the grandparents! No one had any genuine, profound, compassionate investment in the ongoing life of the child. The surrogate and the sperm donor got money, and the grandparents got the thrill of their genetics propagated into the future.

This macabre business is by no means the only such case. Julia, one of my listeners, wrote to me about another "grandmother":

I thought I would send a little note regarding an episode of Oprah *where the topic was alternative ways of making a baby. I am writing to you because one particular guest left me horrified.*

Her nineteen-year-old son had killed himself playing Russian roulette and she refused to donate any of his organs unless the doctors also agreed to collect sperm from her brain dead son. She already has the nursery ready and is in the process of choosing a woman to implant his sperm into. She didn't see

any moral problem with this and shrugged off the suggestion
that she was being selfish. She kept saying that she knew her
son wanted to someday become a father. Nineteen-year-old
sperm does not a father make! Where does it all stop?

There have been other such television programs concerning
this issue. Jennifer, another listener, wrote me about the *Today*
show.

A reporter was speaking with a doctor from Los Angeles,
who, within the past year, impregnated a woman with her
dead husband's sperm. This doctor harvested them from his
corpse. He argues that the woman who asked him to do this
procedure was in such pain that he couldn't refuse her. He said
that having this baby would lessen the pain of losing her hus-
band.

The first part of this story is horrible enough. There was no
discussion preceding his death about having more children. He
obviously could not consent to having his sperm taken from
him. So the doctor, in effect, raped a corpse!! Yet, it gets worse.

The moral nature of this question was limited strictly to this
doctor's conduct, not the fact the child would grow up without
a father!

I am just horrified at the state of morality in this country.
Now it's okay to harvest sperm from a dead man as long as
there is a grieving woman who wants a child? There are no
more standards, no more rules. Everyone has the right to do
what they want and defend their behavior on the basis of feel-
ings and desires. And, what's more, issues such as these are
being popularized by the media who don't take a stand, but
rather, legitimize them.

In our society, reproductive freedom means anyone can
decide to create a life by any means with no, and I mean no,
consideration of what is in the best interest of that new human
being.

The reason there is little societal uproar about this development is that it would imply criticism of popular celebrities,

successful executives watching that biological clock, lesbian couples, and members of other politically correct groups. No one wants to be caught "judging" in this "pro any choice" era!

In other words, to oppose this new version of procreation in the name of the children, the pundits would have to gore oxen they generally venerate. The extent to which society will accommodate behavior is fascinating. One woman used her dead husband's frozen sperm to create a baby girl. She then sued the Social Security Administration for death benefits for the little girl . . . and won! The agency agreed to pay the girl $700 a month, in spite of the fact that the law requires children be compensated to the extent that the award replaces support the father provided when he was *alive* (*New York Times Magazine*, March 28, 1999).

Wow! The mother used the money to pay for her own higher education. Interesting way to arrange a scholarship, don't you think?

The United States is totally unregulated with respect to laws, ethics, and the morality of this sort of reproductive technology, but the Human Fertilization and Embryology Authority, a government agency in England, forbids human cloning and using dead men's sperm without their prior consent.

Our national failure of will in this regard stems from a continuum of callousness about human developmental needs. The modern techno-conception industry is focused on fame and fortune, concerned only with adult participants' emotions, rights, and privileges. The welfare of the children is not even a question.

The Grand Anti-Heterosexism Experiment

Is there anyone left in North America who knows my name and *doesn't* know how I feel about homosexual marriage, childbearing, and adoption? In case there *is*, I'll make a long story short. I'm "agin" it—"it" being the sophisticated, orchestrated campaign to make same-sex marriage and family equal in every way to the traditional mom-and-pop arrangement. The motivation for this movement is to satisfy adult desires, and to hell with the children, if there are any.

The homosexual activists have been very clever. First, they changed the terms of the argument, shifted the focus from abnormal sexual behavior to the apple-pie issue of "rights." They won an influential ally in 1973, when the American Psychiatric Association removed homosexuality from the category of dysfunction, in a demonstration of tolerance.

Since Americans are hypersensitive about individual rights and supersensitive to being seen as prejudiced, societal resistance to the homosexual social and political agenda has virtually collapsed. Political activists have successfully repositioned sexual deviancy as a constitutionally protected "lifestyle," equivalent in every way to heterosexuality. Disagreement on any grounds is evidence of homophobia.

A videotape called *It's Elementary* has been distributed in public schools across the country and has been shown on local PBS stations. The producers say that the intent is to teach children tolerance—a worthy goal. The tape, however, is actually propaganda, presenting homosexuality as normal and no different from heterosexuality in terms of parents and children (ironically, implying stereotyping and demonstrating hostility to those parents who teach their children otherwise).

Though the pro–homosexual adoption activists put forth social science research that favors such flexibility in the definition of family, much so-called research is designed and produced to conform to this agenda.

At least some researchers are honest about their agenda and intent. In "Deconstructing the Essential Father" (*American Psychologist*, July 1999), the authors admit, "our goal is to generate public policy initiatives that support men in their fathering role, without discriminating against women and same-sex couples. We are also interested in encouraging public policy that supports the legitimacy of diverse family structures, rather than policy that privileges the two-parent, heterosexual, married family. *We also realize that some of the research we cite to support our perspective will turn out to be incorrect* [emphasis added]."

Not only is much of what they present incorrect, it's downright silly. The article relies heavily on behavioral studies of nonhuman primates, especially marmosets, to draw conclusions about the character of human families ("marmosets illustrate how, within a particular bio-ecological context, optimal child outcomes can be achieved with fathers as primary caretakers and limited parenting involvement by mothers").

According to Dale O'Leary of the National Association for Research and Therapy of Homosexuality, advocates for reparative therapy for homosexuals:

> Social-constructionist research proceeds in the following manner. Studies are constructed to provide ammunition for the political struggle. Evidence is selectively reported. Conclusions are drawn which are not supported by the evidence. The articles are quoted by others and a body of "uncontroverted" evidence is accumulated. "Uncontroverted" meaning none of the small coterie of advocates for social change criticizes their co-conspirators. Absolutely false "facts" are quoted over and over again until they become "widely recognized."

I have been quite vocal on my radio program about the willingness of psychological and sociological journals to publish advocacy research and the number of universities and colleges willing to hire and promote advocacy researchers. We are being manipulated into accepting the goals and ideals of a small but powerful group of social radicals, who apparently perceive the traditional two-parent, heterosexual home as hostile to the rights of those who won't or can't live up to *Homo sapiens* ideal norm.

A clinician and analyst for Childhood Recovery Resources, Joyanna Silberg, Ph.D., has written an analysis of "Deconstructing the Father." She says:

While this article seems to bend over backwards to "privilege" new kinds of family arrangements for children, no where do they show data suggesting that these new arrangements are better for children, only that harm has not been determined. Before society is ready to discard the values that have evolved to protect and nurture children in families, there would need to be good and compelling reasons for this.

The perceived rights of adults are never a good reason to develop child-based policies. Society should not accommodate to the unfortunate fact that many children do not have the stable and loving homes they need, by discarding the ideal of the traditional family entirely. Within the article, the authors themselves have identified the following factors as significant for positive outcome: two adults, stability, predictability and the availability of bonding with both a mother and a father. While the authors present no data on which arrangements have the best chance of providing all of these, it seems obvious to any one (who is not too fearful of being politically incorrect) that the traditional family has the best chance of providing all of these things that children need.

In 1997, Broward County Judge John A. Frusciante wrote a final order concerning the constitutionality of the Florida statute declaring that no homosexual residing in Florida may be considered as a potential adoptive parent. He said:

> The evidence established that exposure to male and female role models is of particular significance in child development. Traditionally, children receive primary role modeling through the parent/child relationship. The child's gender identity is shaped through years of interaction between the child and his/her parent or parental figure . . .
> The relationship between the mother and father figures also plays a significant role in the healthy development of children. From that relationship, children learn their role

within the family unit and the necessary skills to form meaningful relationships outside the family structure. . . . Divorce, abuse, and domestic violence are just a few of the traumatic disruptions known to cause severe and psychological and emotional conflicts in developing children. The evidence showed that as families deviate from the traditional family model (i.e., one mother and one father rearing the children), the child exposed to that alternative familial environment becomes more prone to develop emotional handicaps and psychological dysfunctions.

The question was raised as to, "who would provide children parented in homosexual environments the necessary male and female role models required for healthy development?" These environments, by their very nature, create a household that is obligatorily motherless or fatherless. An announced homosexual has established a willingness to live in a same-sex relationship; a household relationship which does not provide for both a maternal and paternal figure. . . . Here, the state has determined that the best interest of children cannot be served in an environment which eliminates the primary source of heterosexual role-modeling when the overwhelming evidence suggests that children need male and female role-modeling for healthy development.

This is not about discrimination against homosexuals. Same-sex marriage affects the child's right to have a parent of both sexes. These children are not tragically fatherless or motherless, but *purposely* fatherless or motherless. How dare a society condone or encourage such loss!

Pregnant and Addicted

In an unprecedented action, South Carolina's Supreme Court has ruled that a woman can be prosecuted for child abuse if she takes drugs during pregnancy. The court said a healthy, viable fetus can be considered a "child" or "person" under state law, and should, as a result, be afforded legal protection (*Los Angeles Times*, October 1996).

The dissenting opinion suggested that "a woman would be better off to illegally abort her third-trimester fetus and face a two-year sentence rather than give birth to a baby after taking drugs and face a ten-year sentence for child abuse." In both cases the child is the loser.

Contrast the South Carolina decision with one from a Wisconsin appellate court that threw out a conviction for attempted murder for a woman who gave birth to a child with fetal alcohol syndrome. The opinion stated that "the woman's prenatal conduct does not constitute first-degree intentional homicide and first-degree reckless injury."

Mind you, her blood alcohol level was 0.3. She spent a day in a bar downing White Russians, stating out loud that she wanted to drink both herself and her baby to death. Sounds like intent to me.

An important question about the balance of rights between the adult woman and the unborn child arises, but quickly falls, because we value the freedom to abuse substances without consequences. After all—abusers have a disease. Therefore, there is no personal responsibility.

Joan Ryan, an admitted staunch pro-abortionist, asked in the *San Francisco Chronicle* (June 6, 1999), "How do we balance the rights of a woman to drink and take drugs for the nine months she's pregnant, against the rights of a child who must spend a lifetime with brain damage, chemical imbalances or other debilitating handicaps, as a result of his mother exercising her rights? Let's not dishonor the ideals of individualism and self-determination by invoking them to excuse irresponsibility."

She goes on to suggest mandatory birth control for addicted women until they're off drugs and alcohol. This is just what Barbara Harris of CRACK is doing, and I applaud her, although various special interest groups have relentlessly attacked her as racist and anti-women.

CRACK offers addicted women reimbursement for *voluntary* contraceptive implants or sterilization. Believe it or not, the misery of the approximately 375,000 babies born to mothers using drugs each year in the United States is secondary to those feminist proponents of women's reproductive rights who oppose such programs. Who in their right mind could defend a woman's right to maim and destroy babies inside her body? You'll find their names in the rosters of the American Civil Liberties Union, National Organization for Women, National Abortion Rights Action League (NARAL), and other civil libertarian organizations.

Babies as Lotto Tickets

Further demonstrating the profound indifference our society expresses toward responsible childbearing, there were contests all over the world for the production of the "Official Millennium Baby." Such a contest, organized by a Canadian company, drummed up $2 million in cash and prizes for the first North American baby of the new year.

Supporting my growing disdain for those in the psychology profession, Joachim Krueger, a Brown University social psychologist, is quoted in the *Los Angeles Times* (March 12, 1999) as saying, "It may be foolish, but it's not unhealthy."

What kind of stupidity is that? The creation of life is reduced to a publicity stunt and a race for money and prizes, and he doesn't see that as "unhealthy." The hundreds of thousands of children conceived all over the world by biotechnology, one-time intercourse, and so forth, unwanted on their own account, desired only for fame and fortune, will not suffer. You can't possibly believe that. This "race" produced a boom of ultimately unwanted disappointments.

You're Never Too Old

Then there is the new phenomenon, made famous first in Italy—
in-vitro produced pregnancies in older women, with the assistance of hormone treatments. Now fifty- to seventy-year-old
women can go through their reproductive version of a late-life
crisis, feeling young by virtue of pregnancy and small children.
The small children are ultimately robbed of parents prematurely,
due to illness, aging, and death. As one of my listeners, John,
wrote:

*Please tell your listeners that children do not want old par-
ents. My father was fifty-four when I was born, and my mom
was forty-two. By the time I wanted to play Little League, my
dad could barely move, let alone teach me to play the game.
He died when I was thirteen, and Mom had a stroke shortly
after. People seem to have some sort of need to fulfill themselves by having children no matter what the circumstances.
From the broken heart of a child who grew up without guidance and love from his parents, I'm here to tell your listeners
to consider all the parties involved in a pregnancy—most
importantly THE CHILD.*

I have personal sympathy with this situation as I had our
son at thirty-eight, and my husband was fifty-two. Deryk often
talks to me about his fear of losing his dad. This is one reason
I advise callers and listeners not to have children after forty.
When we're considering making a baby we think mostly of our
needs, passions, desires, in the context of "right now," not
thirteen years from "right now." That's wrong.

Children are not our due. We are not entitled to them. They
are a blessing we have to earn, by providing our best physical
and psychological selves and a proper two-parent heterosexual
home. Children are a gift from G-d, not commodities. They are
a divine responsibility, not property. We have strayed so far
from respect for life, I wonder if we will ever find our way
back. I wonder if we even care to try.

5

Spare the Rod

*One summer day, twenty-two years ago, my
sister and I were sitting on Mom's porch and my
sibling announced, "We've been talking and
we've decided that we're not going to make the
same mistakes with our kids that you and Dad
made with us!" Mom sat quietly for a moment
or two and then gently reached over and put one
hand on each of our well-rounded, pregnant
tummies. "I know, sweetheart," she said. "You're
both gonna make a whole bunch of new ones."*

Lucky and Blessed

"For me," Ms. Lucky and Blessed continued, "the biggest mistake was believing I knew all the answers before I'd even been confronted with the issues. I anticipated problems where none existed . . . and missed the ones that were shouting for attention. I've been both lucky and blessed. I have a wonderful, caring, morally centered, resilient and talented son. But he and I both know I made mistakes. I hope I will remember to lovingly suggest that he learn from my mistakes and listen more, talk less and, above all, that he live the way he wants his child to

be. And, oh yes, I'll tell him he's still gonna make mistakes . . .
a whole bunch of new ones."

Making mistakes in child rearing is inevitable, even with the
most responsible, aware, intelligent, attentive, knowledgeable,
astute, caring, and sensitive parent. Why? Because each child is
unique in appearance, reactions, sensitivities, intelligence, com-
municability, experiences, personality, energy, genetic potential,
health, and so forth. Add to that the combination of maternal
and paternal characteristics and personality; the universal, ongoing, and evolving challenges of life; and the impact of political-
social influences, and there doesn't seem to be enough consistency or reliability to guarantee a continuous optimum of child
rearing appropriate for every child from birth to adulthood.

Granted, the combined impact of all these variables can often
make parenting seem frustrating, impossible, and sometimes
downright hopeless. And sometimes, it is . . . but usually only for
a while. The search for perfect discipline and child-rearing techniques is ultimately doomed. Yet most parents end up doing a
"good enough" job if they:

➤ Are honorable role models

➤ Provide a united mom-dad front

➤ Are consistent, firm, and fair in their approach to rules and
consequences when the rules are intentionally breached

➤ Are basically real, affectionate, and loving with their children

Who's the Boss?

Those first two characteristics, being role models and presenting
a united front, shape children's perceptions of parents as authorities to be heeded. All mammalian animal groups establish hierarchies of power and authority by gender, strength, size, age, and

physical prowess. Though some of the hippie-era mentality might rue the lack of egalitarianism, this instinctive drive toward roles in hierarchies has significant value for creating the order necessary for group cohesion, protection against predators, ongoing peace, division of labor, reproduction, and general feelings of belonging and security.

For all practical purposes, this is just as important in human families. Though social changes have brought men and women, as husbands and wives, into seemingly interchangeable roles, with women sometimes as primary breadwinners and the men as caretakers of the children, the necessity for the adults to establish themselves as authority figures is, in my opinion, the single most important factor in child rearing.

Too many parents today gladly surrender their authority to day care workers, psychologists, schoolteachers and administrators; their kids' demands; what the neighbors are doing; the lifestyles of television families and children; their new or ex-spouse's theories of child-rearing; and even the opinions of their children's peers. They do this for many different reasons—the primary two being a selfish pursuit of their own goals and desires, and the difficulties and stresses inherent in a chaotic life of dual careers, divorce, promiscuity and serial relationships, single-parenting, alcohol and drugs, and a lack of developed talent and skills.

For other parents, guilt about their own bad behaviors as minors or young adults, personal weakness or psychological problems, fear of rejection by their kids, belated rebellion against their own parents' discipline, lack of parenting skills or personal values on which to base a sensible approach to discipline, keep them from becoming the necessary authority figure in their families.

In 1998 the Yankelovich Partners surveyed one thousand teenage daughters and their mothers about their values and opinions. Experts who viewed the results expressed dismay over the huge shift in the attitudes of mothers from one generation to the next.

In the survey, for example, thirty percent of mothers said they simply set the rules as they see fit, while seventy percent of moms said they first discuss rules of expected behavior with their daughters, and then set them.

Leslie Carbone of the Family Research Council, a conservative advocacy group, said in *USA Today* (December 14, 1998), "We're concerned about the lines of authority being blurred. Some rules should be non-negotiable."

Why are these mothers so timid about asserting authority? Many times parents acquiesce because they:

➤ Are tired from a long, hard, frustrating week and don't need the extra stress of arguing with their child

➤ Just don't want to fight the ex-spouse "good guy" game that undermines their attempts at authority with "yes" to all "no's"

➤ Want to take the easy way out and give their child all they want

➤ Are afraid of their children's threats to leave or disobey

➤ Feel helpless in the face of "everyone else is doing/has it!"

➤ Lack the confidence about their rules and consequences being fair and reasonable

➤ Are moved by love and don't want to see their child upset

➤ Are too self-absorbed (new lovers, new work, new hobbies) to devote the necessary time

➤ Buy the professional psycho-babblers nonsense that discipline is psychologically harmful

Eighty-seven percent of mothers responded to the Yankelovich survey by saying they consider their teenage daughters to be their friends and seventy-five percent of moms said a daughter's approval was "very important" to them.

I can testify to this insanity. Many, many parents call me with what seems like an obvious situation with an obvious course of action. Sometimes, in frustration at their apparent cluelessness, I ask, "Excuse me—do you think your grandma or grandpa would have had any trouble whatsoever handling this problem?"

Inevitably the answer is, "No. They'd just take me behind the shed and tar my butt. Then I'd be given more chores and less fun for quite a while. And I'd never do it again."

"So what's the problem here?"

Mysteriously, the fog sets back in when it comes to asserting themselves as parent and authority figure.

"I just don't know. I don't know what to think and what to do. This is different."

No, it's really not a different situation. Children have been children since mankind stood upright on two legs. What is different is that some of the adults never grow up. What we have here is two sets of kids—one young, one old!

My Parent? No, My Pal

"My husband and I have been listening to you for the last six months, and I must say that you are on-target with child-raising. It seems today . . . that parents are afraid to guide their children and want to be friends with them. It is appalling what the parents condone (excess freedom for coed interactions, alcohol, late-night partying, extravagant spending) because they don't want to say 'no' to their children," writes Arleen.

I was sure I was overreacting and overanalyzing a word choice when I read an article in the *New York Times* (August 21, 1999) about colleges and universities helping parents cope with their children leaving home. One sentence caught my eye. It read in part, ". . . and to address the parents, own roller-coaster emotions as they prepare to break away from their companions of the last eighteen years."

"Companions"? I looked the word up in the dictionary: "A person who frequently associates with or accompanies another; comrade; mate."

I guess I didn't overreact, after all. This word suggests a casual rather than causal relationship; i.e., a mother's and father's love and commitment that causes them to bind in a covenant with G-d to produce a child to love, protect, nurture, and teach, over whom they have authority and for whom they have responsibility. How does "companion" describe such a profound relationship? It doesn't; but it does tell, accidentally, how casual we've all become about the sacred relationship between parent and child.

"The Friend Trend—in the too busy lives of today's family, many parents try to make up for lost time by being something experts say they shouldn't—pals to their kids," read a headline in the *Los Angeles Times* (August 31, 1994). Here we have it. Parents who recognize they aren't giving their children what they need relieve their own well-earned guilt by giving children everything they want.

Getting along with your kids and having a positive and happy home environment is an admirable goal, but, if this is accomplished by perpetual informality and false equality, the children lose. "Such relationships," the *Los Angeles Times* article continues, "become detrimental when parents feel reluctant to teach their children morals and manners or to devise and enforce family rules. 'A lot of parents are afraid their children won't like them if they discipline,' said one father. 'But in their hearts they know the last thing a child needs or wants is a true friendship with the parent.'"

The article ends with a quote from a one-time pal-parent who converted to a real parent because, as a social worker, he realized, "kids want discipline even if they don't know it. They need structure and stability. Otherwise, children feel neglected and grow up with low self-esteem."

Amen.

The Psychologists Made Me Do It!

A major source of today's parenting problem is the psychologizing of our culture. In Grandma and Grandpa's time, misbehavior was viewed as a moral issue of right and wrong, acceptable and unacceptable, permitted and not permitted. Simple as that. Basically, kids were kids; that is, narcissistic, antisocial, noisy, nasty, distracted, and so forth.

The old solution would be punishment. The goal of the punishment was to teach accountability, self-control, the consequences of wrong choices, thinking before acting, and the important fact that they are obligated to respect rules of authority.

Then came the shrinks. The psychology community suggested that bad behavior is either the result of some psychological problem (low self-esteem is a favorite) or some biological problem (brain chemistry and food allergies are popular).

The basic notion is that the child ultimately lacks free will. Since he is so upset or so gene-dysfunctional, he cannot consciously choose his actions; he is mysteriously driven by powers beyond his control. It follows that if he is not in control, he is not responsible. This means that discipline and punishment are bad; understanding is good.

The end result of this is disaster. The perpetrator is the victim. (And don't forget, the abused victim is now entitled to perpetrate . . . and so it goes.) The perpetrator need only point some finger of blame at a past experience and, abracadabra, escape wrath and punishment and obtain a perverted sainthood all at once!

Parents are intimidated by this psychological garbage into backing off from disciplining—instead shellacking their children with a coat of overunderstanding, acceptance, and patience.

Zsa Zsa, one of my listeners, experienced this phenomenon firsthand:

Also, in the seventies just about everyone I knew was in some kind of therapy, including all their kids. The basic issue is

*that we were totally insecure about how to raise a kid. The
shrinks told us our parents screwed us up so much we were
afraid to make mistakes. We thought a shrink could tell us
how to handle day-to-day child rearing issues. Although we
loved him (our kid) with all our hearts—this was the era of
"spanking will mess up your kid for life," "don't ever say or
do this or that," "let the kid make his own decisions and have
his personal space," and other such crap. We were pretty busy
with our big house and fancy cars and great careers and private schools . . . always the best for us and the kid. That way
we REALLY thought we were "doing the right thing." We
weren't.*

G-d Died . . .

Why did this happen? The sixties were a turbulent time—
issues of authority, equality, and freedom, blessed concepts,
were twisted, distorted, and thrown away. Part of the rejection
of authority had to do with G-d and religion. Clearly, free will,
accountability, and consequences are biblical precepts. The
idea that all folks are simply inherently good unless something
external occurs (the abuse excuse) is quite secular. The religious point of view is that individuals are not inherently good
or evil—but have the potential for both; and that their soul
depends on the choices they make. Part of this psychologizing
of behavior was a movement to counter religion, hidden under
the veil of science.

"Psychologists, educators—my team—have corrupted parents
with 'happy-think' philosophies, saying that all it takes are
appeals to a child's better side. If the child always feels good there
won't ever be any need to behave badly. Well, it doesn't work,"
said Keven Ryan, Director of the Center for the Advancement of
Ethics and Character at Boston University (*New York Times*,
November 7, 1996).

Well, no kidding, it doesn't work. The Ten Commandments

are basically G-d's demands upon our actions. Nowhere before, after, or within that biblical text do you read any nullification of any one of those Commandments or their consequences based upon someone's self-esteem, quotient of happiness or content-ment. In fact, the very definition of piety precludes such a focus on the "self" and instead concentrates on one's obligations to G-d and, through G-d, to fellow human beings. And therein lies the hint to understanding how thousands of years of wisdom about discipline could be summarily tossed aside for a "feel-good" standard—the rejection of G-d, religion, and a sense of obligation to others.

The "self" became our new G-d to worship and our new preoccupation; my rights, my needs, my feelings, my fulfill-ment, my wants, my way, my happiness, my orgasms, my free-dom, my life, and so forth. Obligation and responsibility to ideals and others were summarily dismissed as oppressive, con-fining, controlling, and the enemy of freedom of expression.

This concept of supremacy of the self is based on the belief that the self is pure or inherently good. How else could the pro-ponents justify such overwhelming respect for inner feelings? That thinking led directly to the construct that since people are inherently good, when they do bad, it must be something in the external world (poverty, alcoholic parents, the neighborhood, historical racial anger, etc.) that forced that person to do evil. Hence all the abuse excuses, from the Twinkie defense to black rage, to explain the evil actions of individuals and groups.

Leaving children to "evolve" virtually on their own is wrong. The reality is that the "brain inside a teenager's skull is in some ways closer to a child's brain than to an adult's. Still being forged are the connections between neurons that affect not only emo-tional skills but also physical and mental abilities. . . . The brain's capacity for growth through adolescence may also indicate that even troubled teenagers can still learn restraint, judgment and empathy" (*U.S. News & World Report,* August 9, 1999).

This means that even as children approach adulthood, their

brains are still in the process of development and they do not as yet have the full capacity for judgment, impulse control, and the wisdom of the ages to tap for direction and solutions. They are still a work in progress. To abdicate being their anchor, weather vane, and compass is to leave them stranded in a sea of their own aimless kind. And this is the formula for disaster.

Lisamarie, one of my listeners, observed, "While cruising the channels on the TV last night, I came upon a scene from a popular sitcom, *Full House*. The teenage middle daughter was rebelling against her father by not cleaning up her room. The grade school age younger daughter was explaining to her why this is a bad idea. The teenage daughter says, 'We've been living by Dad's rules all our lives, and where has it gotten us?' To which the younger daughter replies . . . 'a nice house, three meals a day, and a buck a week. Don't rock the boat!'"

This is one of the main points I make to both parents and their children who call sometimes in unison, other times separately. The power to make the rules is directly connected to the responsibility. Parents are responsible for food, a roof, education, medicine, clothes, and so forth. It is this responsibility, combined with the moral and legal obligation parents have to caretake their children, that gives them the privilege of being "in charge." Not only, however, is that a privilege, it is a necessity. Children can be as or more handicapped when brought up without the loving blessing of discipline as when born without a limb. It is harder to compensate for the former.

In addition to the psychologizing of all behavior, there is another seriously destructive force operating to undermine parental authority—the so-called village that Hillary Clinton popularized.

Where the Hell Is the Village?

The most frequent complaints and issues with respect to parenting that I deal with on my radio program have to do with the parents themselves—and not some technique of punishment or communication. I've already discussed the primary problem too many parents have in their fear, unwillingness, or resistance to being the authority figure.

The second most serious, and related, problem is the profound lack of community support. Parents, struggling to impose standards on their children's behavior, are surrounded by a "village" that discounts their attempts as excessively restrictive, un-hip, unreasonable, or religious zealotry. ("Hey, it's the twenty-first century—kids are going to do what they're going to do.") It's not surprising that they are often cowed into impotence.

Consider the pressure to refrain from judging teenage girls and women who have illegitimate kids, on purpose or "accidentally." Instead of displaying appropriate disapproval for the wrong done to the unborn and the immorality and irresponsibility of the mothers-to-be, the school or family give a cheerful baby shower. I have had too many calls from responsible parents who consistently expect their children to value commitments, the home, and their obligation to G-d, only to deplore their confusion over the societal acceptance of any and all behaviors around them.

The villagers are either too busy, too self-involved, too frightened, too jaded, or too perverse to want to present a united front for the best interest of their children, let alone the neighborhood or community children.

Children are oversexualized in their behaviors, speech, dress, activities, and entertainment. The parents are providing the money and the permission for tattoos, body piercing, inappropriate dress, and activities. Neighbors, instead of maintaining old-fashioned "community values," allow unsupervised coed parties, sleep-overs, and sometimes provide the alcohol or condoms themselves!

Malls, movies, theme parks, and public parks are teeming with kids disconnected from their families. Gangs of all ethnic groups have provided a home away from home for their members. Parents dump kids in libraries, fast-food restaurants, and stores in order to have their own time. Schools are struggling to deal with the bad behaviors of children not disciplined at home to demonstrate self-control. And the wider culture on which parents used to be able to rely when the going got rough is now as unreliable as the neighbors in providing help and support for civilizing our young.

The Attack of "the Village"

Planned Parenthood, SIECUS, and the American Library Association (ALA) give Web site information aimed at teens that is permissive and sexually explicit, with the ridiculous defense that this information enables children to make "informed choices" (*Philadelphia Inquirer*, August 8, 1999).

An indication of the ALA's true agenda, with respect to our children, is the fact that the organization's Web site refers children to Peacefire, an Internet site where they learn to dismantle filters their parents may have installed on home computers. The ALA Web site also refers kids to Go Ask Alice, a Web site that answers viewer questions about health and sexuality, including anal sex, bestiality, and sado-masochistic sex.

Where is a parent to turn when politically powerful, often government-funded, groups with access to our children in public schools and on the Internet are advocating that parents and educators teach minor children about masturbation, mutual masturbation, and oral sex as an "outercourse" alternative to intercourse?

While Planned Parenthood and the Sexuality Information and Education Council of the United States (SIECUS) maintain that our children's sexuality is an unstoppable avalanche, the truth is that "abstinence-only programs for teens are changing the face of sex education today" (*Los Angeles Times*, August 10, 1999), challenging the secular and sacred duo of safe sex and birth control. While the liberal sex educators insist they believe that young people should delay having sex until they are physically and emotionally mature, in reality they leave it up to the physically and emotionally immature child to decide that for themselves and discourage turning to parental authority. Pregnancy, disease, inappropriate relationships, interpersonal problems, and depression due to premature sexual activity are not readily cured by an information blitz. If they were, then the three million new teenage STD cases, and half of all new HIV cases occuring in people under twenty-five wouldn't be happening.

In fact, in 1999, the Consortium of State Physicians Resource Councils released a report showing that the cause of the overall teen birth rate decline in the 1990s is not increased contraceptive use, but a trend toward sexual abstinence. The report also showed that among those teens who are sexually active, the non-marital birth rate has risen dramatically. The conclusions of the study are controversial because they refute statements by the U.S. Department of Health, the Centers for Disease Control and other governmental public health organizations that credit increased contraceptive use for the decline in the number of teen pregnancies (New Jersey Physicians Resource Council).

As I have mentioned earlier, we can't look to the social sciences for any help. Many of these professionals are in the forefront of sexualizing our culture—a movement started by Alfred Kinsey in the 1950s. Among the more egregious efforts is one to erode the barriers to adult-child sex. In 1990, the *Journal of Homosexuality* (Volume 20, 1990) produced a special double issue devoted to adult-child sex, entitled "Male Intergenerational Intimacy." One psychologist wrote that the loving pedophile can offer a "companionship, security, and protection" which neither peers nor parents can provide. Parents should look upon the pedophile who loves their son "not as a rival or competitor, not as a thief of their property, but as a partner in the boy's upbringing, someone to be welcomed into their home. . . ."

This outrageous assertion made its way into the psychology mainstream in 1999, when the *American Journal of Psychology* published an analysis of child-abuse research and concluded that such criminal behavior was not always detrimental to the child! As predicted by legal experts in the child-abuse field, this so-called study made its way immediately into the defense strategy of a pedophile accused of child molestation in an Arizona court.

And let's not forget the legitimization of pornography as a course deemed worthy of academic study by many of our top public and private universities. Homework and class assignments include watching X-rated movies and videos and writing papers on works of "literature" that involve sadism and bestiality. These courses are protected by claims of academic and intellectual freedom and underwritten by the unsuspecting parents of sexually liberated students.

The abdication of parental authority in the home, and the general lack of community support for responsibility and obligation over the exercise of individual rights, has created a chaotic environment for child-rearing. Somewhere, the understanding was lost that children need civilizing; that rules of expected behavior must be presented and enforced; and that children must be taught the meaning, beauty, benefits, value, and technique of self-control.

I remember the challenge from one female teen on my radio program who demanded to know, "Why can't I have sex in a casual way with a number of people if it feels good? My mother couldn't give me any good reason."

I answered that with serial, casual sex, only if the sex partner of the moment were good technically would she feel good physically.

"But," I asked, "can you feel really good if you know that ultimately nobody cares about you, nor you about them, much at all? Isn't that a lonely thought—a lonely feeling?"

She quietly said, "Yes."

"And think about this. Any animal can hump. Only humans can make love within the blessings of a covenantal relationship. Each day you have the opportunity to choose between humping like an animal, or elevating yourself. You choose."

With the village marginalizing such universal values as intact families, parental responsibility, and authority, to whom do children turn for a sense of intimacy, safety, and belonging besides mosh pits; gangs; cults; drugs; sick Internet chat rooms; dysfunctional, sexualized relationships; and radio talk show hosts?!

This is why I call our society the Village of the Damned. Our children, unformed and ultimately directionless, have only popular culture to guide their impulsive and hedonistic instincts. If almost total freedom of expression, sex, drugs, and behavior is so healthy, why do we read daily about our young people killing themselves off at rates unheard of in modern human history? It must be that deriving meaning and pleasure from life isn't solely about experiencing anything and everything at any time. Maybe doing anything and everything isn't enough to make a child want to live. Perhaps the chaos formed by all individuals "doing their thing" provides too little to count on, too little security on which to build a permanent sense of accomplishment or well-being or hope.

Home Alone

Our children have been largely abandoned by how we adults have structured modern society and culture.

Pat Hersh spent three years researching teenage life today. In an interview for *The Washingtonian* (July 1998), she said, "Adolescents can't state their independence by leaving us because we've already left them. We've become a nation of working people. It takes adults to raise children. There's no getting around that."

Ms. Hersh also came up with this startling calculation: "By the time a girl (typical latch-key teen) turns 18 and graduates from high school, she may have spent six to eight years of her life without consistent, meaningful adult contact. One recent study found that half of the adolescents' time may be spent entirely on 'discretionary activities,' meaning basically on their own. That in turn means loneliness and opens opportunities for loads of problems. They have easy access to car keys, liquor cabinets, and beds."

Since parents are basically "not at home," where are children learning about ethics, family values, sex education, and G-d and morality? Most of these values used to be conveyed by adults at home, extended family, or the "village." Now our culture seems to look to schools as a source of instruction in these eternal verities. But that is a big mistake, because schools are now propagandizing young people into believing that tolerance requires acceptance and that deviancy is diversity. The ACLU is ready to sue anyone who teaches religiously based sexual abstinence, although abortion and bisexuality are OK.

So now we have the most unbelievably lax school policies for behavior and dress, to give that all-important leeway for self-expression, individuality, and personal comfort and well-being. B. K. Eakman, executive director of the National Education Consortium, wrote an opinion piece in the *Washington Times* (April 26, 1999) that criticized this philosophy:

Trench-coat Mafia? Heavy eye makeup? Black hats and knee boots? What on earth did we expect when we started allowing kids to come to school permanently decked out in Halloween costumes? When we stopped giving youngsters more to do than primp, preen, strut, intimidate, and spout filthy song lyrics, what we reaped was swastikas and vampire cults.

Curriculums and activities that revolve around psychological calisthenics instead of serious learning fuel a morbid preoccupation with self. They don't increase self-esteem or instill self-respect. It doesn't take a psychiatrist—or, for that matter, a priest—to figure out that youngsters who are allowed to spend the largest part of their days acting out fantasies, who are drilled with "antiauthoritarian" theology, and who can get easy A's under phony "standards," are eventually going to unleash an environment of social chaos that in 10 years will transform even a United States of America into a Kosovo, Iraq, or Bosnia.

The "village" is a scene out of Mad Max and the Thunderdome. Parents—you better get back home!

In the absence of adults at home or in the family or in the neighborhood, children satisfy the basic human need for attachment and belonging, and the feelings of acceptance and intimacy that brings, by forming their own world.

Remember *Lord of the Flies?*

Peer Predators

Dr. Gordon Neufeld calls it peer orientation (*Southern Newspapers*, Vancouver, July 7, 1997). "It is rampant among juvenile delinquents, but it is evident in every school and on every playground. This is scary because as the kids age and their orientation to peers strengthens . . . parents and teachers are left in the dust, incapable of reaching their children, morally and intellectually."

Parents today want their children to have the best opportunities to learn—so they enroll them in school programs almost from birth, put them in umpteen after-school lessons, or put them in day care so Mom and Dad can work for the goodies they believe are in their child's best interest. This seemingly well-meaning behavior is destructive to the psychological health of youngsters.

The kids are busy, busy, busy, but they lack the closeness of a parent. Instead, they are surrounded by other children and end up bonding with them. As the approval and attention of peers becomes more significant and powerful than that of adults, behavior problems inevitably appear. Studies show that the worst-behaved kids are those who spend the most time with other kids.

It should be obvious that parenting styles, in which the parent is present, loving, and actively providing discipline and direction, are most likely to result in less peer orientation, therefore less involvement in sex, drugs, and antisocial and violent behaviors. In fact, a study conducted by the University of Maryland School of Medicine (May 3, 1999) noted that "especially among Caucasian, middle-class families, but essentially across all ethnic groups, parenting styles in which the parent is warm but demanding are the most likely to yield high achievement and low risk involvement."

"We can emphatically say that parenting makes a difference . . ." said one of the researchers. Like . . . no kidding.

Many lawmakers and mental health analysts assume that the high level of crime in America must have its roots in material conditions, such as poverty, unemployment, and a shortage of social programs. "But since 1965," according to a 1996 Heritage Foundation study, "the number of major felonies per capita has grown to roughly three times the rate before 1960, while welfare spending has increased 800 percent in real terms."

The study also disputes the notion that race or racism is a key cause of crime. "A closer look at the data shows that the real variable is not race but family structure and all that it implies in commitment and love between adults. . . . Most delinquents are children who have been abandoned by their fathers and are often deprived of the love and affection they need from their mothers."

Here are some important facts from this Heritage Foundation research:

1. Neighborhoods with a high degree of religious practice are not high-crime neighborhoods.

2. More than ninety percent of children from intact, stable homes do not become delinquent—this is true even in high-crime inner-city neighborhoods.

3. The mother's strong affectionate attachment to her child and the father's authority and involvement in raising his children are the best buffers against a life of crime.

Just listen to my radio program for one week and hear how often somebody from the broken-home triangle (child, parent, stepparent) complains about the chaos in disciplining and the behavioral/emotional problems of the child. New loves for the parents usually end up in pain for the children, who have no say in these events and no recourse to show their suffering and displeasure.

Dust Off the Rod . . .

For the last three decades, parents who disciplined their children—in other words, who consistently trained, taught, and punished them with consequences for transgressions—have often been admonished for being controlling, dictatorial, tyrannical, oppressive, destructive, confining, unloving, overly protective, old-fashioned, inflexible, authoritarian, and even abusive.

Consequently, parents became paralyzed into believing that any kind of structure or punishment would psychologically or emotionally scar or destroy their children forever. What I have heard time and time again from listeners is the fear that adherence to proper guidelines and consequences will either hurt or alienate their children, pushing them into rejection or rebellion. Of course, at this point in the degeneration of standards, values, and adult authority, that latter fear becomes more of a reality. More and more callers tell me that their recalcitrant children threaten to go live at a friend's house whose parents are more "accepting," or shack up and form their own immature, fragile new family so they can do what they wish.

I am not the only one seeing this decline in intergenerational responsibility and authority (parents) and respect (children); so is the military. A survey conducted by the Congressional Commission on Military Training and Gender-Related Issues was reported in the *Washington Times*, August 10, 1999. It concluded that the current generation of inductees are "lazy, selfish, out of shape, undisciplined, lacking in morals, challenging every order or decision or rule, having no respect for authority . . . and unwilling to shift from an individual mentality to a team orientation."

The military trainers see the pathetic degradation of the character of our young people and are handcuffed in being able to repair what mostly absent parents and a fragmented community have wrought. According to that same study, "Trainers expressed anger that they could not fail or expel recruits who did not meet standards . . . that they could not raise their voices or curse to motivate recruits verbally and that they had no recourse when recruits 'talked back' or refused to do what they were supposed to do. Respondents also argued that boot camp has shifted from a focus on preparing youth for military service to avoidance of scandals and/or hurting the feelings of recruits or impinging upon their rights."

I figure that those same young people, who can't tolerate rules, regulations, yelling, cursing, hurt feelings, or any compromise of what they imagine their rights to be, are probably going to be very upset when they are shot at, sniped at, mutilated, bombed, assaulted with chemicals and biological weapons, captured, tortured, and so forth. Think they'll cope? I doubt it. Actual warfare will probably hurt their feelings, damage their self-esteem, and diminish their immediate experience of happiness—all the values we hold most dear. This country better pray we never have to defend our land. We may no longer have the warriors to do so.

Ultimately, if parents do not teach their children the value of self-discipline, how will those children function in the real world, which requires individuals to exhibit self-control, to fit in, and to direct their creativity into something credible, useful, and valuable? If parents do not teach their children values and ideals, how will those children find meaning and purpose in their lives? If parents do not teach their children respect and cooperation, how will they learn to successfully work and play with others? If parents do not teach their children sacrifice, how will they learn to give and absorb the joys, blessings, sorrows, and challenges of a family life? If parents do not teach their children that love means suffering through difficulties, how will their children ever feel secure and confident in what life and relationships have to offer?

The answer is that they won't. Discipline is an essential feature of the parent/child relationship. It is an integral part of parents' love for their children. Children without discipline often become adults with temper tantrums, defiance, rage, depression, anxiety, poor school and work adjustment, drug and alcohol abuse, and criminality.

Does this all mean that a child's feelings don't count? No, of course not. Loving, attentive listening and compassion are also an essential part of parenting. However, children need to be clear on what's right and wrong, what's expected of them, and what the consequences are for being mean, destructive, self-centered, or out of control. That doesn't preclude ongoing or specific discussions as to why something is right or wrong or necessary. That doesn't preclude listening to a child's point of view. That does, however, preclude the child controlling the parent with manipulation, threats, tantrums, or obstinacy.

Children often do bad things because it is the only way they have of exerting power in powerless, hurtful situations. For instance, it is not unusual for a child to behave badly during visitation to his own divorced parent's house when there is a new marriage, a new stepparent, and a new baby. Since this child may feel marginalized by being a visitor in his own parent's home, he may resort to disrespect, rebelliousness, or even violence. I have spoken to some of these children on my radio program. They are devastated by the tragedy of their home lives, angry that they had

no say in subsequent events, and upset that their lives seem to be
at the mercy of what's convenient for adults. I tell them that their
feelings are entirely justified, but that still does not entitle them to
behave badly, which won't change reality, make them feel better,
or get them any goodies from this point on.

This, in essence, teaches them that life can be upsetting and
devastating. Their feelings are a reasonable response to an unreasonable course of events, but they still are responsible for maintaining internal control and dignity for the sake of their own
souls, psyches, and functional life.

Even in the healthiest of homes, children always complain
about not getting their way and feeling unfairly punished and
restricted. Although I counsel adults to be open to discussion,
while maintaining their position of final authority, I remind children that their dependency on their parents for all things puts
total responsibility on the parent for their entire well-being. This
responsibility comes with a perk: power. I tell them that when
they are entirely responsible for themselves (job, car, home,
insurance, food, and so forth) then they have that power. Until
such time as they are independent, their gratitude for their parents' efforts and responsibilities, their awareness of themselves as
"works in progress," and an acknowledgment of their parents'
superior experience and wisdom ought to lead them to respect
their parents' authority in spite of urges to the contrary. Most
important, children must trust that their parents are functioning
with the child's best interest at heart.

The parents who negotiate too much usually do so out of
guilt for their excessively busy lifestyles (be it work, play, new
lovers). They also want to make their children "happy," as a
way of reducing the parental stress of dealing with typically
demanding and argumentative children.

This letter from Jim, one of my listeners, tells a story of a
parent who learned the hard way:

*I have been a long-time listener, and your comments the
other day about raising children in this "feel good" age really*

struck home. We have two sons, eight and twelve. When we had our first son, we read all the latest. He was praised for everything, no spankings, and we explained why he should do what we asked him to do—and then helped him do everything because the poor darling couldn't be allowed to fail—it would hurt his feelings and damage his self-esteem! We saw doctors (medical and psychiatric), had him diagnosed as ADD and ADHD and put him on various drugs (Ritalin, Dexedrine, Imiprimine) because we knew that it couldn't be our child-rearing because we had done everything by the book.

Well, we finally came to our senses early this year. We looked at all the unacceptable behaviors and realized that WE HAD CREATED a selfish/spoiled brat. He also had a deep rooted fear of failure and very little self-esteem with no concept of consequences for his actions. Our son now has limits, has a progress chart of acceptable behaviors (loses TV and is grounded if he doesn't keep up his B+ average)—and tension in the house has mostly diminished. Additionally, we are trying to instill in him a sense that doing the right thing should not be to gain praise, but because it is morally correct and that the praise and good feelings should come from within—only when earned.

By the way, our second son was raised just the opposite of the first—he has high self-esteem, is full of confidence, and has true caring for others.

Dr. Spock is dead . . . Long Live Dr. Laura.

"NO!"

Some parents use the word "no" to simply avoid dealing with their child because they're too tired, too distracted, and too out of touch with their parenting responsibilities. This often results in a child who is completely compliant without thought, or else a child who has a strategy for ongoing war. The former child will likely always find a place in life in which to hide, get approval, and take orders. The latter child will likely always find an angle, an opportunity to "win," a person to control or beat.

"No," out of the mouth of a reasonable, sensitive, involved, loving parent, is a necessity in teaching children important lessons about life's limitations, the blessings inherent in self-control, the essence of values, and how to avoid danger.

Clinical psychologist Patricia Dalton wrote in the *Washington Post*, July 20, 1997, "I've talked to many parents who are so influenced by psychological theories about child rearing that they disregard common sense. 'No' is a dirty word. Children should be given choices and provided with explanations; punishment and adverse situations should be avoided as much as possible because they might harm the child's fragile self-esteem. There is an unspoken assumption that a child who feels good will never need to behave badly."

All in all, this is a formula that kills children with excessive, inappropriate kindness, because it shields them from frustration. Saying "no" will likely cause tension, but it will in no way permanently damage the bond a parent has with a child. Saying "no" is not the antithesis of love. It is the very proof of the love that a parent has for a child. In setting limits on possessions, experiences, activities, behavior, and words, parents help their children become centered (as opposed to self-centered), secure, confident, and able to negotiate life in a healthy and productive way.

The teaching has to start early. Andrea, one of my listeners, wrote:

When I quit my full-time teaching job last fall to be my kids' mom, the decision was scary for financial reasons, but I was clear as a bell that it was the best thing for my kids.

When I take my children grocery shopping at our local market, my four-and-a-half-year-old constantly asks for special treats. I always have the same matter-of-fact response: "No,

Mommy doesn't have any extra money for special treats. We're shopping for groceries today."

As we walked through the store the other day, I heard a boy whining for stuff and his exasperated mother (in go-to-work clothes) giving in. My son also listened and watched and asked me why that boy was acting that way. I said, "He hasn't learned his store manners yet."

We walked on and my son saw something neat he wanted and asked for it. (Hey, a kid's gotta dream!) I gave him my standard response. He said, OK. A few steps later he said, "I love you, Mom. This is fun."

But it doesn't always stay that easy. Kelly, one of my listeners, wrote about her thirteen-year-old son getting very upset with her after she told him that she wouldn't give permission to go to a movie until she knew the name of the movie, the rating, and who else was going. Her son threw a major screaming fit, blaming her for being too strict and making his life miserable. He decided that the world would be better off if kids didn't have parents.

It went on and on, she writes, *and he ended up getting grounded for the week-end. That evening my husband and I went to Bible study and listed him in the group's prayer concerns at the end of the lesson. When we arrived home, all the children were sleeping. Just as I was going to bed I found a note on my nightstand—from my thirteen-year-old: "To Mom and Dad—I am very sorry for the way I was acting the past few days. I wanted to write this on a note because I didn't want to get into an argument again. If you would, please give me a second chance. If you don't I'll be upset, but will understand. I really do mean this! I love you! Love, Your delinquent teen-age son, Drew."*

Being a mom is definitely a tough job, but certainly the most rewarding I'll ever have. P.S. He's not getting the second chance for this movie.

One of the most insidious problems for decent parents clarifying limits by saying "no" is the undermining of their good sense, morality, and protective wisdom by the laxity of most other parents. If I told you how many times a parent called me after saying "no" to her child about coed sleep-overs, parties in hotels, alcohol at parties, and R-rated movies to complain about how she was the only parent to say "no," you wouldn't believe me!

Here's a letter from Nancy, a listener:

My high-school senior son is a responsible, adorable young man—every mother's dream. However, this dream turned into a nightmare at prom time when his sixteen-year-old date's parents were just fine with the plan to have a post-prom party at a hotel room—without adult supervision.

Mom said, "No." She said that even if there was no sex, no drinking, and all good behavior, having underage girls in a hotel room could invite arrest. However, she remarked, the chances that there would be no sex, no drinking, no drugs, and all good behavior were unlikely.

Life has been difficult since, to say the least . . . I am now controlling, manipulative, will never let him make his own decisions and will never let him grow. After all, all his date's dad said was "go out, spend money, and have a wonderful time." I am the one who ruined their night and his life.

Her son did come home as he was told—but Mom feels bad that *such a good, responsible child, who has worked hard, achieved a lot and deserves all the wonderful things that life has to offer . . . had to be the only one.*

Even if it is "right" or "reasonable," kids do not like to be the only one, left out to feel stupid and geeky and oddball with crazy, repressive parents.

No Truth—No Consequences

It is especially troubling to me when parents respond to their child's misbehaviors by defending and protecting them against truth and consequences. One recurrent factor in bad-behaving children, who inevitably turn into bad-behaving adults, is the failure to hold them responsible for wrongdoing, and to scapegoat other kids or institutions. Someone or something else is always to blame, and punishment of almost any degree is deemed too damaging, traumatic, or unnecessary because these are basically "good kids." G-d save us all from these parents, these courts, these administrations. This is the most fertile ground for the production and nurturance of sociopaths known to man.

I literally have thousands of examples of these incidents from newspaper accounts and personal letters from listeners. Here are just a few.

According to an Associated Press report, August 4, 1999, a seventeen-year-old teenager in Saratoga Springs, New York, pleaded guilty to demanding protection payments from a schoolmate. His offense won't go on his permanent record. The victim in the case, another seventeen-year-old student, allegedly paid the extortionist $2,000 over a two-year period. He was arrested after investigators witnessed him accepting $300 from his victim, whom he threatened in order to collect payments. The perpetrator's father said that the case had been blown out of proportion by the media. "'I don't like the way he has been portrayed,' the father said."

This teenager admits to, and is caught red-handed, making threats and extorting money over a two-year period, and his father says his public image is distorted. What? Is this father incapable of separating his own image from that of his child's?

The parents of eighteen Provident High School prom-goers are suing a Lockport, Illinois, limousine company owner for refusing to drive their children back from the dance after finding three flasks of alcohol in the two cars the teens had rented (*Daily Southtown*, June 29, 1997). The parents' lawsuit acknowledges that flasks of alcohol were discovered inside the limousines, but asks for a reimbursement of the amount of money paid for the car service, plus, get this—an additional $5,000 for "mental suffering."

"'They were stranded,' said one of the parents. 'Their prom was ruined.'"

Their good time was ruined? Oh my. It gets worse! This same parent said the teens had not intended to drink in the limos or at the prom. "'They had no reason to,' she said, 'because they had all been invited to attend a supervised all-night, after-prom party at her home, where alcohol was to be made available to them. . . . All the parents agreed to it.'"

Here we have it—a communitywide conspiracy to subvert the morals of minors—under parental supervision! Swell.

My favorite lousy scapegoating parent quote comes from one of the parents of the fifteen Pope High School students serving ten-day suspensions after flunking breath-alcohol tests at their senior prom (*Atlanta Journal-Constitution*, May 13, 1998). Outraged parents and students contacted lawyers over what they called selective prosecution and a penalty, which might have affected their children's admission to college. While a school spokesperson is quoted as saying, "We're just grateful that fifteen students are safe and alive today," one of the parents countered, "They (school officials) don't give a damn what they've done to these kids."

A parent of a Pope High School graduate, who was afraid to be identified lest those scapegoating parents come after her, wrote me, "Thank you Cobb County for reinforcing what we teach at home!"

I became personally involved in one such situation. This was the case of Justin Swidler, a teenager in Bethlehem, Pennsylvania. According to numerous articles published from 1998 to 1999 in the *Morning Call*, the local newspaper, he created a Web site that contained vile profanities. On a Web page called "Why Should She Die?" he offered to pay a hit man to kill one of his teachers. The site also had interactive displays showing a distorted likeness of the principal being hit by a cartoon bullet.

According to his father, who sued the school over his expulsion, "The Web site was a way for his son to vent his frustration at allegedly being belittled in class each day. He found an outlet and began feeling better" (July 24, 1998).

As we know, it's very important for children to "feel good."

I became involved when folks in Bethlehem sent me the news articles about this event. People were outraged that the parents, instead of apologizing and accepting the expulsion, were suing for Justin's reinstatement in school. They were also alleging First Amendment protection for his Web site (which subsequently was denied in court) and for "embarrassment, ridicule, humiliation, isolation, and severe emotional distress," as well as "substantial pecuniary loss and inconvenience."

Are we as a society to accept that threatening the lives of other human beings is a simple matter of free speech?

This information came to me just days after the Columbine High School massacre in Colorado. The newspaper report indicated that Justin was transferred, ironically, to a school in Colorado, and was given a position of responsibility for the school's Web site. Frankly, because of what appeared to be parental accommodation to their child's terroristlike behavior, I was frightened for the children, teachers, and administration of this new unnamed school and revealed that part of the story on the air to warn those folks. Soon afterward, Justin left that school.

I read a letter from Justin's principal on the air, which was summarized in the *Morning Call* (May 24, 1999). The principal wrote:

You are totally correct in your impressions of the parents of this student. From the beginning, the parents had initially denied any involvement with the Web site and then attempted to make a mockery of the process that our school district took. The parents have continually challenged our position saying the site was only a joke. This was not the first conflict we had with these parents. . . . It has disrupted our school community and for a time tarnished the excellent reputation that we have earned through the years. The morale of our students and staff

*has been affected. . . . A sense of "nothing will ever be the
same" pervaded our hallways.*

A report by the Associated Press (June 21, 1999) stated:
School officials who are pushing to get unruly students out of
schools are finding that the students and their parents are pushing back. . . . Connecticut does not compile data on total numbers
of expulsions. But state education officials say expulsions—and
parental challenges to them—have become more common in
recent years because of zero-tolerance policies on drugs and
weapons. . . . "In days gone by, parents who were contacted by
administrators were more likely to respond by saying, 'I'm very
sorry my son or daughter did this, is there anything we can do to
address this issue?' " State Department of Education spokesman
Tom Murphy said. "Now, the response oftentimes is, 'How dare
you. You'll hear from my attorney.' While parents have a right to
protect their child, the predominant attitude is that we can get you
off if we're sharp enough."

When the "best defense is a good offense" tactic isn't
employed, you can be sure to find some pop-psych rationale to
excuse the bad behavior. As Sandra, one of my listeners, wrote:

*As I watched 20/20 on TV last night I was so upset by what
I heard. I watched as they showed how children were throwing
50-pound rocks over bridges into oncoming traffic. People all
over the U.S. are being injured and killed by these bored children. As the report went on I watched as a 21-year-old man,
called a boy, cried as he told how sorry he was and that he
never thought that it would hurt anybody. Now I will get to
the bad part . . . there was a psychologist from California that
was defending the children, saying that they need help not
punishment. He said that they were "Type T personalities and
they are just after the thrill." This is the kind of thrill that I
think should have punishment but I thought you'd like to hear
what more the media is doing to promote kids and crime.*

On the other side are those intrepid parents who still believe in accountability and character. As Stan's mom wrote to me, "By forcing our son to own up to full responsibility even when others may not require it of him, it is our hope this practice follows him through his life. I hope this is another building block for a foundation of integrity and honesty in a world that seems to discourage and minimize the importance of these qualities."

Karen, another fearless parent's senior high school daughter, was caught doing something she shouldn't have with six other seniors. "The school meted out their punishments which we supported and thought were fair. The other six parents were vocally and obnoxiously against the punishments. One mother even got a lawyer because she was afraid it would jeopardize her son's college. She called me for support and I told her that while I understood how bad she felt, I was more concerned about my daughter's future as a good, decent and responsible human being."

And that's the crux of the difference in parent types with respect to punishment and accountability. One set of folks sees material things, position, and power as ultimately important in life. Anything that threatens those opportunities (like school records, and other legal documents) is the enemy to be vanquished. The other set of folks sees character, integrity, honesty, ideals, and values as of the utmost importance in the lives of their children, and figure that loss of opportunity and status are of secondary importance.

Finally, Dana, a former assistant prosecuting attorney and district court magistrate, wrote to me in response to my on-air advice to a mother to press charges against her daughter who used her credit card without permission. "When I was a prosecutor, in cases where parents declined to be the complaining witness in a case where their child committed a crime against them, I could always count on seeing the child again in court, whether for the same crime or for something far worse."

Learning How to Hang Tough

Children will try to manipulate, intimidate, and basically threaten their parents into a fearful retreat from consequences—or even the pronouncement of rules in the first place!

In response to questions to adults on my Web site (www.drlaura.com) concerning the biggest mistake their parents made with them, Greg wrote:

A mistake my father made with me when I was a junior in high school is that he didn't carry out his edicts. I had ditched school four days in a row, and the school called my mom. She told my dad, who took my car keys away from me and said that I wouldn't get them back for a week. This happened on a Thursday. He relented and gave the keys back to me by Monday.

At the time I felt that I had been let off the hook too easily. At the time I wish he had kept them. He was right, and I was wrong. Actually, he should have kept the keys for the entire semester. I would have felt a lot better if he had because I know I needed a kick in the ass to make me more disciplined, responsible, and productive.

I felt shortchanged by his leniency. Kids know when they're wrong and they really want someone to give them boundaries. Providing boundaries and enforcing them is an act of love that too few parents have the balls to insist upon.

Indeed, according to neuropsychologists at McLean Hospital in Belmont, Massachusetts (*U.S. News & World Report,* August 9, 1999), their research "reinforces other new findings suggesting that the average teenager's prefrontal cortex isn't ready to take on the role of brain CEO. . . . Until the prefrontal cortex has been pruned, most young teenagers don't yet have all the brain power they need to make good judgments. . . . One of the last parts to mature [in the brain] is in charge of making sound judgments and calming unruly emotions."

Bottom line is that teenagers may look as though they've

grown into their feet and ears, but until their early twenties, they just haven't grown into their brains. For parents to abdicate guiding their children's lives for any reason is to leave children to the chaos of their peers, the psychosocial environment, their own impulses, and immature emotions. These are not the happiest children.

Missy wrote in response to my Web site question:

The biggest mistake my parents made is they did not trust themselves to follow through on enforcing the rules. When I was 15 years old, I truly believe my parents would give in to my complaining or moaning. The few times they did hold the line, I know I was a better person for it. As a parent of a 4-year-old, I try to provide him with an environment that says these are the rules—this is what happens if we break the rules—and I follow through. And he knows what is OK and what is not OK to do. And he is a very happy and outgoing little boy!

Children are happier when they know what is expected. Clarity and structure breed a feeling of security. Nonetheless, some children will always push the envelope, and that is where consistency and a sense of humor come in. Mary, one of my listeners, shares her story and gives evidence to the fact that good parenting builds a stronger bond between parent and child than laxity:

I too had my eleven-year-old daughter try to use psychological guilt to get her own way. My rules are not dating until she's 16, and then only with a group of friends. Well, now the love of her life has asked her out and she decided to try to make mom feel bad.

We were both putting groceries away and she said to me, "Ya know, I'm gonna end up mentally scarred when I grow up because you won't let me go out with Mike."

I looked at her in surprise because of her adult terminology. Realizing immediately what she was up to, I returned to putting the food away and used my quick-witted mom sense of

*humor by replying, "Well, I guess I'll just have to carry that
guilt with me to my grave."*

*I then looked at her and smiled a knowing smile back at her.
We both ended up laughing with each other.*

Swift and Terrible

I've had parents call me on my radio program days and weeks
after their child committed some outrageous offense. One of
the questions I ask them is, "Why have you waited so long to
deal with this?" The usual answer? "I don't know." When I
push more, they might add, "I wasn't sure what to do."

Over my years in broadcasting, I have been amazed at the
growing sense of impotency in parents. Often when I make
concrete suggestions the response is, "But isn't that kind of
tough? I mean—doing that will have a long-range effect on
their lives."

As will the results of their acts of defiance! This is why I always
recommend creative, swift, and terrible action so that children
take their parents seriously and learn "the lesson" permanently.
This technique works wonders with children used to continuous
pouting, arguing, negotiating, manipulation, and who easily tolerate feeble consequence and continue to behave badly.

Diane, one of my listeners, followed through on a technique
I've recommended:

*My daughter is almost twelve and was having a bad day. She
screamed at me and I told her in a quiet voice that we could
talk about this after she calmed down a little. She didn't like
this response and slammed her bedroom door so hard that the
house shook. A couple of minutes later she did it again.*

*Now, Dr. Laura, I don't like slamming doors. So, I took the
most logical and peaceful action I could think of. I went to
the garage, got a hammer and screwdriver, walked to our
daughter's room and popped the hinges off the door and carried
the door to our bedroom closet.*

My daughter was stunned and appalled! "You can't take my door! What about my privacy! Without my mirror, my clothes will be mismatched!"

The door remained in our closet.

Two days later, she and a friend were trying to listen to music in the privacy of her bedroom, which now had a chair wedged in the doorway. She sent her friend out to ask me if I could put the door back up. I looked up and simply told her, "No."

"WHY NOT???!!!" came my daughter's voice from her bedroom. I told her because I wanted to make a deep, deep, DEEP impression in her brain that it was not okay to slam doors in our home and if you did there would be serious consequences. I also told her that she could visit her door and mirror whenever she wanted to (she did, too!).

I put up the door five days later. There have been no further incidents.

Clearly, Diane's daughter learned to take her mother seriously—not only with slamming doors, but with any other infringements. The daughter realized that her mother wasn't going to tolerate inappropriate behaviors, and would not argue and fight about it for days or hours. Diane was swift, and to her daughter, terrible in the choice of consequences.

And that's the main point of swift and terrible. Children learn quickly that their parents mean business. I have suggested that for children with seemingly out-of-control behaviors, drastic measures often have to be employed, so that the parent regains control—without which the child will not likely learn the value of controlling himself.

These actions have often been employed when out-of-control children have been diagnosed with ADD/ADHD and medication is suggested. Child development expert John Rosemond describes such a case in his private practice (*Fresno Bee*, April 19, 1998).

A certain young man was a major behavior problem in

school and at home . . . disruptive, disrespectful and disobedient . . . it was repeatedly suggested that the young man had attention deficit disorder. It was suggested that ". . . his behavior wasn't their fault—he needed medication to help him control his impulses." The parents resisted this well-intentioned hogwash for months.

"Finally," the mother told me, "we reached the limit of our tolerance for his shenanigans. He came home from school one day to discover a padlock on the door to his bedroom, which houses his TV, computer, video-game unit, sports equipment, models and so on. We told him he'd be allowed in his room for 15 minutes in the morning to dress for school and for 15 minutes in the evening to get ready for bed. His bed was going to be the sofa in the living room—most comfortable, if you ask me."

It seems that the boy was stunned and threatened to report his parents for child abuse. They didn't back down. They told him that this situation would go for six weeks, and couldn't be shortened, but could be lengthened one week per each incident of misbehavior at school or at home.

"It was amazing," his mother continued. "His teacher called us several days later to tell us he'd become a completely different child . . . polite, cooperative, talkative, a general pleasure to be around."

Nonetheless, the padlock remained for the full six weeks. One year later, things remained as pleasant at their home.

Drug 'Em Up

"Every school day, more than a million children line up at nurses' stations to get their midday dose of Ritalin, a stimulant used to treat Attention-Deficit Hyperactivity Disorder. Studies show that Ritalin use as nearly tripled since 1990" (*Investors Business Daily*, October 16, 1997).

Though many argue that most of the hike stems from greater

awareness of ADHD among parents and teachers, and that many children still go undiagnosed and untreated, the article points out that the data suggest a link between money and Ritalin use, and that the federal government might be driving the trend.

In 1990, a series of regulatory and congressional changes, along with a Supreme Court ruling, opened the federal Supplemental Security Income program (SSI) to low-income families with an ADHD-diagnosed child, providing cash benefits and access to Medicaid and food stamps.

Also, according to this article, the Education Department might have played a role in the rapid rise in Ritalin use through federal special education grants (IDEA program), which allowed schools to receive more than $400 annually for each child diagnosed with ADHD.

In spite of these concerns, and the serious side effects of Ritalin (loss of appetite, sleeping problems, stomach pain, weight loss, fast heartbeat, fever, joint pain, uncontrollable body movements, blurred vision, and violent behavior), some psychiatrists, educators, and parents are convinced that Ritalin is essential in some cases to help a child get his behavior under control. But some worry that many children are misdiagnosed with ADHD and put on Ritalin when they might have other problems, or simply be bored, highly creative and gifted, or require serious discipline, structure, and consequences to motivate them to develop control.

Some observers are convinced that ". . . harried teachers and counselors have learned to recommend an ADHD diagnosis to parents in order to get their more rambunctious students Ritalin, an easy way to quiet them down," writes John McGinnis in the *Wall Street Journal* (September 16, 1997). Mr. McGinnis says:

> In short, ADD kids are learning an early lesson in the mores of 1990's America: Don't take responsibility for your own conduct; instead, declare that you're in the grip of uncontrollable impulses,

seek professional help, and start making excuses. . . . Aren't parents, teachers and doctors shirking responsibility for raising kids by substituting a phony therapeutic approach for old-fashioned discipline?

Although this issue is controversial among professionals, and sensitive with parents, I generally recommend on my program that before parents consider medications, they find a behavioral specialist to help them with the tools they need to cope and deal with their child. One mother, in response to one of my on-air suggestions, wrote that her daughter was correctly diagnosed at five years of age as seriously ADHD. She didn't want to medicate her; she became expert in the technique and attitude necessary to deal with difficult children. She came to the following conclusions about what these children need:

➤ *Absolute boundaries. Any exceptions made are viewed by the child as nullifying the rule.*

➤ *External environment structure. These children lack the internal structure to provide external boundaries for themselves so they violate other people's space, have a poor concept of time, and get frustrated by a change in routine.*

➤ *Social rules. These children don't learn social skills readily from observation, nor do they generalize from one experience to another. Therefore, constant counseling and clarification are needed to help them relate and get along with peers.*

➤ *Small, quiet learning situations to promote concentration.*

➤ *Consistent reinforcement of rules and expectations—due to the children's difficulty in paying attention and absorbing information.*

What I learned from getting help for my daughter and attending group counseling sessions for parents is tremendous empathy as I began to appreciate how terribly confusing and frustrating life is for these kids. Yes, it is hard to have and help these children, but within six months (!) of starting the behavior program, my 5-year-old daughter was not hitting her father, myself, teachers or peers. She no longer had temper tantrums in the middle of the store, she sat in the time-out chair without being restrained, went to bed when told to—and I was not exhausted emotionally and physically at the end of every day. Even with the extra time it took to run the behavior modification program and see the behaviorist, I had more time to enjoy her because it took much more time and energy to fight with her. When given the tools to understand her world and respond to it appropriately, she absolutely blossomed.

It is axiomatic that some children are more difficult to deal with than others. Nonetheless, it is an absolute moral imperative that parents acknowledge their responsibility to do their best to help their children become functional, spiritual, responsible, and joyous adults. At the center of that loving action is discipline.

As one parent wrote to me after her struggles with her son, "We are very proud of him and know that he may not graduate with honors, but he will graduate an honorable man."

And that's everything.

To Spank, or Not to Spank . . .

Some folks have just gone nutty over the debate about old-fashioned spankings. They don't seem to be able to tell the difference between the proper use of corporal punishment and violent child abuse.

The *Wall Street Journal* (February 4, 1997) published some interesting statistics about preferred discipline methods between the year 1962 and 1992. For example, this newfangled "time-out" concept was unheard of in 1962. By 1992, 35 percent of parents preferred it. Cutting allowances and sending to bed have changed very little in popularity, remaining at unpopular single-digit percentages. Scolding has remained virtually the same, 17 percent in 1962, and 15 percent by 1992. Limiting TV has dropped more than half in preference from a 1962 high of 38 percent. However, spanking showed the largest change, 59 percent in 1962, dropping to a mere 19 percent in 1992.

However, when kids themselves are asked, the picture is quite different. *USA Today* (April 11, 1995) polled middle and high school students about whether corporal punishment should be used on guilty teens for some crimes. The middle and junior high school students said "yes" with a resounding 51 percent, while 60 percent of high school students approved!

The change in preferred methods of discipline is obviously due to the professional psychobabblers who intimidated parents from using the time-tested technique of spanking to make an impression, get kids' attention, reassert authority, teach a lesson, and ward off even the mere thought of the misbehavior repeating itself. The threats from the psychological community were horrifying. Parents who spanked would turn their children into angry, violent, self-loathing, depressed juvenile delinquents, and someday, neurotic adults. This was part of the post-1960s absurd notion that children should be treated as equals, and that parents should discipline by appealing to the child's better or rational side.

Good luck.

In fact, the notion advanced by many American child-rearing authorities that a couple of well-placed swats on the tush of one's small child (from two years to adolescents) irreparably harms him is essentially a myth. The so-called research upon which much of this silly thinking was based was inconclusive and badly flawed—but spread with ignorant enthusiasm by the uncritical media anyway.

Typically, studies on spanking have been carried out by retrospective interviews with adults, who are asked decades later to talk about their spankings as a child. Researchers then attempt to link the spanking with current behaviors (like spousal abuse, depression, drug use, and so forth). Other research generally aims at correlating a mother's description about her children's behavior with the pattern of spanking.

Neither technique is objective on the part of the interviewee or the interviewer. It is impossible to demonstrate the accuracy of retrospective studies. It is impossible to know if the spanking led to the misbehavior or the misbehavior led to the spanking. Researchers also failed to adequately control for other variables: degree or type of spanking, age of child (teenagers are generally considered too old for corporal punishment to be effective), other behavioral problems, family problems (broken home, substance abuse, etc.), the age of the mother (often anywhere from fourteen to twenty-four years old—hardly representative), and so forth.

Nonetheless, journalists reporting on child-rearing trends rarely bothered to scrutinize the claims of anti-spanking forces, perhaps due to their own personal bias or just plain old sloppiness.

One of the main arguments of those who oppose spanking is that it is a form of child abuse and will lead to further child abuse.

According to a report in *U.S. News & World Report* (April 13, 1999), "no study demonstrates that spanking a child leads to (parental) abuse—indeed, it may be the other way around. Parents who end up abusing their children may misuse all forms of discipline, including spanking. Sweden, often cited as a test case, hasn't borne out the spanking prohibitionists' fears either. After Sweden outlawed spanking by parents in 1979, reports of serious child abuse actually increased by more than 400 percent over ten years . . ."

In 1997, the *Archives of Pediatrics & Adolescent Medicine* published two articles with research about spanking. One, by sociologist Murray A. Straus, concluded that spanking children, ages six to nine, three or more times a week increased a child's antisocial behavior, measured in activities like cheating, bullying, or lying. The same issue carried another, longer-term study by psychologist Marjorie Lindner Gunnoe, which came to different conclusions. According to the *U.S. News & World Report* article mentioned above, "Unlike Straus, Gunnoe used data that tracked more children (just over 1,100) for five years (not two years), sampled older parents as well, and relied on reports from both children and adults. The researcher concluded that 'for most children, claims that spanking teaches aggression seem unfounded.' Gunnoe found that children ages four to seven who had been spanked got in fewer, not more, fights at school."

It is fascinating that the Straus anti-spanking conclusions made all three TV networks and at least 107 newspaper and magazine stories. The Gunnoe pro-spanking report didn't make one TV network. Only fifteen of the 107 newspaper and magazine stories on Straus's research mentioned Gunnoe's contrary findings.

So much for counting on the media for unbiased and thorough reporting about sociopolitical issues.

Finally, according to *U.S. News & World Report*, in 1996, psychologist Robert Larzelere from Boys Town (which does not allow spanking) did a review of all the spanking literature. He dropped those papers that were not peer reviewed, in which the spanking reached the level of abuse or the behavior did not clearly precede the spanking. He ended up with thirty-five studies that failed "to find any convincing evidence that nonabusive spanking, as typically used by parents, damaged children." His review also "revealed that no other discipline technique—including time-out and withdrawal of privileges—had more beneficial results for children under thirteen than spanking, in terms of getting children to comply with their wishes."

Bottom line. Parents should use spanking (when they're not enraged or hysterical or using an object that can cause bodily damage) as a backup to other disciplinary techniques (reasoning, time-outs, rewards, withdrawal of privileges, and natural consequences). If they have a loving relationship with their child, spanking can have a beneficial role in extinguishing inappropriate behaviors or at least in cutting down on repeats.

6

Give Them What They Want

*The number one worst thing my parents (more
so my mother) did that caused me difficulty was
to never let me feel anything but happy ...
Everything I did was perfect—I was never disciplined, never spanked, never told "no," never
grounded, never made to do my homework.
There were always excuses for me and blame
was placed elsewhere. I lived with unrealistic
expectations and perceptions of who I was ... I
eventually became very angry ... to the point of
violence.*

Jacqueline, 1999

Unfortunately, indulgence is currently in our societal blood—a
deadly mutant of identity and selfishness that appeared with
the loss of *guilt*. Actually, guilt wasn't lost. It was accused,
tried, convicted, and sentenced to death by a generation who
invented a philosophy of *total* freedom of expression and
behavior—without limits and without judgment—destructive
to both self and society.

Before the 1960s, children learned from their intact, nuclear, religious families that there was right and wrong, that wrong should and would be punished, and that a guilty conscience was a healthy and necessary internal warning system alerting us that we were doing something wrong. The principles of morality, reinforced in large part by civil laws, taught each child that there were clear boundaries around sexual acting out (deviant sexual behavior, unmarried sex); aggression (violence, extortion, intimidation); acquisitiveness (stealing, manipulating); character assassination (vicious, vulgar gossip); and so forth.

When folks stepped over those clear demarcations, there would be hell to pay in the form of personal and societal disappointment, disapproval, rejection, admonitions from one's clergy (with the appropriate repentance and repair), and a bad reputation.

While all of these pressures were not 100 percent effective in controlling the lowest human instincts and impulses, they were reasonably effective in setting a tone, laying a foundation, and establishing expectations about punishment and reward. They embraced an ideal to which the majority aspired.

All that changed with the "sexual revolution" of the sixties. The results are evident in our children, who display problems related to a lack of values, a lack of self-control and discipline, and no sense of meaning to life in general, or theirs specifically. This is why we see such a difference in pre- and post-sixties abuse of drugs and alcohol, sexual promiscuity and deviancy, eating disorders, self-destructive behaviors, suicide, violent acting out, and relationship problems, just to name a few!

Too many children today are morally and philosophically aimless as well as behaviorally and emotionally out of control. The crux of the matter is society's intense focus on individual *rights*. Think about it. Isn't the perpetual wanting machine an indication of an infantile, egocentric personality? And isn't the adamant and insistent focus on personal rights an example of minimum empathy and sympathy for the needs and rights of others?

Narcissism Is a Killer

Right after the massacre at Columbine in Littleton, Colorado, the eighth school shooting spree in two years, pundits racked their brains to figure out what was making kids more viciously and (more frighteningly) coldly violent.

Barbara Lerner, a writer and psychologist, wrote in the *Orlando Sentinel* (May 2, 1999) the truth about these kids. She explains that the shooters, counter to conventional wisdom, were generally from nice, intact families in good neighborhoods. In fact, many of the parents were either in therapy with their children, or sending their children separately for counseling for self-esteem and aggression issues. Both Columbine shooters graduated from therapy some two months before the crime, with glowing reports!

From Dr. Lerner's point of view, the problems of those two boys, and most of our children these days, is a very different form of abuse: indulgence that leads to narcissism.

> A narcissist is a person who never progressed beyond the self-love of infancy, one who learned superficial social skills— narcissists are often charming—but never learned to truly love another, and through love, to view others as separate persons with a worth and value equal to their own. To the narcissist, other people have no intrinsic worth; their value is purely instrumental. They are useful when they satisfy his desires and enhance his self-esteem. . . . Only he matters, and because his sense of self-importance is so grossly inflated, his feelings are easily hurt. When they are, when others thwart him or fail to give him the excessive, unearned respect he demands, he reacts with rage and seeks revenge, the more dramatic the better.

Psychology cannot fill the void where morality and conscience ought to be. This hole needs to be filled by the example of parents, who walk the moral walk themselves, establish in the home clear-cut rules, and demonstrate the will to enforce them. Children need to learn that there are limits to what will be expected and accepted. There will be judgment, consequences, and even punishment when those limits are exceeded.

In psychological terms, the parents' standards and values and the child's desire for acceptance and approval from the parents will function to override his immature wishes, so that he internalizes those standards and values, eventually making them his own. This is the development of a conscience.

With the pop-psychobabble insistence on equality of children with adults, self-esteem over conscience and rules, unconditional love over moral training, and freedom and rights over judgment, our children walk around as the center of their own universes, lacking in an ability to truly care for other people. This philosophy is ultimately more destructive and abusive to the psyches and characters of children than any one spanking could ever be. As Dr. Lerner concludes, "These experts have no real solutions to offer, when the problem is overindulgence rather than abuse, as it so often is in the 1990s."

Indulgence Creates Kids Who Crumble

When children who murder classmates are queried as to their motivations, there is a numbing realization. The reasons are often mundane—they broke up with a girlfriend, jocks made fun of them, they were treated like geeks, and so forth. Yet these artificial hierarchies are as old as civilization itself. They are nowhere more evident than in the schoolyard.

I was actually harassed, excluded, and even beaten up (way, *way* before my martial arts black belt!) because my mother was an "immigrant," an Italian Catholic married to "a nice Jewish boy," living in a predominantly Jewish neighborhood. Did it hurt? You better believe it. Did I shoot anybody? While hurting them back was often high on my agenda, revenge, my father taught me, was best delivered with dignity through personal accomplishment.

When children are indulged, never challenged, never taught to deal with real life and adversity, they become weak. This weakness often leads to identification with some movement or group that readily accepts them and makes them feel strong or important, like neo-Nazis. The next step is labeling others as bad (athletes, girls, Jews, blacks, teachers, and so forth) *and* the cause of their own problems. Then they act out, usurping the ultimate power—of life and death—becoming godlike.

These murders take many forms. Look at the rise in infanticide by girls and young women who want to avoid embarrassment, their parents' anger, or the inconvenience of having to raise a child. Have you noticed how feminist groups and liberal pro-abortion spokespersons talk only about the girls' probable low self-esteem? They never admit to the heinous quality of the crime.

Leonard Pitts Jr. writes in the *Detroit Free Press* (June 10, 1999):

> Our children are the children of entitlement. These are the children who were never shamed enough, blamed enough, held accountable enough or told 'no' enough to understand that the world does not orbit around them nor exist for their immediate gratification.
>
> These are the children of the new age, the one wherein parents worried so much—too much . . . —about bruising self-esteem. As a result, they fall apart like a house of cards in a hurricane the moment life deals them a hard slap or two.
>
> If we continue to smooth the way; if we continue to protect our children from the consequences of their wrongdoing; if we persist in eliminating judgment and morality as too confining; if we don't teach our children that the earth moves around the sun (*not* around them), we will continue to make frail, frightened, emotionally and psychologically compromised, morally vacant, dangerous, aimless, self-indulgent, confused, lost children.

Where Are the Role Models?

The day I began writing this chapter, I read Maureen Dowd's column in the *New York Times* (August 22, 1999). I was struck by her assessment of the problems presidential candidate George W. Bush Jr. was having with the media nagging about his youthful drug use. In the midst of this analysis she brought up an important point about the differences in role models before and after the 1960s.

> John F. Kennedy, Bob Dole, President Bush, and John McCain offered traditional conquests. They fought real enemies in war.
> But boomers like Bill Clinton and George W. Bush, who *avoided Vietnam*, needed to create domestic dragons and internal giants to kill. Mr. Clinton dramatized his teen-age confrontation with his alcoholic, abusive stepfather.
> Yuppie candidates play up painful odysseys of *self-discovery*. They slay the Gorgon of addiction and the Hydra of *self-indulgence*. They present themselves as redeemed, reborn (or born again) with the Arthurian virtues—temperance, loyalty, courage.

I found Dowd's comments to be right on and insightful. The baby boomers and their children had little in the way of external challenges to fight—no Great Depression or World War. They were indulged by prosperity and technology and by parents who wanted them to have better/easier lives. They believed tasting all of the fruit from previously forbidden trees was an entitlement and a certain route to life enrichment. Only later was there the realization that this was not the best route to build character, reputation, healthy relationships, or success in life. Hence comes the "painful odyssey" back to "oldies" values.

And with Clinton, at least, we know that this "painful odyssey" did not result in self-control or strong character with respect to marital fidelity or honesty. However, the most telling point about the Clinton story, and most relevant to this book, is that America said his immoral behavior "didn't matter."

Parents of America—your children heard you loud and clear!

Fruits of the Tree

While many children fantasize about total license, they realize its damning nature when experienced too soon. Barbara, one of my listeners, wrote about this very issue:

I was allowed to date at thirteen and the clothes my mother gave me to wear made me look like a woman. The youngest man was eighteen; the oldest, twenty-six. I was thrown into too many situations I didn't understand, therefore, didn't know how to handle. I didn't even know what sex was, but I would before it was all over with.

By the time I was sixteen, I was allowed to go to college games and dances for weekends without a chaperone or my parents knowing what my sleeping arrangements were. I was so experienced and jaded by this time, I found the things the other kids my age did childish and boring.

College was not any better because I had done that scene in high school. Peggy Lee's blues song . . . "Is that all there is . . ." are the lyrics that come to mind. So the next step was to end up pregnant, married—in that order—then, the one after that, divorced.

My life has been so messed up because I continued to create even more drama in it. I asked my mother why she let me do all those things, and all she'll say is she was young and didn't know any better. How did she ever get the idea I would know better than she did?

Jacqueline, whose quote begins this chapter, went on to relate that she "grew up believing I was perfect, the center of the universe, and had no comprehension of reality. The rules that pertained to everyone else did not pertain to me, because I was perfect and could do no wrong. If a sign said 'DO NOT TOUCH,' I touched it because it didn't mean me."

The result of this "indulgent parenting" was that she became angry, even violent, when others did not treat her according to her self-image and sense of entitlement. She became physically abusive to her boyfriend if he did not fulfill her every need. After almost seven years of psychoanalysis, she learned to express her emotions in a healthy manner, and to find her rightful place in G-d's universe, not Jacqueline's.

Stupid Trusting

If there is one serious concept most parents have wrong, it is this issue of trust. For some reason parents have gotten the impression that "love means always having trust." That is both a silly and a dangerous notion.

Many parents call my radio program, having heard something serious about their child's behavior from one of their child's friends. Or perhaps they read something on a piece of paper that slipped from the pocket of their child's jeans during the spin cycle, or snooped in their child's journal, backpack, dresser drawers, or closet floor. They are immobilized to follow through lest their child accuse them of *not trusting*!

The fear of that indictment virtually paralyzes some parents into ignoring problems concerning illegal behavior, drugs, sex, cheating, skipping school, sneaking onto Internet pornography sites, smoking, and eating disorders.

One mother was virtually hysterical on the phone after having found blatantly vulgar e-mail on her fourteen-year-old daughter's computer from her sixteen-year-old boyfriend. The message was rather graphic, describing in detail the sexual delights in store for her little girl.

I asked the mother what she intended to do about it. She said she didn't see how she could do anything, because she'd have to admit prying into her daughter's privacy. She said, "Tina would never trust me again."

I challenged her with "So, Mom, rather than risk her getting mad at you, you'd risk her becoming sexually active at an age when she certainly can't handle the psychological ramifications of sexual intimacy, getting pregnant, acquiring a sexually transmitted disease, being used as a sex toy? Are you kidding?"

No, she wasn't—and that's downright scary.

This dopey mentality reflects a belief that children are the equals of their parents—just shorter; that children, whose every need is met by their parents, are somehow entitled to equal standing when it comes to their own opinions, decisions, activities, and *privacy*.

As I've said many times, those who accept the responsibility are entitled to the power. Since the parent shoulders the entire responsibility for the life and continued well-being of dependent minor children, the parent holds the power. Children have power only by the dispensation of the adult—who metes it out to the child as a function of maturity (the ability and willingness not to be impulsive and to follow rules), trustworthiness (gained by opportunities handled appropriately), and circumstance (people, places, and things involving minimum risk).

Trust is a very different concept as it relates to the child or the parent. This is the point of error in most families. When a child in a typical family speaks about trusting a parent, he generally means that the parent will give or do whatever she's promised, in spite of any or all intervening circumstances. I spoke with one fifteen-year-old boy who complained to me that he could no longer trust his mom. It seems she promised him extra money for doing some specific chore and didn't pay up. Of course, the fact that money became scarce in the household due to financial troubles was irrelevant to him. And that's the point. For children, trusting a parent means getting what was promised—a *self-centered* concern.

This is in contrast to the essence of a trustworthy parent. A parent must be trusted to be alert and aware of her child's behaviors, emotions, activities, and problems. A parent needs to be responsive to the child's needs and events in her life. A parent must be trusted to discipline, teach, direct, and even punish when necessary, to help his child develop character. Notice that the things that make a parent trustworthy are not self-centered but child-centered. That is because the parent is responsible *for* the child, while the child is responsible *to* the parent.

To that end, the responsible parent must use any and all means to gain the information she needs, if there is concern that the child may be off track. I have told parents that daily snooping in their child's things is wrong, destructive to the relationship with their child, and indicative of some psychological problem of their own that needs attention. However, where there is an indication that something might be wrong, or where there is the intent to follow up to make sure things stay on track, the parent has a moral responsibility to that child to get that information.

I just love it when a parent and a child call my radio program together and the child is complaining about *his* things and *his* space and *his* privacy being invaded. First I determine that the parents are not compulsively bugging the children for no good reason. Once that is determined, I remind the children that the possessive pronoun "mine" is not completely accurate. All the children have, including their own lives, is by the grace of their parents and G-d.

I suggest they consider their things and space more like rental property, since it is by their parents' hard work that these things even exist. When they challenge that they bought something or other with baby-sitting or part-time job money, I remind them that this money is "extra" only because everything else is provided for! I tell them they must show respect and gratitude, not attitude and resentment.

Maggie, a broadcast journalist from North Carolina, sent me a copy of a "man on the street" column from the *Fayetteville Observer Times* (February 5, 1994).

I was appalled by the answers of three teenagers. I can't

*believe, when asked how their parents would feel if they were
dating someone three or more years older, they responded, "I
don't think my parents would care"; "My parents trust me
enough to know that concerning dating, I would make the
right decision"; and "I think they would question my dating
someone older, but they would trust me."*

*We have an incredible number of unwed pregnancies and
statutory rapes in this country because parents leave that decision to their kids to make.* They are kids!!! *That's why we call
them that. It's not a matter of trust. Kids generally don't have
the wisdom or experience to make those decisions!*

*If we are ever going to see kids with two parents as the norm
and not the exception, kids not getting beaten or killed by step-
fathers or boyfriends who have no emotional connection to
them, parents are going to have to wake up and take responsibility for their children until they see them out of the house as
adults. The newspapers are full of domestic incidents that start
out with young girls and boys sleeping with older people or getting pregnant by their boyfriends, because their parents were
uninvolved with their lives. Many of those broken families go
on to domestic abuse when the next boyfriend comes along. It
all starts with a parent "leaving that decision to my kid."*

Trusting a child does not mean abdicating responsibility. It
does not mean turning over power to the child. It does not
mean getting on with your adult life because they "look"
grown and argue too long and annoyingly. It does not mean
giving in to the community status quo so that you don't look
mean and your child isn't mad at you.

Trusting a child is a carefully designed effort to immerse him
into the real world with lessons, support, rules, expectations,
and supervision. In the *Antelope Valley Press* (June 5, 1999),
Los Angeles County Sheriff Sergeant David Sauer wrote:

Parents who allow their children to be in situations where
they are likely to have to make a choice that could affect their

entire lives are not paying attention. How many times do you want your child to make a choice under peer pressure about drinking, drugs, sex, stealing, or any of the other myriad of things that could screw up his or her life?

We have adults who can't make the right choice every time. Are you willing to bet your child's life that he or she will? Our job as parents is to protect our children while they are vulnerable to the dangers of this world, not subject them to the dangers and hope they make the right choices and live through it. We protect them, not from the consequences of their choices, but from having to make the choice before they are ready.

There are certain things your children need to trust you will teach them:

➤ How to know right from wrong (this is where religion and G-d come in).

➤ How to make appropriate choices in friends who share values and are less likely to act out impulsively and get into trouble.

➤ How to make wise decisions about places to go and things to do so that problem situations can be avoided.

➤ How to handle a situation gone bad or inappropriate (leave, call home or authorities).

➤ How to have the strength of conviction to stand up to peer pressure or serious temptation.

Now—Don't Overwork the Little Darlings . . .

It may be spiritually superior to "give rather than receive," but it sure isn't parentally superior to give, give, give to children. Angelique, one of my listeners, explains why:

As a child I had it pretty good. I got what I wanted most of

*the time. I never had any chores. I hardly had any rules to fol-
low. The problem with something that is spoiled is that it eventually rots. It was great being a kid in a way—imagine never
having to earn or work for anything. It was when I reached
adulthood that the indulgence of my childhood began to rear
its ugly head. I lacked any sense of responsibility. I was inso-
lent. I was rebellious. I was dependent. I was lazy. I had a
problem with rules and authority. I had unhealthy and sometimes destructive relationships. I lacked the essential mental
and emotional tools needed to be an adult.*

*If my parents had given me more rules, structure, chores,
and responsibilities, I believe that I would be much better off
and farther ahead today. I am now twenty-six, and only now
am I figuring out what I want to do with my life. I seem to be
about five years behind my peers in terms of "life experience"
and career, but I am grateful that I am figuring things out now
and not at forty-six or fifty-six. I could have easily married a
man to "take care of me" and spoil me like my parents did.
My true self—the responsible, self-sufficient, person of character—may never have surfaced.*

Some parents excessively cater to their children because of a
need to be loved, important, powerful, and necessary. Others
do it because they are so controlling and such perfectionists
that they can't endure the trial-and-error, less-than-perfect
attempts of a child to do anything. Whatever the motivation,
constantly indulging children, as Angelique describes, is injurious and destructive.

Sometimes I wonder if some parents aren't simply evil. I
have gotten so many letters and calls from young people
whose parents actually introduced them to inappropriate
behaviors like drugs, alcohol, sex, and illegal activities. The
rationale was often "they're going to do it anyway—at least
we can show them how to do it right." It may be that some
of these parents are just bad people in need of company, but
their behavior doesn't go unnoticed by the children who

finally pull themselves out of that ugly, dangerous vortex.

In *Parade* magazine (August 22, 1999), one young person, answering the question of the day about telling parents the truth, described a parent who let every bad behavior go unchallenged. "Finally, I turned myself around—with no help from my 'understanding' father. You may think it would be great to have no rules and to be able to do whatever you want. But trust me: I've been there, and it's a lonely road when nobody really cares what you do."

And that is the ultimate message. While a child may kick, yell, and scream as Mom or Dad imposes rational rules and follows through against infractions with fair but serious consequences, it ultimately tells them that they are cared about.

Parents are so busy, busy, busy these days that they cater to their children's whims without question because it's quicker and easier. It is also probably because parents are so wracked with well-earned guilt for their divorces, workaholism, affairs, remarriages, new children, stepchildren, and reliance on child care that they indulge their children in the hopes of "making it all up to them." All it does is further alienate them behind a wall of gifts, undeserved privileges, and inappropriate freedoms.

A survey released by Massachusetts Mutual Life Insurance Company (*Orange County Register*, July 7, 1994) showed that most eight- to twelve-year-olds do two chores a day, far fewer than their parents did. The article also revealed that "the money kids get for household chores has grown—both in dollar terms and as a percentage of their total take."

For example, in 1998, kids received 53 percent of their money as no-strings-attached allowances and 15 percent as payment for services. In 1994, those percentages were 45 percent and 21 percent, respectively.

Additionally, children have been given control over family spending! "They pick out about 80 percent of their clothes, a total reversal of the 80 percent impact Mom had a generation

ago. They get sent to the store to pick up their own school supplies and rent their own video games."

What's the problem with this? Easy. The children are not
taught the connection between responsibility and earnings.
They have financial power without responsibility or effort.
They have independence and a sense of importance unearned
by experience or striving.

The result is spoiled, bored children.

"I'm Just So Borrrrrrred!"

Dr. John Rosemond reported on informal polls of parents from
foreign countries (*Hemisphere Magazine*, December 1992). He
asked these parents, "Do children in your country frequently
complain of being bored, of having nothing to do?"

In every instance, the answer was "no." In fact, foreign parents were amazed that children would have such complaints.
"Frequent feelings of boredom," he wrote, "have nothing to
do with being a child, but everything to do with being an
American child. . . . Feeling bored is only epidemic in the most
recent generation of American children."

In America, parents seem overly committed to easy, external,
and artificial stimulation. This usually requires the purchase of
many toys and amusements, often too many structured activities,
and excessive media input. All in all, this makes kids less able to
take care of themselves. I've always been impressed by children
who could engage, entertain, and amuse themselves, who would
invest creatively in their own activities and environment. These
children will never be the drones.

One of the impediments to children being allowed to impro-
vise and use their imaginations is the competitiveness of parents
who need their children's accomplishments and acquisitions to
shine as a measure of their own worth and success. Another
impediment is the maniacal schedule of parents. After a frenzied
day of work, traffic, errands, pulling together a fast-food dinner,

and complaining about their day, these parents can't possibly model simple pleasures like writing, reading, painting, bike-riding, sewing, conversing, or cooking. Instead, they go brain dead in front of the television set and so do their kids. Also, these busy, exhausted parents often give their kids too many things in exchange for some peace and quiet. So-called quality time turns into just keeping them happy and quiet.

Children need to grow and develop as creative, self-sustaining people. They can't do that if every whim is satiated and their sense of happiness depends on what inanimate object is put before them. All parents know that new toys have a short life.

In the hit movie *Big*, a boy is transformed into an adult in looks only—inside he is still that small boy. He gets a job in a toy company where he is responsible for concept development. In one telling scene, he is highly critical of a competitive col-league's new toy because it does things. He tells the company president that kids like toys they can do things *with;* in other words, that give opportunity for independent thought and action. Toys that limit those possibilities get boring fast.

Children are most absorbed by situations in which they can express themselves and discover something about the world. That is why pots and pans and everyday things in drawers can engross a child for hours as they come up with new uses for mundane objects—the function of which they may not even know.

The key to healthy development in children is providing opportunities for them to experience an expansive universe and affect it. Perpetual stimulation is dulling. Action is perpet-ually thrilling.

This is why I am so impressed with the function of religion in the family. Having children learn from a young age to share and to do for others is such an opportunity. It develops charac-ter and compassion, and demonstrates vividly that a life spent looking toward what you can *do* rather than *have* is the true key to eliminating boredom.

Having children give their old toys to charity, or give part of their allowance and birthday money to relief programs, is a good start. The more personally involved they are, the better.

The *Los Angeles Times* ran a major story on June 8, 1999, about the Mormons' tradition of missionary work. "How the Mormons manage to take young people fighting raging hormones and competing preoccupations with romance, college and career, and redirect their energies into two years of selfless, self-paid spiritual service is the key to one of the remarkable expansions in modern religious history."

These young people have learned some life-altering, essential facts. One is that while happiness can be pursued, it can't be bought, and it isn't constant. Another is that happiness comes from contentment with life, an appreciation of G-d's gifts, gratitude for our relationships, acknowledgment of what one owes to others, and an understanding that our personal talents and abilities are to be used with generosity in order to be truly enjoyed.

Missionary Work Begins at Home

The answer to the question posed by the *Los Angeles Times* as to how young people with powerful self-focused drives could be induced into selfless service is that these young people are raised in a community of shared values. They are greatly influenced by their peers, who tell them that the greatest high they can ever experience comes from being of service to others, not from taking drugs!

In other words, a decent concept of values begins at home. The nuclear family is the basic unit of civilization and of civilizing the young. One of the toughest lessons for children to learn is that everyone is not there to serve them—that something is required of them in return for all the gifts, blessings, advantages, protection, nurture, and love they receive.

Civilizing a child is not easy, especially when the so-called child development experts push their agenda of self-esteem, happiness, fulfillment, and personal rights as the main objectives of life. In 1997, the syndicated cartoon strip *One Big Happy* showed a mother talking with her mother about whether she is a good parent. The grandma says, "Ellen, honey, there's a good way to find out!

"Ruthie," she says to her small granddaughter, "Would you describe yourself as a deliriously happy child?"

"Me? Happy?" the little girl responds. "Gosh, no! There are way too many rules around here, and I work too hard, and I never get to do everything I want to do!"

"See?" says the grandmother to her adult daughter, "You're an excellent parent!"

"And the food is too healthy," continues the grimacing granddaughter.

As Carl, one of my listeners, wrote somewhat tongue-in-cheek, "Parents who insist on chores, responsibility, homework, manners, eating right, sleeping right, and chaperones really mess up their kids by producing hard working, responsible, polite, healthy adults. If that isn't making a kid into a new age freak, what is?"

When children are told and taught that they have to participate in life in ways that are not personally or immediately gratifying, they often rebel in anger and annoyance. This doesn't necessarily mean they are "bad seeds." It is completely normal for the young human being to be self-absorbed, self-centered, and selfish, primarily focusing on pleasure, gratification, enjoyment, and avoidance of discomfort. It is the solemn duty of parents to expand their children's repertoire of attitudes, motivations, and behaviors—ultimately building a sense of social responsibility.

Ellen, one of my listeners, experienced one of those moments. During the first day of spring break in 1999, her two boys, ages twelve and fourteen, were expected to mow the front and back yard and blow off the dirt and debris. When morning came, however, her older son slept in until 10 A.M. and woke with an "attitude" about how this was his vacation time—and work was not part of his vacation activities.

Ellen assumed that even with the griping, her boy would do the task as told. Later in the day she found him in her car listening to the radio, while his younger brother was doing his part of the work for $5 extra. Ellen was furious. Her boy thought he was brilliantly entrepreneurial: "The work got done, didn't it? He wanted the money, so I'm paying him to do it."

Getting the lawn mowed was *a* goal but not *the* goal.

Ellen asked her son if he understood why she and Dad were upset. He said, "No. It just seems like you want to control my life!" Ellen answered:

I do control a large part of your life. As long as you are under age and dependent on us for all the things you need, we will control a part of your life. From our point of view it seems that all you want to do is take from us. You want privileges, privacy, money, to play on the computer, but you don't want to help out in the family.

Helping is part of giving back. Building relationships requires a give and take. You give of yourself because you care about the relationship. This is how you build it. The giving back from the other person is how you nourish it. There is a back and forth of giving and receiving in relationships that are happy. This is true with friends, co-workers, family and that special person you find to love. Helping out in our family is a way of practicing to build future relationships. We are teaching you to find real happiness. We love you and want you to find deep happiness in your life.

And this is precisely the lesson learned by having children do chores and be responsible to the family—how to build bridges between people, bridges which bring security, love, a sense of usefulness, bonding, and ultimate meaning and purpose.

All that just from doing chores. Amazing.

The Endless Excuses

Parents come up with lots of excuses for indulging their children's weaknesses, whims, and weirdness. While some of them might be worthy of more sympathy or respect than others, do not think for a moment that all these roads don't lead to hell.

I recently took a call from a forty-one-year-old father of a nine-year-old daughter. They had moved into a new area about nine months ago. His daughter begged to join the swim team. He and her mom agreed. She went to the tryouts and was good enough to win a place on the team. It's a few weeks later and early-morning practices are to begin the next morning.

His daughter is begging again—this time not to go!

It seemed obvious to me from our discussion that the little girl was simply avoiding hard work. I asked the father if laziness or tantrums were typical behavior, or if anything happened at the tryouts that might explain her reaction.

He said he had some history to tell me. When she was three, they had her in full-time day care. At some point she began to beg and scream and cry about not going back. Since they couldn't figure out from her or anybody at the day care center why she was so upset, they continued bringing her there.

One day, the mother of their little girl's friend overheard her say that a day care teacher had spanked her and told her not to tell her parents lest she be sent to jail. The mother told my caller. My caller and his wife were overwhelmed with guilt.

Since that time, anytime their little girl wails away they have flashbacks to having forced her to go someplace "bad" and wimp out completely in handling the moment as a new circumstance. Consequently the child has total control and manages to avoid anything uncomfortable, stressful, or demanding by tapping into that emotion without even knowing why it works!

I explained to the dad that his guilt was inappropriate, since the "error" was inadvertent and ancient history. Secondly, it was causing him to opt out of his responsibility to help his daughter develop strength, courage, persistence, and character.

By making sure he'd never be accused of making another boo-boo, he was supporting her weakness.

I have also had many parents pull back on their appropriate parenting responsibilities out of a sense of compassion because their child has an infirmity or handicap. These parents will tell me that their child has "suffered enough" with whatever the medical problem is. They feel bad not giving the child what he wants or disciplining the child when she needs it because that only adds "hurt." I remind them that a well-behaved, thoughtful child will get much further in life with that physical limitation than one who is self-centered, spoiled, uncivilized, bratty, demanding, and irresponsible. That usually gets them!

This issue of guilt also enters the picture when parents realize or imagine that their child's behavior is basically their fault! Sometimes a parent will, in exasperation or uncertainty, simply ignore inappropriate behaviors. Often, parents refuse to face the influences and problems at home that contribute to their child's behavior. Jen, one of my listeners, found herself facing both issues.

She wrote:

I was confronted today by my son's teacher who was concerned about his behavior at school. She said he is scratching and pinching his friends and using bad language. I am very embarrassed about my son's behavior mostly because I know I am responsible. My mother always uses bad language around him, and he does scratch and curse at home. I sometimes ignore these behaviors in the hopes that no attention will decrease them.

Other times the parents wish to hear no evil and see no evil that would interfere with their fantasy of a perfect child, a perfect family, a perfect marriage, and a perfect self. Melody, one of my listeners who works with law enforcement investigations, deals with these kinds of parents all the time.

I find that most parents don't want to know who and what their child really is—they want to just believe in their fantasy.

They believe their beautiful little girl is just popular, and not that she is being passed from one gang member to the next. They believe that her pupils are big because of her contacts and that the clothes she wears are just what all the kids are wearing (yes, that is true, all of the gang whores wear the same look) and it doesn't mean anything. Well, let me tell you, it does mean something. It is called "dressing for death." That is what the gang members call it, because they are always ready to die ("being down") for the gang and it shows identification. Not only that, but the lifestyle means death—death of a future. Please parents, wake up! By the time you are calling me, it's usually too late. Face reality or reality will be in your face.

The flip side of fantasy requires real commitment. If parents want to save their child from a life of crime, prison, drugs, illegitimate children, and so forth, they must take a stand and make tough changes in all of their lives. It will require refocusing attention on the children, assuming the dominant role in the home, clarifying rules and consequences, following through on punishments, and becoming willing to take stands on issues.

Forget this nonjudgmental nonsense. It gives children the impression that acting out on every desire is ultimately okay. The problem is that today's children aren't safe from one another or their own impulsive immaturity. The problem is that too many of today's parents, confused by their ultra-liberal upbringing, are soaked in a culture that dissolved all tradition and rules of decorum and modesty.

In an interesting editorial in the *Wall Street Journal* (July 30, 1999), Midge Decter pointed out that the problem is safety and meaning. In contrasting and comparing Woodstock '69 to Woodstock '99 she wrote:

> The original celebrants were young people who had been encouraged by both parents and the press to declare that their life of self-indulgence was in truth the higher idealism, whereas the young rioters of today are simply victims of plain parental

neglect. Sex and drugs and rock 'n' roll are for the kids of the nineties no longer the components of a much-heralded and cheered-on liberation, as they were for the young of the sixties; they have become rather, an almost inescapable form of oppression . . . nudity and public sex. For the kids themselves, it was just the same old obligatory routine as can be found at their parties . . .

These kids are from earliest adolescence left entirely at the mercy of the dictates of their social milieu. On the one hand, their parents being busy retaining that sense of liberation for which they have so relentlessly praised themselves, there is no one to assume the burden of keeping the children safe. But neither is there anyone, as there once was for their parents, to help them pretend that their lack of discipline is the higher virtue. No wonder they end up piercing their tongues and navels and painting their bodies like so many savages—anything to call attention to the fact that they are, underneath all the simulacra of worldliness, still needy and unformed children.

Some parents use their children for their own ego gratification. This is especially true in the areas of power and success. Here are two examples:

➤ "Four ninth-graders who published an underground newsletter at the Portola Highly Gifted Magnet School have been suspended and ordered transferred from the Tarzana school for writings that administrators called abusive and offensive. The parents said the newsletter was a 'misguided prank' and described the punishment as too harsh" (*Daily News* [San Fernando Valley], May 26, 1994).

The newsletter ridiculed students and administrators by name, using racial and gender-based slurs, and encouraged students to abuse them verbally and physically. It also described ways to cheat on tests, how to make napalm, and how to sabotage graduation ceremonies. The father of the boy predominantly responsible excused him because of his intelligence. "I don't think they should have kicked them out of the school. They have IQs over 160 and are gifted students. They should have used an educational approach."

Educational approach? Throwing them out is the best kind of education to give these arrogant and hostile young people. The lesson is that no amount of IQ points substitutes for goodness and accountability. We've got a lot of smart people . . . what we need are more good people.

➤ "A yearbook signing party planned for tomorrow is up in the air after it was discovered that several photos in the publication were monkeyed with by the captain of the cheerleading squad, an honor student who is on the yearbook staff. The published pictures show four members of the squad, their eyelids and eyebrows branded with a clownish swath of blue" (*San Diego Union Tribune*, June 1996).

The mother of the offending girl is quoted as saying, "My daughter has 100 friends to their one. She's a young, professional lady and she's drop-dead gorgeous, and they're just jealous. . . . She's just superior, I'm sorry. She outshines these girls and is way more mature."

When children are bright, talented, and accomplished, and have great potential for success, their parents and society tend to bend the rules too much—valuing the superficial over the profound issues of character and citizenship. In fact, I've felt that many parents who call me in these situations are both vicariously enjoying their child's "superiority" and downright intimidated by their child's talents.

The problem is that when these children are perpetually forgiven for their mounting sins, without accepting responsibility, demonstrating remorse, or making an effort to repair the damage done, they become monsters who can't see or sympathize beyond the borders of their own lives, desires, and ego. These are children who become uncaring adults unable to respect the needs or feelings of others. They become people who see others as objects to be used, abused, removed—as necessary. And, my friends, that's a danger to all of humanity.

Perhaps no mother knows that better than Dottie Belman, the mother of one of the so-called Spur Posse members (*Los Angeles Times*, March 22, 1996). "On March 18, 1993, Los Angeles County Sheriff's deputies arrested nine Lakewood High School boys on a range of allegations including lewd conduct and rape." These boys were "star athletes, powerful young men worshipped by peers and parents." The district attorney's office declined to prosecute and they were "greeted with a hero's welcome at Lakewood High staged by some of their classmates. . . . Several swaggering Spur members soon appeared on national TV to boast of their sexual conquests."

On one of the talk shows, one of the Spur members said that his parents bought him condoms by the boxload. He bragged that he was the high scorer with sixty-six points for having various forms of sex with minor girls, three more than Posse founder Dana Belman.

"Dana's dad, Donald, told a reporter at the time, 'Nothing my boy did was anything any red-blooded American boy wouldn't do at his age.' Dottie, the mother, said, 'Those girls are trash.'"

However, reminiscing three years after the scandal, Dottie, whose son was now in prison, serving a ten-year sentence for thirteen fraud and burglary convictions, admitted that "she gave her kids too many material things, too much praise, not enough responsibility. She closed her eyes to the drinking, the gambling, the swearing, the violence on TV, the socks on the floor, the condoms in the car ashtray, the overdeveloped pectorals—and egos.

"With a wry chuckle she says, 'Dana went from no spankings to maximum security.'"

Shortly after the original arrests in 1993, Dottie left the family home. "'I should have stayed and faced the music,' she says now. 'I felt like a failure . . . I let my kids get away with murder and I knew it . . . I never made them accountable. If they got me a touchdown, that was enough. I covered everything up. I gave, gave, gave, gave, gave. I expected nothing in return. I wanted all of their friends to like me. I wanted to be the coolest mom in town.

"'All of our energy went into sports. . . . We made heroes and stars out of our children, and we became stars. It felt good. But it goes to your head. You get a big ego. You begin to feel better than everybody else. My kids were going down the slow drain of specialness.'"

Dana is in jail. Another member was gunned down. Others were arrested in connection with a near-fatal stabbing at a party. Many had illegitimate children. No parent wanted to hurt their self-esteem. Real life did that.

Finally comes the important issue of hypocrisy. I had a concerned caller who found that his son was involved with pornographic material. The father was unsure of what to do about it. He didn't feel he could say a lot because he had done the same in the past. He wanted to be so sensitive and understanding that, ultimately, he was unable to fulfill his parental duty to teach morality and enforce correct behavior.

Angela, one of my listeners, responded to that call:

Chances are the father's real dilemma is that he enjoyed his experience with pornography, even though he knew it was wrong. Thus, his confusion and guilt blocks him from being a responsible parent.

This really bothers me because this allows him to shuck his responsibility and justify it because of his own guilt.

I too have been in similar positions with my children. And whenever I "parent" them I have a wonderful sister-in-law who tells me I am too strict and kindly reminds me that I too made the same mistakes. She believes that because we made the mistakes, it is okay for our children to make the mistakes.

She also believes that we become hypocrites if we parent our children in these situations.

No Way!

My answer to her and your caller is "Just because we did it, doesn't make it right." As parents it is our responsibility to help our children not to repeat our same mistakes. It is our job to guide and assist our children to form their own conclusions and outcomes. Parents who live by their own guilt do a great disservice to their children by not allowing them to learn. Basically, it was wrong then, it is wrong now and two wrongs don't make a right. So get over it and deal with it for your children's sake!

Do for Me

Whether parents are greedy, fulfilling their own fantasies, or attempting to repair their own parental loss, they harm their own children by overindulging them with possessions, experiences, and inappropriate opportunities.

➤ A parent caller complained that his teenage son refused to stoop to driving the family car because it wasn't "cool." He actually didn't know what to do. In response, Michelle, a listener, wrote:

As a teenager I too received the offer of the family car. It was a white '68 Oldsmobile which, due to rust and a minor collision, sported a purple driver's door that didn't open, and a brown passenger door through which all entries and exits were made. Unlike this ungrateful young man, I was thrilled. After years of pedaling my bicycle to school, this was a major upgrade. Perhaps, like so many other arrogant youth, the caller's son simply had too many things given to him.

In fact, that is exactly what I told that father—"Let your kid ride his bicycle and figure out where you went wrong in teaching him about gratitude."

➤ "Seventeen-year-old Srinu Yeshwant had a problem. He couldn't get a parking spot at Barrington High School. His father had the solution—buy the kid a house—not to live in, but to use as his own personal parking lot. A few of his friends use it too . . . [the parents] plunked down $180,000 cash last year for a one-story, white bungalow. . . . As doctors, [the parents] work long hours and are not available to drive their son back and forth to school. . . . Students who want spaces must arrive well before the 7:25 A.M. start of classes. . . . 'I don't like getting up at 6 A.M.,' Srinu said" (*Chicago Tribune*, May 5, 1999). Of course not.

➤ The *Los Angeles Times* reported the following on May 21, 1999: "Driven by vanity, self-esteem issues and society's fascination with breasts, teenagers are having implant surgery in increasing numbers . . . receiving breast enlargements as graduation gifts from their parents . . . 'There is enough affluence in Southern California that [parents] say you can have both the BMW and the breast implants,' said an anesthesiologist. . . . Increasingly, daughters are being encouraged by mothers, who are themselves veterans of the surgeon's knife." In spite of the good common sense of one plastic surgeon, who said he has "'mixed feelings about teenage surgery because teens' views of themselves are manifestations of immaturity. They are extremely unstable, and their narcissism is legendary.'" A psychologist is quoted, saying, "'It's healthier to create internal mechanisms—rather than seek external change to cope with such stress. Teens should develop a greater sense of confidence and comfort within themselves because that improves the quality of life for years and years.'"

➤ "Kids think tattooing and piercing are fashion statements, and they do it because they think it's cool. Some kids do it to fit in more with the crowd. 'I just like how it looks. It's decoration. And it's my body; if I want to decorate it, what's wrong with that,' said one teen. His parent commented that 'I was very upset, but there wasn't anything I could do at that point except hope things would be all right.'"

The corker of this article is a so-called child expert advising parents who object to these sometimes dangerous, often obscene decorations, "Get off your parental high horse, come down to earth, and don't be judgmental. You want to keep communication channels open"(*Milwaukee Journal Sentinel*, August 8, 1999).

The reaction of Peggy, one of my listeners who read this article, was incredulity. "The idea that we need to give in because they'll do it anyway is ridiculous. Children and young adults need boundaries they believe are real, beginning, when children are very young, with bedtimes, allowances, and respect for siblings and obedience to the family rules."

The reality is that children need to understand that their bodies are not "theirs." They are on loan from G-d and are not to be desecrated on a social whim. The reality is that children need to understand their uniqueness comes from the expression of their special gifts in life—and not from the conformity to a current style or fad.

I took a call from a mother and her nineteen-year-old daughter who was demanding to live in an off-campus apartment, fully paid for by her mother, while she was rooming with guys and gals. The girl was disrespectful toward her mother and toward any notion of personal responsibility or morality. The mother seemed absolutely incapable of setting down the law and the options: Take the dorm or surrender the family financial subsidy! The daughter was trying to con the mother into believing it would be cheaper to do it her way.

Karen, one of my listeners, wrote a lengthy fax, analyzing the truth of the situation:

As my son would say, the nineteen-year-old arrogant, disre-

spectful, exasperating twit on the phone with you yesterday was "blowin' smoke!" Her analysis of costs included rent, utilities, miscellaneous, food, cleaning supplies, paper products, furnishings, dishware and pots, parental co-signature for rent, security deposit, cleaning deposit, maintenance, repairs, the financial burden when one of more roommates didn't cough up their part, and so forth.

My sons know that they could kiss my money, my signature on any papers, and my emergency rescue services goodbye if they came up with this one. And, as for the daughter, I'd tell her, "Contact the rental agency and find out how many thousand dollars you need to put up in lieu of a co-signer, quit school, work full time and save up the deposit. Then, you can live anywhere you want because you're risking your own hard-earned money." And, parents, "JUST SAY NO!"

On February 7, 1999, the *New York Times* wrote a story about sweet sixteen-year-olds:

> Girls are asking their parents for everything from formal parties at private clubs, to parties in downtown lounges like Jet and Chaos, with price tags that run from $5000 to more than $25,000.
>
> Nick Raynes, fourteen, said, "The rule in the whole entire thing is that the adults totally don't care, and they can't stop anything that's happening."
>
> A child psychiatrist is quoted as saying that children are "speeded on their way to adulthood by willing parents, [who] on the privileged end of things are giving too much and requiring too little . . . they are providing too few challenges. What happens is that the children later have trouble figuring what their worth is."

By the way, the photograph accompanying the article showed a mother bursting out of her low-cut dress, drinking champagne with sixteen-year-olds. A little bit of youth envy?

Aiding and Abetting

I want to be generous here and not so critical of many parents, but I am too furious. There are innumerable examples of parents who, whether out of weakness, a vicarious charge, a mistaken notion that supervised illegality or immorality is better than the unsupervised version, contribute to the destruction of their children's moral and spiritual lives. They might as well be putting them on the railroad tracks as okaying drinking parties, coed sleepovers, premature dating, and early sexual exposure via film, TV, music, and the Internet.

Coed Sleepovers

"Propelled by changing mores, insistent teens and indulgent parents, the slumber party, once a treasured rite of passage for girls, is going coeducational" (*Wall Street Journal*, January 28, 1995). Sickeningly, as the article reports, many counselors and therapists are practically sanctioning the notion. One absurd guidance counselor is quoted as saying that coed sleepovers are the norm and a safe way to learn how to interact with the opposite sex. In the same article the teens themselves show him to be an idiot—"stuff happens," they say.

We all know what motivates these parents who want to seem enlightened and "with it," wanting their children to be popular and wanting also to believe their children's stories that nothing is going on.

The family section of the *Chicago Tribune* (May 23, 1999) had a debate between an eighteen-year-old girl and her father. The girl said, "Coed sleepovers can give rise to these wonderful experiences—sexual or platonic. The bonding that occurs in the early morning hours and perhaps in the arms of your significant other can last a lifetime. Why take away these precious opportunities because of the unjustified fears of adults."

Frankly, I'd be ashamed if my son wrote or thought this. Equating physical closeness with profound interpersonal intimacy is precisely the kind of immaturity that parents are there to protect their children from! However, the father's response was too pathetic to repeat.

Fortunately, Kevin, a listener, had the better response:

During my high school years, our English class went on a trip to the Shakespeare Festival in Ashland, Oregon. We stayed in a youth hostel, which was normally segregated by sex, women upstairs and men downstairs. As there were more girls than boys in our class, there was not enough room for all girls to be housed upstairs, and we ended up with both male and female classmates sleeping together downstairs, side by side, in separate sleeping bags. To me, at the time, this seemed really cool, because first, while I was not a boyfriend of any of the girls there, I did have sexual thoughts about them on a regular basis, and it was very thrilling to be able to sleep next to them. This of course was the planting of the seed, not only in my mind but also in all of us. That very day a boy and a girl, who were sleeping side-by-side, became a couple.

In later years, I began sleeping over with other "friends" who were girls, some that I wanted to become my girlfriends, and some that I just wanted something to happen with. . . . This is not how I saw it at the time. I recall saying to friends who asked about these sleepovers that they were harmless and nothing happened. I believed this, not realizing that the roots were growing deeper.

The sleepovers became more and more frequent, and I started having girls over to the house when my parents were out of town. We were a very religious family, and my parents would have disapproved had they known. Actually the sleepovers became so frequent, my parents did find out, but by this time I had lost my virginity to my girlfriend and had started fooling around with other girls too. My entire life was changed for the worse with this chain of events as my parents kicked me out. I could not serve a mission for my church; I dropped out of school and did not obtain a degree—a decision that affects me to this day. I got married much too soon and caused irreparable damage in the lives of many people I came into contact with.

For your caller, and any others who contemplate sleepovers with boys and girls, it may be innocent now, but think of the fruits that are borne—quite literally—from the idea they plant in these children's head that it's okay for boys and girls to sleep together.

The coed sleepovers breed a brand of familiarity that is inappropriate in the immature minds, bodies, and souls of minors. It is irresponsible and shortsighted of parents to underestimate the powerful impact of physical proximity on the developing psyches and sexuality of minor children.

Dating Older Men

I can't tell you how many girls and young women are flattered out of their minds by the experience of having an older man want them in a sexual relationship. Perhaps it's just the easy, warp-speed version of feeling like a real woman and a real grown-up. Perhaps it's the pleasure of being taken care of. Too many parents just seem to go along with this. Our ever-growing societal sexual permissiveness and sexual obsessiveness has permeated our children's cultural experiences in ads and the media, which, in turn, has erased any stigma or shame about children being sexual, getting pregnant, having illegitimate children or abortions. Recent studies reported in the *Family Planning Perspective* (August 1999) indicate that the rate of pregnancy increases as the age gap between the girl and her guy increases beyond two years. To whom does this not seem obvious?

According to the *Los Angeles Times* (August 13, 1999), the researchers were reluctant to discuss the policy implications of their study. "Some pregnancy-prevention groups said the message to parents is clear: 'They really need to take a stand against their daughters dating older guys.'"

Well, it would be nice if the law and society in general would back up these parents. Instead, parents call me complaining that statutory rape charges against adult males for having sex with their minor children generally are not prosecuted, especially when the girl says she consented. I thought that was the point of the statutory rape laws—a determination that minor children could not, by virtue of their age and immaturity, consent to sex.

All this free information and sexual freedom turns out to be deadly, oppressive, and destructive. So much for freedom without an ethical and moral context.

Contributing to the Delinquency of a Minor

"A male stripper accused of fondling at least four teenagers during his routine at a chaperoned girls-night-out party was arrested Thursday on felony lewd conduct charges. The girls—including one who allegedly performed oral sex on him—apparently were willing participants . . .

"'His hands were on bare breasts, under bras, down pants,' said the Deputy District Attorney. . . . The mother helped hire and pay for the stripper. . . . She said she only let him continue his act to avoid embarrassing her daughter." (*Los Angeles Times*, November 27, 1998).

"A man convicted of hiring a prostitute to provide his thirteen-year-old son with his first sexual encounter was placed on five years probation . . . at the time, the father was separated from the boy's mother. They are now divorced" (*Milwaukee Journal*, January 29, 1999).

"In a December, 1998 poll conducted for Maclean's by the Strategic Counsel, 57 percent of Quebeckers said they would let teens in a steady relationship sleep together. That's compared with 18 percent of Canadians nationally who would permit sons, and 16 percent who would allow daughters to have sex in the family home" (*Globe and Mail* [Toronto], February 25, 1999).

The twelve-year-old girl who sent me this article wrote: "The majority of parents in the article think it's OK for their kids to do that in their home. I find this sick, and certainly below my family's values."

This is just more of the same determined, degenerate philosophy that, since children have functional bodies and sexual feelings, they should be permitted to act on them. Too many parents have bought the lies that sexual acting out is inevitable, a right, a natural and healthy activity for teens, necessary for the development of a positive attitude about sex. That's nonsense. By allowing teens to have sex in their home, parents are promoting sexuality without commitment, adult intimacy without maturity or responsibility, and physical intimacy without any sacred context.

Susan, one of my listeners, whose mother was "supportive" of her teen sexual behavior, put it this way: "By abusing this sacred act, I have demeaned and diminished it. My past promiscuity and the emotional damage that I inflicted upon myself has been a very difficult hurdle in my marriage. I have practically ruined the idea and feeling that intimacy and sex are related."

According to radio listeners Eric and Denise, "Parents used to say 'no' to what kids *wanted*, and 'yes' to what kids *needed*. When parents began to say 'no' to what kids *needed* (intact marriages, at home parents), they also began to say 'yes' to what kids *wanted*."

Right on!

Alcohol and Other Drugs

"Alcohol remains a key fixture on the high school party landscape. . . . There's nothing new about teens consuming alcohol, but there are some disturbing trends on the partying front. . . . There seem to be more parent-sponsored drinking parties, and teens say there is much more peer pressure to drink when parents are supplying the booze" (*Denver Post*, April 28, 1999).

Did you read that last admission slowly and clearly? If not, here it is again: *"teens say there is much more peer pressure to drink when parents are supplying the booze"*! It is *not* that parents are simply providing a safe situation for the inevitable. It *is* that adult participation is, itself, pressure on kids to drink. Put that in your pipe . . . and try not inhaling. This is just another one of the stupid mixed messages: "It's not okay to drink, but since you're probably going to do it anyway—let's party!" Never mind that this kind of drinking can lead to serious problems later. Young people who begin drinking at fifteen are four times as likely to develop alcoholism as those who begin drinking at age twenty-one, according to the National Council on Alcoholism and Drug Dependence.

It seems as if kids are pushed to party harder and harder. Unfortunately, they're being pushed off cliffs. The *Fort Worth Star-Telegram* (May 14, 1999) reported on a Catholic high school after-prom bash given by two parents who "may" face charges over the teens' binge, which resulted in their own child as well as others being hospitalized. According to the police report, the mother told the police, "'This was her house and if she wanted to have all the kids over and give them alcohol it was her business.' A week later she denied making that statement."

The basic problem is that with so many parents justifying their stupid and destructive behaviors by permitting drinking, there's no longer a clear consensus about what our values are. It is increasingly difficult for those who hold traditional values to talk about them in a public way without being discounted or attacked as ignorant. When values are not clear, there are infinite choices *and* many more repercussions and risks.

You may have noticed the main thesis of this book is that our society has lost communal values and standards, and too many adults have regressed to immature behaviors and attitudes, supporting unfettered freedom for themselves and for their kids in place of traditional parenting. Many parents have given up parenting to take on the simpler role of "hall monitor."

Participation in a child's immoral or illegal activities is not the only way parents contribute to the delinquency and destruction of their children. Failing to say anything at all is a problem that can result in drug experimentation and abuse.

According to a *Washington Post* article (March 21, 1999):

> The majority of teens enter substance abuse treatment only after they have gotten into trouble with the juvenile justice authorities. . . . Studies show that teens who drink alcohol and use drugs are more likely to engage in other risky behaviors that increase the odds of early pregnancy, contracting sexually transmitted diseases, and exposure to violence or involvement in car accidents.

The national Hazelden Foundation survey, published in the *Milwaukee Journal Sentinel* (July 20, 1999), unveiled the irresponsibility of parents with respect to drug use. For example, even though 41 percent of parents have smoked marijuana themselves, most do not communicate the consequences to their children, even though 98 percent said they'd be upset if their children smoked marijuana. The study also found that although 84 percent of parents believe marijuana can be addictive, only 19 percent voiced that concern to their children.

"In some cities like Minneapolis," says senior research analyst Carol Falkowski, "treatment admissions for marijuana outnumber admissions for cocaine, and half of the patients are under the age of eighteen."

According to the National Institute of Drug Abuse, marijuana is a hemp plant that contains a chemical known as THC, which alters neurons in the brain that are crucial for learning, memory, and the integration of sensory experiences with emotions and motivation. Frequent users may experience coughing and wheezing and are at a greater risk of developing pneumonia. Marijuana today is much stronger, and with increased potency comes the increased likelihood of faster progression from first use to problem use. Marijuana often is mixed with crack cocaine, PCP, or formaldehyde without the user's knowledge.

Denise, one of my listeners, wrote of her family's experience with "just one puff."

I just heard a woman on your radio program who said that her son was smoking marijuana and that she felt it was just experimental and not that bad. Talk about a parent not wanting to read the handwriting on the wall! You were perfectly correct in telling her she sounded like a twelve-year-old. My brother started "experimenting" with marijuana when he was nineteen, and he then went into "experimenting" with other types of drugs and alcohol. He is now forty and still struggling with drugs and alcohol. We haven't seen him for three years. Our family is heartbroken. The problem was that my parents waited too long to do anything or admit that he had a problem. They kept saying, "Oh, he's a good boy, it's not that bad. . . ." When they finally tried to get him help he was thirty-seven and couldn't accept their help. If they had nipped it in the bud, we would have a complete family today. It's never too early to deal with it. I would say to that woman exactly what you said. She doesn't realize that she should take this very seriously. I wish someone would have been strong with my parents.

Many parents avoid the issue of drug use out of guilt for their own past use or fear of finding out the worst about their kid. If and when they *do* introduce the subject, the child is likely to condemn the hypocrisy of parents who risk cancer, lung disease, and heart disease by smoking; or alcoholism, cirrhosis, or drunk driving by drinking. Frankly, the kids have a very good point! How can you teach self-discipline and avoidance of mind-altering substances if you, the parent, are addicted to nicotine or dependent on a daily drink (or two!)? Being a role model is everything.

Well, almost everything. Taking care of business as the authority figure is the rest of the story. Ralph, one of my listeners, is such a parent.

We had a problem similar to one of your recent callers, and we handled it much as you suggested. I found our son, who is generally a great kid, smoking pot and decided that, although my wife and I had grown up during the sixties and made some pretty silly mistakes, I would not permit our children to do the same.

We sat our son down, and firmly explained to him that, as a dependent minor, he has absolutely no rights but only privileges granted to him by my wife and me. We explained that his recent behavior simply would not be tolerated and if he felt inclined to challenge my authority that I would be glad to focus my every activity on making his life miserable (clear out his closet and drawers except for two outfits, take out all the fun stuff, have only a mattress on the floor, leave his room only for meals and school, etc.). I am the oldest of seven children, well known for being "in-charge," and my son knew that I could do just that if I were challenged. I also informed him that he would be taking a drug screen every month as long as he chooses to take advantage of the life-style my wife and I provide.

He was absolutely shocked at first. After a short period of acting angry, I think our son was actually relieved. He has since turned completely around. He is a straight A student and is getting exceptional reports from his teachers, and he is a total pleasure to be around.

Too often I get parents who say they know they should change their own habits and get control of their kid's drug/drinking problem . . . but . . . they don't want to be too tough. One mother forbade her son to go to his prom . . . then called me waffling because his girlfriend was upset since she had already bought a $200 dress. Better that he doesn't go to the prom than that he ultimately ends up in the morgue.

Pornography

Pornography has become so mainstream that it's difficult to alert parents to the dangers of sexually explicit and vulgar materials. It's impossible to watch prime-time television without viewing crass, casual, promiscuous sex. The daytime talk shows, once the venue for learning about social issues, are now the venue for deviant behavior presented as commonplace. While I tell parents they should probably epoxy their TV dials to either the History Channel or the Discovery Channel, the reality is that most television is devoid of families, committed attachments, religion, and values—all in the name of either free speech or "we're just giving the audience what it wants!"

Well, there was once an audience for watching gladiators fight to the death and Christians being consumed by hungry lions. That was entertainment? Well, the house was full, we're told!

The sexualization of young people is widespread. Frankly, it's almost impossible to get away from it. However, the most insidious source of material is often the parent.

George wrote:

My life is a testimony to the effects of pornography on a young child. I plead that all parents will not take this subject lightly as it can destroy innocent minds. At six years old, I discovered some pornography magazines under my father's bed. You see, my parents had a relaxed attitude about this. These images had a powerful effect on me and peaked [sic] my interest. I quickly formed the opinion that women were objects for my pleasure. Later, I snooped, and found some tapes. At ten years of age, a male friend and I experimented with sex. At twelve, I experimented with a six-year-old female neighbor. I started having long-term sexual relationships at thirteen and cheated on my first serious girlfriend with another girl who was easier.

My eighteenth birthday present from my mother was a subscription to Playboy. What a cool mom! By twenty-one, I was dating a girl that looked and acted like one of your typical Playmates and together we made a porno tape.

I was predatory, but had everyone around me convinced that I was the nicest guy in the neighborhood. For the longest time, whenever I looked at any woman, it was to determine what she would be like to have sex with. Watching porno tapes became a habit, then an addiction, and by the time I had met my wife, an obsession. Although I desperately tried to hide everything, I couldn't. My lack of appreciation for her and my thirst for variety were soon discovered.

Although I am responsible for my actions, the early exposure to pornography and the attitude of my parents didn't give me a fighting chance at developing a healthy perspective toward women and love. I hate to think of what my life would have become if I hadn't met someone with the courage and integrity to take a stand on this issue. I am living proof that pornography and the indifference toward it can lead you down a road of exploitation and destruction. Pornography incessantly promotes objectification, promiscuity, and perversion. We are raising a generation of sexual deviants and victims by not doing something about this issue.

I am reminded that this is largely what Ted Bundy said on public television just before he was executed for the multiple rapes and murders of young women. It also occurs to me that calls from women frustrated, guilt-ridden, confused, and hurt by their husbands' obsessive use of Internet pornography has escalated in recent years, as pornography has become the fastest-growing industry on the Internet! It used to be embarrassing to buy a brown-wrapped magazine, or go to girlie bookstores to rent tapes. Now it's delivered free to your home computer screen.

The Ma Barker Syndrome

REVA: "I am the mother of Melissa. She is seventeen. Melissa and her little sister, who is sixteen, went with another girl and Melissa's boyfriend to a carnival. The only thing is that they didn't go to the carnival. Instead they went to a house that belonged to another friend."

DR. L: "Wait . . . you have too many people involved here and I'm not sure I have them straight. Your two daughters went someplace with your daughter's boyfriend, but they didn't get there. They went to somebody's house instead. And what bad thing happened there?"

REVA: "Well, they didn't go to the other friend's house—they picked up that friend."

DR. L: "Just tell me the bad thing that happened . . . wherever they were."

REVA: "Breaking and entering, possession of alcohol and marijuana, criminal trespassing . . ."

DR. L: "That's what your two daughters did?"

REVA: "That's what they all did. There was a group of five."

DR. L: "Wow, your daughter had illegal drugs and was involved in a break-in. Kids don't go from zero to one hundred. She's been in trouble before?"

REVA: "Yes, but not the sixteen-year-old."

DR. L: "So now your older daughter is corrupting the younger one."

REVA: "Right."

DR. L: "Great."

REVA: "I got all the charges dropped. I made all the kids go back to the house and clean it up."

DR. L: "What? You got the charges dropped!? You think this is all made okay with a clean-up? How is your daughter going to learn accountability if she doesn't have to pay the piper?"

REVA: "Did I make a mistake?"

DR. L: "I'll say. Now your daughter knows she can get away with anything because Mommy will protect and serve. Gee, I am sure that's making her stay on the righteous track."

REVA: "Yeah, she says I am overprotective, and she is meeting the boy behind my back."

DR. L: "Reva, you did the wrong thing and you have to clean it up. Have them arrested."

REVA: "Oh, God . . ."

DR. L: "You did the wrong thing. You are overly protective, and you've raised one monster because of it . . . and she's now recruiting your younger daughter."

REVA: "I don't want her to go to jail."

DR. L: "Well, thank you—just let her prey on the rest of us."

REVA: "If they would give her community service and give her a chance . . ."

DR. L: "You admitted that you'd already given her chances. The community service would be to protect the community from her and her friends. She'll get whatever punishment she's earned. And how do you raise children with the mentality to be decent citizens and have character and conscience? Don't turn into Ma Barker—you know how her kids ended up? With toe tags after having their bodies well ventilated by FBI bullets."

REVA: "I know you're right."

DR. L: "You're her mother. You take care of this. Her future ultimately depends on you being stronger and more resolute about right and wrong and consequences."

Reva is the all-too-typical story of a mother who doesn't want to understand the deeper implications of her daughter's choices—and the strength she'll need to counter them. There are other parents who get even more aggressive about protecting and defending their children. I believe these actions are a form of child abuse. Instead of hitting the child's body or pummeling her psyche with hostile words, these parents indulge their child's sociopathic behaviors to protect themselves, as well as their child, from the ugly truths, embarrassment, and punishment.

Two favorite techniques of irresponsible and ultimately abusive parents is scapegoating and "law-suiting." A prime example of scapegoating took place in Schenectady, New

York. According to a story in the *Daily Gazette*, June 18, 1997, Jeremy McNamara was one of five high school seniors who broke into the school early on New Year's Day. They carried tools that they apparently planned to use to commit major vandalism. However, state police had been alerted, were waiting in the school, and arrested all five. McNamara and three others pleaded guilty, were sentenced to five years' probation and two hundred hours' community service, fined $1,500 in restitution, and expelled from school.

I think they got off easy. I think his parents should have been grateful, but, no, they were not. McNamara's parents sued, basically claiming that since the school knew the event was going to happen *they should have prevented it*. Thus, there would have been no crime.

Huh? The parents are shifting the blame from their son, the criminal, to the school for knowing about the crime in advance and not stopping it, so their kid would not be in trouble? *Oy vey.*

Then there is the case of two Carbondale, Colorado, parents, who took the town board to task and complained that their two daughters were being unfairly targeted by police, after they were stopped, yet again, for violating curfew. It turns out that both times one daughter was pulled over for breaking curfew, the mother didn't know she was out of the house.

According to the *Glenwood Independent* of April 30, 1999, the mother admitted "she didn't know her daughter's whereabouts at every moment of the day. And she resented having been called to get out of bed and come down to the police station." *Oy vey, again!*

Bruce and Jacqueline Davenport's sixteen-year-old son was caught with marijuana at West Bloomfield High School. The *Oakland Press* of June 14, 1996, reported that later that day he carjacked a BMW. The Davenports sued the school district, claiming the district should have told them immediately about the marijuana at school, rather than calling at 7:30 P.M. As a result, the Davenports say, "their son, a sophomore at the school, was left unsupervised for several hours at a time when he was disoriented, upset and confused, and that he committed a car-jacking while in this state." Where were the parents when there son wasn't home at night?

Parents who don't take the time, or protest they don't have the time (same thing), to properly supervise and raise their children, protect their own failures and the shortcomings of their children by accusing, attacking, suing, harassing, and scape-goating. These parents create monsters who destroy their own lives, their relationships, and their community. These parents are raising children to become just like dear old mom and dad.

And then there are the good guys. Lyndsay Beal performed hundreds of hours of volunteer work, earning a citywide Out-standing Character Award. The YMCA sent out a news release; the Dallas Children's Advocacy Center threw her a cel-ebration party.

She was one of about 150 teens at a warehouse party raided by police. When the YMCA president asked her whether she had attended the party, she admitted honestly that she had. The award was revoked. The president said, "This young lady is an impressive individual and a real outstanding person. But when we look at our standards for the character awards, we look at the whole person. She knew there was going to be drinking, she bought the ticket to go, and we just didn't think that was showing responsibility."

Neither Lyndsay nor her parents defended her decision to attend the party. "I know that it was wrong to go," she said. "I've never made a decision that I took so lightly that had such severe consequences. I definitely learned some lessons."

Lyndsay said that friends and family offered a lot of empa-thy and pity. Only her father gave it to her straight. "Why would any organization want to give a character award to a minor who had attended such a party?" he asked. She is sad at having disappointed so many people who believed in her.

Frankly, my friends, this is, for seventeen-year-old Lyndsay's soul and future, and for the community of other parents and children, a very happy ending.

Hang the Parents—Hang 'Em High!

A current trend is holding parents legally responsible for their children's actions. Many state statutes specifically authorize civil damages against parents of kids who do harm.

A Kentucky judge allowed a lawsuit to proceed against the parents of fourteen-year-old Michael Carneal, who killed three students and wounded five more at his high school. According to an account in the *Wall Street Journal*:

> Mr. Carneal's grades had plummeted and his mother had found knives and pictures of dead pigs in his room. Several students said he brought guns to school repeatedly. In addition, he had written two disturbing stories, including one called "Halloween Surprise," in which he and a fictitious brother gunned down preppies and then detonated a nuclear device.
>
> "There were a litany of warning signals that should have alerted the parents," claims the lawyer.
>
> In court papers, the Carneals say . . . "Kentucky law doesn't recognize a parent's duty to prevent children from harming others."

Nice defense.

In 1995, authorities in Silverton, Oregon, began issuing citations to parents whom authorities said failed to supervise children who ran afoul of the law. Parents are not jailed, but can be ordered to pay restitution. Youth crime dropped after the law was approved. It's interesting how having to pay up money is a powerful incentive for proper parenting (*Seattle Post Intelligencer*, March 4, 1997).

The *Los Angeles Times* (April 24, 1999) reported that the
parents of seven teenagers accused of bank robbery are being
sued by the bank for the loot and damages. The lawsuit was
filed under the Illinois parental responsibility law, which is
most often used to collect from parents whose offspring have
caused damage, through carelessness or mischief.

"A mother who knew her son was having sex with his teenage girlfriend had a legal obligation to stop them, according to
parents suing to collect damages for their daughter's pregnancy" (Associated Press, February 25, 1999). According to
the parents' attorney, "The boy's mother knew the two were
having sex but did nothing to stop it because she wanted a
grandchild."

Parental responsibility is a controversial legal issue. In press-
ing their cases, lawmakers and attorneys frequently draw on
the "arguments that, along with their rights to raise children
free of government meddling, parents bear the responsibility to
provide adequate oversight. In 1988, California amended its
statute to target parents who do not 'exercise reasonable care,
supervision, protection and control' over their children. Penal-
ties can include a year in jail and a $2500 fine.

"'There are a whole lot of parents out there who act as if
being a parent is just their right, and it doesn't come with
responsibilities,' says Donald Pasulka, a Chicago attorney.

"There's a difference between moral culpability and legal
culpability. Drawing a firm connection between what children
do and what their parents could have done to stop it remains
difficult and constitutionally problematic, say lawyers and
almost any parent who has tried to tell a teenager, 'Don't'"
(*Los Angeles Times*, April 30, 1999).

There is not one parent alive who has not failed to adequately supervise a child at *some* moment in time. But when
parents do not hold themselves and their children accountable
for their actions, they teach the children that there are no limits and no consequences.

While I agree with holding parents legally responsible for a child's major misdeeds, I appreciate that society seems to want it both ways. This is exemplified by the following cartoon by Trever that appeared in the *Albuquerque Journal* (May 20, 1999). Each frame shows an expert spouting "wisdom":

➤ "Parents should never spank their children."

➤ "Parents don't have to stay home—kids do just as well in day care."

➤ "Overly controlling parents stifle creativity and self-esteem!"

➤ "Kids need to experiment and clarify their values . . . just provide condoms."

➤ "Teens shouldn't need parental consent to get an abortion."

And finally:

➤ "Parents who can't control their kids should be held legally responsible!"

In speaking about this subject, Thomas Sowell wrote in his May 7, 1999, syndicated column:

> What all these efforts have in common, aside from an arrogant presumption of superiority, is a drive for power without responsibility. They don't even take responsibility for their own activities, which are hidden, denied or camouflaged. Above all, they are not prepared to be held accountable for the consequences of their playing with children's minds. . . . But it is truly galling to have those who have been undermining both morality and parents for years now demand that parents be held legally responsible for the acts of their children.

Although I wholeheartedly agree with Mr. Sowell and the cartoon, I still hold parents ultimately responsible for what they have allowed in their schools, their communities, and their homes. It is true that so-called liberal, progressive activist groups, well ensconced in the fields of psychology, education, religion, and communications, have been tremendously destructive to our society by advocating "freeddom" from values and the family. But, individual parents, you still have the power to make decisions about the rules governing your family life and the behavior of your children. It is your secular and sacred duty. Get busy! Go do the right thing!

7

Child-Free Parenting

Nancy Horwich appreciates that we're all rushed and distracted these days, but she recently observed an extreme case on Lexington Avenue. A young man came out of a shop pushing a toddler in a stroller at a quick pace. He caught up to a woman loaded with shopping bags about a block away. "You forgot this, ma'am," he said. To the amazement of Ms. Horwich, he then handed over the stroller. As he returned to his store, the shocked mother leaned against a wall repeating, "Oh, my God, oh, my God!"

New York Times, August 8, 1999

I often despair for the future. Families are fast becoming whatever anyone *says* a family is. The concept of family as a sacred vessel, strengthened by a committed, covenantal relationship between a man and a woman, for the safe passage of moral, generous, and loving children, is no longer venerated or even aspired to. It is, instead, mocked and denigrated as old-fashioned, patriarchal, and exclusive. At worst, it is ridiculed as an emblem of religious bigotry and intolerance.

The new family is any one or more adults doing their own thing and leaving the child rearing to paid help—nannies and baby-sitters at home or paid day care workers, coaches, librarians, tutors, teachers, and so forth. Child-free parenting is *very* twenty-first century!

Although I deplore the fact that so many affluent parents hire round-the-clock in-house child care providers, rather than put aside high-powered careers for the sake of their children, my main concern is the growing consensus that parents have a "right" to government-funded child care. This issue is a favorite of politicians and will continue to take center stage in our public policy debates.

It is important to note that we are speaking about the "rights" of parents, rather than the "rights" and inalienable needs of children. The latter's "rights," much less needs, are not even part of the equation. In fact, much effort has gone into proving that it ultimately doesn't matter to children how and with whom they spend their formative, dependent, vulnerable, and innocent years. So let's take a closer look at this burgeoning child care industry, which is touted as equal to or better than an attentive, loving mom or dad.

Dr. Mark Genuis, director of the National Foundation for Family Research and Education (NFFRE), wrote in a letter:

Our latest analysis examined over 25,000 children in studies covering from 1957 through to 1996. Numerous considerations were made regarding the year of the study, quality of study, and so forth. The bottom line appears to be that regular separation of more than approximately twenty hours per week places young children at significant risk of impaired development in areas of bonding, cognitive development, behavioral development and social development.

All of this is precisely why child development expert Edward Zigler of Yale has gone so far as to call day care "psychological thalidomide. Research beginning in the early 1970s has found that such children are more likely to be violent, antisocial and resistant to basic discipline" (*Wall Street Journal*, January 9, 1998).

In addition, there are medical consequences to institutional child care. The incidence of diarrhea, ear infections (which may lead to hearing loss with the concomitant problems of learning disabilities), and respiratory illnesses occur with higher frequency for children in day care. "Overall," according to a 1989 estimate by Dr. Ron Haskins in the *Bulletin* of the New York Academy of Medicine, "the excess illness attributable to day care costs American families and society $1.8 billion and the lives of at least one hundred children each year."

Mike Thompson's cartoon in the *Detroit Free Press* (March 2, 1999) shows a well-heeled mom and dad popping into their child's day care center. "Quick!" yells Dad, "Tell our Jimmy that a new study says our career obsession isn't bad for him."

"OK," says Mom, "But, which one's Jimmy?"

In his extensive article on day care in the May/June 1998 issue of *American Enterprise*, editor Karl Zinsmeister quoted a letter from a mother with a master's degree in social psychology on her visit to what she considered one of the best day care chains. "What I saw broke my heart. Babies were lined up, six in a row, crying, waiting for their meals. Toddlers were still in their cribs, some with tear-stained cheeks . . . with looks of having given up any hope of personal attachment a long time ago."

Also profiled in the same magazine were William and Wendy Dreskin, who operated a "good" day care center in San Francisco for five years. Its ratio of children to workers was low. It had ample equipment and an excellent curriculum. Teachers all had degrees plus at least a year of graduate training.

They wrote a book about their experience called *The Day Care Decision*. In it, they concluded, "For two years we watched children respond to the stress of separation from their parents with tears, anger, withdrawal or profound sadness. We found, to our dismay, that nothing in our own affection and caring for these children would erase this sense of loss and abandonment." The Dreskins eventually closed their quality center.

I have received hundreds of letters from day care workers that attest to these sad observations. Here are only a few of them:

➤ "I have been a licensed day care provider in my home and was a foster parent for nearly four years. As a day care provider and, I might add, one of the good ones, every day I saw children yearn for their parents. Some children cried when dropped off. Some cried for their mom at naptime. I have been told by some older children that they wish their mom would stay home so they could be with her. I had one baby, whose mom went back to work when he was eight weeks old, who refused to eat for me. It took weeks of Mom coming to my house on her break to feed him before he adjusted and finally took a bottle from me."

➤ "We are both stay-at-home moms and day care providers in Salt Lake City, Utah. We felt strongly about mothers staying home with their children before, but the feeling has doubled and tripled in intensity as we have taken care of children ten to twelve hours a day, who spend only two to four hours each night with the people they really want to be with—their parents. All of this, plus the desire to be full-time moms to our children, has helped us make the decision to quit providing day care."

➤ "We got in some financial hardship, so I decided to work in a day care center, just so I could stay near my baby. It was a nightmare. Most of the children are depressed, afraid, and they do not understand time or when Mommy is coming back (or is she *ever* coming back). It seems like the teachers were always trying to make the kids behave and control the crowd. So there is no time for personal attention. I was in the best day care in the region, and I got a scolding for giving one-on-one attention to a boy who cried every day, all day long, and was depressed. I was told that he should be punished—put in 'time-out'—whenever he cried. And not allowed to play. This is not a childhood! I quit and am very happy at home with my beautiful and loving son and very, very proud, even if we live in a very low-income neighborhood and have many financial troubles. How many people do you know who would drop a brand new Mercedes in a garage for all different people to drive all day long and pick it up at the end of the day? I bet that no one would do that with a car, but with a child . . . ?"

➤ "After ten years of work in a quality center, countless certificates, seminars, workshops, and a B.Ed. in Early Childhood Education, I find myself in full agreement with your urging parents to stay home with their children. Turnover rates due to illness, leave of absence, retirement, vacations, quitting, and part-time help are quite high. The children always have to adapt to new people on a continuous basis, thus inhibiting the bonding process. Even with government sanctioned teacher/child ratios, no matter how qualified or caring the staff, there is only so much time workers can spend with each child. The health, welfare and safety of the group become a priority, making it impossible to attend to each child's needs. What children need are mature parents, who provide a consistent, nurturing, quality of care, and a home that is more than a pit stop between the car and day care center."

➤ "I am a stay-at-home mom and a former day care worker. A particular episode of *Sesame Street* stunned me. There was a 'grown-up' rabbit named Benny, who was complaining bitterly to those around him that there were no day care centers when he was little and therefore he felt like he had missed out on all that fun other kids have. Feeling sorry for the rabbit, they allowed him to visit the local day care center so he could participate in all the fun, games, snacks, and friendships the other children have. As a former day care worker, I can assure you that I never met a child who opted for day care over staying home. Now children's shows are *promoting* day care over the care of their own mothers?"

➤ "I am a child-care provider. Over the last nine years I have seen a change in the children I take care of and their parents. The younger children seem to have more emotional, behavioral, and attention problems. *My* problem is that the more I am willing to do, the more the 'parents' are willing to let me. Parents, more and more, seem not to want to be with their children or interact with them. 'I don't know how you do it,' some have said. 'I can't even stay home with my *own* kids all day. They drive my crazy.'"

➤ "I have worked in five highly regarded day care centers in a middle and upper middle class large town. What I have seen there makes me plead with new mothers or mothers-to-be. Please, do not put a child in an institutionalized center (babies left crying, bottles propped up instead of held, scolding children who need attention and love, etc.). . . . Lastly, let me share with you what one little girl said to me. As I was explaining why their teacher would be leaving soon to stay home with her new baby, one two-year old girl looked up at me and asked, plaintively, 'Why is she staying home?' I said 'Because she wanted to hold her baby and take care of it, feed it, and love it.' The little girl looked up at me and said, with a confused look on her face, 'Why? We *have* a baby room here!'"

➤ A friend of mine owns and operates a day care center. She recently told me a story, which left me speechless. My friend often held one baby while he went to sleep. A few weeks later, the mother of this child asked my friend if she was doing this—because her son seemed to want to be held more often. After my friend responded, 'Yes,' the mother asked her to stop holding her son because she does not have time to hold him at home.

Nonetheless, we have a daily media diet of social service propaganda promoting the virtues of nonparent care, although every now and then the truth seeps through. The Sunday *Boston Herald* (December 5, 1999) published an article entitled "Familiarity Breeds Contentment." It was intended to reassure parents that their children's pain at being left in day care would subside as it became routine. The accompanying photograph was pathetic. It showed a mother looking at a window against which her obviously agonized three-year-old daughter's nose and hands were beseechingly pressed.

Yet another mother is quoted as saying, "My husband and I reluctantly toughed it out for three months as Ally continued to have trouble adjusting. She spent most of her early days at day care crying for mommy, taking small breaks from her tears when she was distracted by snack time or an activity she liked."

Two things about this quote enrage me. One, this woman talks about her own "toughing it out" experience, as though we are to feel for *her*. Why does it not occur to her that her angst might be an internal message that she is doing something wrong? Two, since when does a child's acquiescence to a situation means everything's fine?

Every psychology major has read about the animal experiments wherein monkeys are put in a cage with an electrically wired floor. At first, when the electrical shock is administered, the animals jump and scream and try to escape. After repetitive shocks, the animals realize that their screams of pain do not bring relief or assistance, and their attempts to escape are hopeless. They just sit there and take the pain. Would you call that a successful adjustment to the situation?

The end of the article is most telling, as Ally's mother keeps wondering if it would be better for Ally if she had stayed home. The reporter gives lip service to some "recent findings" about the negative effect of the loss of mother care on children. According to a researcher at Temple University, "when we're around people more, we know them better. . . . We used to believe that quality time was all that was needed, but now we're learning that maybe some quantity of time is needed."

Now, doesn't this sound like an important statement about the needs of children? But wait! In the very next quote, the "expert" shifts from objective scientist to feminist ideologue: "but my own personal sense is that whatever we choose to do as moms, so long as we're happy in what we do, we're not going to hurt our kids."

Another example of the canonization of selfishness—what feels good to mom automatically dictates what's good for the family.

The extent to which adults will go to maintain their child-free lifestyle is astounding. The *Washington Post* (November 28, 1999) reported that a North Arlington home day care owner admitted to exceeding the county's limits on children at family day care homes and cheating the IRS out of the additional income. She had forty-two children inside her house instead of her license limit of five. This all came to light with the death of a four-month-old infant, who had recently been adopted, and had been left alone for at least an hour and a half in a small office area at the day care center. While the owner is not being accused of murder in the infant's death, she could receive up to three years in prison for the other offenses.

Do you think the parents of the forty-one surviving children are upset? Of course they are. They are upset with the authorities for interfering with their day care arrangements. They banded together to plead for leniency and get her back in their busy, important lives. In February 2000 the court put her on probation.

Kristen Terrell, a news anchor at WPTY, wrote me about a story she was covering.

On Wednesday, July 22, two Memphis Tennessee babies were overlooked inside their respective day care transportation vans. Temperatures reaching into the nineties, the hot sun heated both vans to the 150-degree range. In one case seventeen-month-old Darkish Slater was left all day. In the other case, two-year-old Brandon Mann was left for five hours. Day care workers at the two separate facilities did not realize their "mistakes" until parents arrived looking for their children. I cannot get out of my mind that these two little children literally simmered to death inside those vans.

The story gets worse. The next day both day care centers in separate parts of town were open for business. With the exception of only a few, the parents actually left their children in the hands of the centers again. I submit to you that this country gets what it deserves. We already kill over a million unborn children in abortion each year. It only follows that the disrespect for life will migrate to older post-birth children. May God forgive us.

The *Seattle Post Intelligencer* reported on June 18, 1999, that four sets of children, all younger than age ten, were dropped off in front of their home day care, and the parents drove away. Unfortunately, the day care provider, her adult daughter, and her granddaughter lay dead in the home, murdered the night before.

Our cultural imperative of career and money, combined with the almost universal validation of hired care for children, is devaluing and seriously endangering the children who were given to us to protect and cherish. Nor does the attitude of many parents change even when the kids are older.

"Seventeen cases of syphilis . . . More than 50 teenagers experimenting with group sex . . . At least 200 middle and high schoolers exposed to sexually transmitted diseases" (*Atlanta Journal-Constitution*, October 19, 1999).

These were the opening sentences of a shocking article about the children of Rockdale County, Georgia, who were immortalized by a PBS special for reconstituting syphilis as a major health issue in the United States. Syphilis has been a disease of poverty and poor health. Rockdale's children, affluent, privileged, and indulged, have changed all that.

> Rockdale's teens were infecting each other with chlamydia, herpes and human papilloma virus, the cause of genital warts and occasionally of cervical cancer. . . . Surprisingly, there were only a few pregnancies, possibly because multiple infections impaired the girl's fertility.
>
> "Kids need parenting," said Cynthia Noel, a county public health nurse who treated most of those infected. "They want a family. They want rules. They want someone to be in charge. If they can't get that attention from their parents, they will seek it somewhere else."

At Memorial Middle School, counselor Peggy Cooper was hearing . . . teens having sex with multiple partners at home after school and before parents came home, and sleepovers where imitating sexually explicit movie scenes on cable television was the chief entertainment. . . .

The investigators found the adults were pursuing their own agendas. Many worked long hours—often, ironically, to fund their kids' label-conscious clothing and consumer goods. Some had allowed their kids to move out—in one case, into a pool house behind the family home—or to live with family friends.

The disconnect between Rockdale's parents and teens is a central theme.

The out-of-control behavior of Rockdale's children is not unique. It is a symptom of the larger problem of our society, which does not support the proposition that adults should sacrifice for their children or that adults have a G-d-given responsibility and obligation to put family welfare above personal desires.

This is not just an issue of American society. "The dark flipside of economic power, many experts say, has been the gutting of family life and playtime in the name of workplace performance and school achievement," writes the *New York Times* (October 12, 1999) about Japan's troubling trend: rising teenage crime. "A consensus is emerging that the long work hours of many Japanese, followed by long commutes and job-related social engagements, has stripped many children of almost any meaningful contact with their parents . . ."

As long as some parents *feel* as if they're actually involved in their kids' lives, it *appears* to be just fine. S. B. from Phoenix wrote me about a special kind of report card an acquaintance of hers accidentally left at her house.

It is rather explicit testament to the method by which many children today are being raised, i.e., dropped off at the kiddy corral. Apparently, after dropping the child off at 7 A.M. and picking him up at 6 P.M., the parents are informed about their child's life through a checklist of sorts. This laissez-faire method of child rearing is somehow legitimized by the apparent "care" and "attention" given to the individual child throughout the day, as described on the report card.

On this report card, the times of urination are noted. Each entry is in a different handwriting—exactly five. That means that over the course of the day, at least five individuals were in charge of caring for this child. The ten arms of these five strangers are not necessary, but rather the two arms of one familiar, nurturing and loving mother are. Contrary to popular culture, it does not "take a village."

A small checklist in the bottom right-hand corner of the report card reads four choices: happy, talkative, quiet, and played well. This list falls a little short as I do not see included in the choices such descriptions as: abandoned, irreparably scarred, forsaken, discarded, rejected, and generally sad—but I suppose that wouldn't be good for business.

"Chilling is the large number of studies that link early, extensive day-care with psychological, social, and behavioral problems," writes Maggie Gallagher, summarizing the vast and growing body of knowledge concerning day care's detrimental impact on children.

An affiliate scholar at the Institute for American Values, Gallagher is also a nationally syndicated columnist. "Studies increasingly confirm the common-sense intuition that day care poses dangers to small children. An emerging body of research suggests that children in full-time day care are less likely to be firmly attached to their parents and are, on average, more disobedient towards adults and more aggressive toward their peers than children cared for primarily by their parents. In certain circumstances, daycare also puts children's cognitive development at risk" (National Review, January 26, 1998).

Julia, from Jerome, Idaho, wrote to me about her father, who is the director of a college family learning center, which is a day care center for students' children as well as an educational center for those getting degrees in early childhood education.

While we were eating, my father asked my twenty-two-year-old daughter exactly how old her son was. She replied twenty months. My father responded that in about two years her son would be able to attend the center. I spoke up and mentioned that you, Dr. Laura, wouldn't agree. "Dr. Laura and I would prefer that he remain home with his mother until he is ready to go to school."

The conversation continued, and my father agreed that the best thing for a child is to be with a parent while in those early years, but then he said that most of the kids in his center do not have parents who would stay home with their kids. He said that it seemed to him that most of the parents didn't even care much for their children, so he felt they were better off at the school where they were loved and given the attention they were not receiving from their parents.

Julia's letter ends with a question to me: "The point of this fax is to ask your opinion. Do you think that children are better off in a day care setting when they aren't nurtured at home?"

Depending on the day care situation and the true level of love and attention at home, maybe so. However, situations of extreme deprivation are the *only* ones in which kids might be better off in day care. How would that be for parental stigma?!

If this society could reverse its love affair with parenthood by proxy, there would be more loving parenting at home and more essays like this one, written by seven-year-old Meaghan to her mommy:

I LOVE MY MOM

I love my mom because she stays home with me. She is always there when I need her. My mom is the best mom in the whole world. My mom should be in the Hall of Fame!

Meaghan's mother wrote me about an incident that occurred around Mother's Day.

Yesterday my seven year old daughter got off her school bus and fell apart. I took her up to her room and found that during the three days she had missed school leading up to spring break, another child had made her Mother's Day present for me. She was crying and distressed that her present would not be something she made. I told her she was right to feel sad and said I would get a new pot she could paint. When she brought home her present, we could transplant the flowers.

She felt so much better and went off to play.

I wondered what she would have done had she gone to "after school care" until 5:30 or so or had come home to a baby-sitter. I quietly thanked God that I picked a husband who sees so much value in my job as mom.

Today she came home with the pot that we transplanted. She also wrote me the enclosed letter. I had a good cry. She didn't mention the violin lessons, skating lessons, baseball clinics, roller-blading, bike riding or the fact that I coach her softball team. She just loves me because I'm there for her. Working women do not know the price they are paying to work.

Rather than sacrifice and compromise their own personal goals and desires, too many adults expect the kids to do the sacrificing. "Becky Brouwer is delighted with the program at Hamilton Heights Middle School, the one that allows her two children to skip homework," reported the Associated Press on November 11, 1999.

"A one-time voucher excuses students from the homework assignment of their choice as long as they spend a night with their family—doing anything or even nothing."

The director of the Center on Work and Family at Boston University, commenting on this project, is quoted as saying, "many of today's families need a break like this in their heavily scheduled lives."

The answer to the problem of the breakdown of adult investment of time and energy in their children is for the children to give up their education? What next? Eating and sleeping? I guess so.

➤ "Iowa's first childcare center at a casino opens next Monday at Ameristar in Council Bluffs (9 A.M. to 11 P.M. or midnight). Though critics say the service could encourage problem gamblers, organizers say it will prevent children from being left alone while parents gamble. For five dollars per hour, parents can feel secure. . . ." (*Omaha World-Herald*, June 11, 1996).

"I wonder," writes listener Tony, in reference to this news, *"if Sodom and Gomorrah had a childcare center. What happens if you go belly up at the craps table and don't have any money left to pay the childcare bill?"*

➤ Plano, Texas, has come up with the Disneyland of all day care centers, according to the *Dallas Morning News* (June 26, 1998).

About $4.5 million is being spent on the facility, [which] will offer a full-day nursery and preschool program for children from ages six weeks through kindergarten.

Called "Crème de la Crème," this center houses computer labs, dance studio, gymnasium, library, tennis courts, baseball park, trike garage, barbershop, dry cleaning, tutoring, music classes and more. It is obviously very expensive.

"But," said a spokesperson, "parents often spend about the same amount if they factor in the cost of such outside programs as dance or music lessons and the time they spend driving their children from one activity to another. They won't have to take their kids other places for dancing, theatre, water park activities, sports, etc."

Not everyone was impressed. Gloria Dedman wrote a letter to the paper saying of Crème de la Crème, "It will even eliminate the need for parents to bother driving the little buggers around to all those time-consuming activities. The parents can work longer hours and spend even less time with their children. What's next— a place parents can deposit the baby on the way home from the hospital and arrange to pick it up when it turns 18?" Well, maybe!

➤ "The 'Six-O'Clock Scramble' to pick up kids before clos-
ing time is the most stressful part of the day for many
busy moms and dads . . . but [the stress] should abate as
more and more 24-hour day-care centers open up for
business" (*Los Angeles Times*, August 1, 1999).

That's just what we need. Round-the-clock day and
night child care.

Obviously, any parent or family can, from time to time, run
into trouble and need back-up support in an emergency. Historically, this back-up has been relatives, neighbors, and friends.
What is frightening to me is the ongoing conspiracy to normalize
institutionalized care as *the* best situation for children, period.
Listen to Shelley Waters Boots, research director for the California Child Care Resource and Referral Network (*Los Angeles
Times,* August 1, 1999). "Although convenient, those options
may lack the social and educational benefits that make center-
based care so appealing." Those "options" include relatives, nannies, or family day care providers—all of which obviously can
provide more intimate relationships than a large center.

It seems to me that the natural next step to child-free parenting
is none at all. This would naturally limit the stress on adults. And
what to do with those fleeting twinges of desire to be a mom or
dad? Buy Babyz, the latest virtual pet product from Mindscape.
They're sold like Cabbage Patch dolls or puppies at the pound.

The *New York Times* (December 9, 1999) says of this new computer game, "Adoptive parents of Babyz can keep busy by feeding,
teaching, tickling and cajoling their infants" and "peruse a search-
able database of new Babyz to add to their collection. Hair color,
eye color, sex, complexion, you name it—it's Gattaca in booties."

This is a Brave New World in which Babyz can simply be
turned off when inconvenient, annoying, or demanding. How
about that!

Of course, unlike listeners Tom and Stacy, you won't have
anything like the following happen to you.

The attached letter is from our daughter, Tonya. Today is her twenty-second birthday. As we left for work this morning, this letter and a beautiful bouquet of flowers was sitting in the front seat of our car. We have been married twenty-five years and this is what parenting is all about. We hear parents on your program all the time say they have to work. We are self-employed and ALWAYS were done for the day when our daughter was out of school. If we had something to finish, we would pick her up and she would come with us. Money was tight at times, but we did fine! Our motto: enjoy and spend time with your kids, as tomorrow they will be getting married! They grow up too fast.

This is Tonya's letter:

This year, instead of celebrating my birth, I want to celebrate you, my parents, my best friends—because without you . . . I would cease to be. I could never begin to express my gratitude for all that you have done and put up with. I have so many wonderful memories.

Thank you for sitting in the bathroom with me playing Barbies, trying to keep me in the cold water in an attempt to get my fever down, in our old house on Railroad Avenue. For all the birthday parties thrown for my cabbage patch kids and for going to all the trouble to bake the cakes. . . . Thank you for getting me through the teasing in grade school, near fights in middle school, and the largest crisis I had as a child . . . losing a friend. Thank you for believing in me, especially in my swimming. It always amazed me that you never failed to get me to competitions across the state; that you were always there for the most important swims (even for the not so important as well). Thank you for dumping way too much money into our wedding, for lending so much money for groceries, clothes and so much more . . . knowing that we couldn't possibly pay you back for all of it. I only hope that someday I can return the favors. For everything that you have ever done, I thank you from the bottom of my heart. God blessed me so much on my birthday; he gave me the both of you. Thank you, God.

Epilogue

I have personally come through the fifties, when family life was secure and healthy; through the sixties with its turmoil over authority, tradition, and the overblown emphasis on the self; through the seventies, eighties, and nineties, watching great social experimentation bring forth some incredible advances, as well as devastating assaults on respect for authority, personal responsibility, religion, morality, and obligation to family and community.

I am finishing my fifth adult book on the edge of a new century. Each of its predecessors stimulated various passions and moods, encouraged self-exploration, and precipitated philosophical struggles within me. And each was generated by a desire to explore, challenge, and inspire.

This book is decidedly different. The genesis of this one was anger, which the process of researching and writing only heightened. I am angry with the historically esteemed professional organizations (medical, psychological, sociological, educational), so adamantly committed to secularism and total individual freedom that G-d, sexual fidelity and holiness, marital vows and family obligations have all become targets of derision and destruction.

I have received thousands of letters, faxes, e-mails, and calls during just the past year from women who feel stupid and wrong for having made sacrifices to center their lives on their children and family. Parenting and child magazines inundate them with heroic tales of powerful women who manage to squeeze in some late night "quality time" with their kids (when they're in town). Lately, the social science professionals have weighed in with so-called research suggesting it's better for kids to be in day care than at home with Mom.

On December 24, 1999, I read this letter to the editor in the *New York Times*, from Peter F. Worms of Parsippany, New Jersey.

> Two articles on Dec. 23 speak to an issue pervading our world. An AT&T executive, Kathleen B. Earley, writes in *Business Day* that she misses seeing her children grow up because she sees them only in the morning, if at all. Quoted in a sports article, John Fox, a Giants coach, talks of watching three hours of videotape of his 7- and 9-year-old boys playing football, which he enjoyed because "usually I only see them asleep."
>
> It appears that our children are continually placed at or near the bottom of parents' priorities.

Notice that Kathleen B. Earley "misses" and John Fox "enjoyed." It is with compassion and without judgment that these statements are generally presented in the media—compassion for what the selfish and neglectful *parent* is *missing* or *accomplishing* or *enjoying*. Don't Kathleen B. Earley's children miss her? Wouldn't John Fox's children have enjoyed his being at their games? Does any of that matter anymore in this frightful era of self-gratification at the expense of our children's needs?

In lamenting the supposed dearth of wonderful acting roles for mature women, Christine Lahti is quoted in the *New York Times* (December 19, 1999), pointing out that actresses like Sally Field and Diane Keaton are directing now. "It's a fabulous avenue," she said. "I love acting, but if I'm going to play supporting, under-written mom parts in a movie that I can do in my sleep, I may as well be home with my kids."

There it is. If I have nothing really fun, great, or challenging to do, I may as well be home with the kids. Until something more stimulating and important comes along, that is.

Smack in the middle of an article in *U.S. News & World Report* (December 20, 1999) entitled "World-Class Workaholics—Are Crazy Hours and Takeout Dinners the Elixir of America's Success?" is a small bullet: "In 1900, men in America worked ten-hour days and six-day weeks." I don't know if this was meant to convey the impression that nothing has really changed in one hundred years. But something has. For turn-of-the-century children, Mommy was there. Since then, we have moved into the feminist era, which, while reasonably asserting that women are capable and entitled to fair compensation for their work, downplayed and even denigrated women's feminine and maternal desires for marriage and the blessing of hands-on mothering. Instead, the feminist lie that women could "have and do it all" has seriously weakened the cohesive family fabric in America.

It is not an accident that one of the beginning prayers for each Friday night's Sabbath dinner in observant Jewish homes is one of gratitude and just praise for the mother. Thousands of years of Jewish tradition acknowledge the special spiritual place of women with respect to G-d, life, civilization, home, husband, and children. It is a terrible calamity that modern civilization seeks to replace that very special role with materialism and worldly accomplishment.

Some women, some very powerful women, admit this truth openly. The front page of the *New York Times* (November 28, 1999) carried the story of Colonel Lois Beard, America's prime candidate to become the army's first General Mom.

> On top of her typical twelve-hour workday, Colonel Beard, forty-five, was the mother of her three children, raising them with her husband, Glenn, another Army colonel. . . .

But then Colonel Beard called it quits and retired. After holding every job and attending every school required to be selected as general, she decided she could no longer be both a mother and a commander. "I certainly would have kept going if it wasn't for the family," she said. "I loved being a commander, but I found myself saying I would be a better commander if I wasn't a parent and a better parent if I wasn't a commander."

I pray this book will encourage more women to follow Colonel Beard's brave sacrifice for her children. I deeply hope reading it will awaken our consciences; ignite our compassion toward our children; and prompt a reconsideration of the ultimate cost of coveting more money, more things, more power, more sex, more pleasure, more experiences, and more success. The inestimable rewards for turning away from those temptations and toward the expectant faces of our children are clear in the following letter from Cheryl from Caliente, California:

I am writing you in response to the comments you made about gratitude. You told the story of how you forgot to "up" your son's allowance as you always did on his birthday. He never made any demand for more money. You rewarded him with a raise because he was grateful for what he had.

Seven years ago we moved to the country. The house we bought was shabby and somewhat in distress, but the location was simply beautiful. My husband, who is a general contractor, assured me that we could fix it up. We still have a lot to accomplish toward that goal to say the least. I noticed that over the last several months I had become more and more demanding of the completion of this seemingly eternal project, even to the point of making ultimatums to "cut our losses" and sell the house as is and move back to the city.

Last night our family sat together on our bed reading, laughing and having a great time. After the kids were in bed, I was reflecting on our good time and I realized that I had healthy, happy children and the warmth of my wonderful husband—

things so many people will never experience. I thanked God at that moment for the priceless gifts He so graciously gave me.

No longer will I make petty demands. Regardless of the way my house looks, my home will lack nothing if I honor my Heavenly Father and my family by living every day from this moment on with joy and gratitude for all they bring into my life. It makes me sad to think I was willing to give up all we've worked for because I wanted what was "due me" now!

Dr. Laura, thank you—and your son—for giving me a new attitude.

No, Cheryl, thank you!

In conclusion, I'm hoping to either never see the following two types of insanity again, or at least see them attacked as shameful if they appear in print.

The first is taken from a book by James Gleik entitled *Life in the Fast Lane,* which is recommended reading in *Readers Digest.* "Even reading to children is under pressure. The volume of *One Minute Bedtime Stories* consists of traditional stories that can be read by a busy parent in only one minute."

Whew! Talk about streamlining "quality time"!

The second was an ad in the California *Contra Costa Times* on February 16, 2000. "Household. Domestic worker clean 12 rm house. Take care of 4 children. Wash dishes, wash/iron clothes/linens, straighten rms, change diaper, clean up mess, make beds, prep/serve meals & snacks. May wake up at night for toilet needs. Watch phys/emot. health, depression, fear, anger, cuts, bruises, sores, inspect health hazards/furn./equipment. Report unusual/uncommon behavior to parents. If hired, must speak/read/write Eng.; legal right to work, live on premises, avail. on-call 24 hrs./day, O/T paid, 3 mos. exp., Mon–Fri, some Sat/Sun, 6 a.m.–9 a.m. & 3 p.m.–9 p.m. (40 hrs). $1808.53/mo., free rm/bd. Job site/intrvw. Send ad/resume."

Can you imagine? How less connected could human beings be to their offspring?

Don't have them if you won't raise them.